*Thomas F. McGovern, EdD*
*William L. White, MA*
*Editors*

# Alcohol Problems
# in the United States:
# Twenty Years
# of Treatment Perspective

*Alcohol Problems in the United States: Twenty Years of Treatment Perspective* has been co-published simultaneously as *Alcoholism Treatment Quarterly*, Volume 20, Numbers 3/4 2002.

*Pre-publication*
*REVIEWS,*
*COMMENTARIES,*
*EVALUATIONS . . .*

"SHOULD BE REQUIRED READING at every alcohol treatment site and for all individuals involved in the treatment of alcoholism and alcohol abuse. . . . CAPTURES THE FULL SPECTRUM of alcohol treatment issues. By presenting a wide range of treatment perspectives, weaving them into a pattern of human experience, and relating personal perspectives of veterans in the field, McGovern and White have brought together the knowledge and experience of twenty turbulent years in the treatment of alcohol abuse and addiction."

**Rick Seymour, MA**
*Editor,* Journal of Psychoactive Drugs

The Haworth Press, Inc.
New York

# Alcohol Problems in the United States: Twenty Years of Treatment Perspective

*Alcohol Problems in the United States: Twenty Years of Treatment Perspective* has been co-published simultaneously as *Alcoholism Treatment Quarterly*, Volume 20, Numbers 3/4 2002.

# The *Alcoholism Treatment Quarterly* Monographic "Separates"

Below is a list of "separates," which in serials librarianship means a special issue simultaneously published as a special journal issue or double-issue *and* as a "separate" hardbound monograph. (This is a format which we also call a "DocuSerial.")

"Separates" are published because specialized libraries or professionals may wish to purchase a specific thematic issue by itself in a format which can be separately cataloged and shelved, as opposed to purchasing the journal on an on-going basis.

"Separates" are carefully classified separately with the major book jobbers so that the journal tie-in can be noted on new book order slips to avoid duplicate purchasing.

You may wish to visit Haworth's website at . . .

## http://www.HaworthPress.com

. . . to search our online catalog for complete tables of contents of these separates and related publications.

You may also call 1-800-HAWORTH (outside US/Canada: 607-722-5857), or Fax 1-800-895-0582 (outside US/Canada: 607-771-0012), or e-mail at:

## getinfo@haworthpressinc.com

---

**Alcohol Problems in the United States: Twenty Years of Treatment Perspective,** edited by Thomas F. McGovern, EdD, and William L. White, MA (Vol. 20, No. 3/4, 2002). *An overview of trends in the treatment of alcohol problems over a 20-year period.*

**Homelessness Prevention in Treatment of Substance Abuse and Mental Illness: Logic Models and Implementation of Eight American Projects,** edited by Kendon J. Conrad, PhD, Michael D. Matters, PhD, Patricia Hanrahan, PhD, and Daniel J. Luchins, MD (Vol. 17, No. 1/2, 1999). *Provides you with new insights into how you can help your clients overcome political, economic, and environmental barriers to treatment that can lead to homelessness.*

**Alcohol Use/Abuse Among Latinos: Issues and Examples of Culturally Competent Services,** edited by Melvin Delgado, PhD (Vol. 16, No. 1/2, 1998). *"This book will have widespread appeal for practitioners and educators involved in direct service delivery, organizational planning, research, or policy development." (Steven Lozano Applewhite, PhD, Associate Professor, Graduate School of Social Work, University of Houston, Texas)*

**Treatment of the Addictions: Applications of Outcome Research for Clinical Management,** edited by Norman S. Miller, MD (Vol. 12, No. 2, 1994). *"Ambitious and informative. . . . Recommended to anybody involved in the practice of substance abuse treatment and research in treatment outcome." (The American Journal of Addictions)*

**Self-Recovery: Treating Addictions Using Transcendental Meditation and Maharishi Ayur-Veda,** edited by David F. O'Connell, PhD, and Charles N. Alexander, PhD (Vol. 11, No. 1/2/3/4, 1994). *"A scholarly trailblazer, a scientific first. . . . Those who work daily in the fight against substance abuse, violence, and illness will surely profit from reading this important volume. A valuable new tool in what may be America's most difficult battle." (Joseph Drew, PhD, Chair for Evaluation, Mayor's Advisory Committee on Drug Abuse, Washington, DC; Professor of Political Science, University of the District of Columbia)*

**Treatment of the Chemically Dependent Homeless: Theory and Implementation in Fourteen American Projects,** edited by Kendon J. Conrad, PhD, Cheryl I. Hultman, PhD, and John S. Lyons, PhD (Vol. 10, No. 3/4, 1993). *"A wealth of information and experience. . . . A very useful reference book for everyone seeking to develop their own treatment strategies with this patient group or the homeless mentally ill." (British Journal of Psychiatry)*

**Treating Alcoholism and Drug Abuse Among Homeless Men and Women: Nine Community Demonstration Grants,** edited by Milton Argeriou, PhD, and Dennis McCarty, PhD (Vol. 7, No. 1, 1990). *"Recommended to those in the process of trying to better serve chemically dependent homeless persons." (Journal of Psychoactive Drugs)*

**Co-Dependency: Issues in Treatment and Recovery,** edited by Bruce Carruth, PhD, and Warner Mendenhall, PhD (Vol. 6, No. 1, 1989). *"At last a book for clinicians that clearly defines co-dependency and gives helpful treatment approaches. Essential." (Margot Escott, MSW, Social Worker in Private Practice, Naples, Florida)*

***The Treatment of Shame and Guilt in Alcoholism Counseling***, edited by Ronald T. Potter-Efron, MSW, PhD, and Patricia S. Potter-Efron, MS, CACD III (Vol. 4, No. 2, 1989). *"Comprehensive in its coverage and provides important insights into the treatment of alcoholism, especially the importance to the recovery process of working through feelings of overwhelming shame and guilt. Recommended as required reading." (Australian Psychologist)*

***Drunk Driving in America: Strategies and Approaches to Treatment***, edited by Stephen K. Valle, ScD, CAC, FACATA (Vol. 3, No. 2, 1986). *Creative and thought-provoking methods related to research, policy, and treatment of the drunk driver.*

***Alcohol Interventions: Historical and Sociocultural Approaches***, edited by David L. Strug, PhD, S. Priyadarsini, PhD, and Merton M. Hyman (Supp. #1, 1986). *"A comprehensive and unique account of addictions treatment of centuries ago." (Federal Probation: A Journal of Correctional Philosophy)*

***Treatment of Black Alcoholics***, edited by Frances Larry Brisbane, PhD, MSW, and Maxine Womble, MA (Vol. 2, No. 3/4, 1985). *"Outstanding! In view of the paucity of research on the topic, this text presents some of the outstanding work done in this area." (Dr. Edward R. Smith, Department of Educational Psychology, University of Wisconsin-Milwaukee)*

***Psychosocial Issues in the Treatment of Alcoholism***, edited by David Cook, CSW, Christine Fewell, ACSW, and Shulamith Lala Ashenberg Straussner, DSW, CEAP (Vol. 2, No. 1, 1985). *"Well-written and informative; the topic areas are relevant to today's social issues and offer some new approaches to the treatment of alcoholics." (The American Journal of Occupational Therapy)*

***Alcoholism and Sexual Dysfunction: Issues in Clinical Management***, edited by David J. Powell, PhD (Vol. 1, No. 3, 1984). *"It does a good job of explicating the linkage between two of the most common health problems in the U.S. today." (Journal of Sex & Marital Therapy)*

# Alcohol Problems in the United States: Twenty Years of Treatment Perspective

Thomas F. McGovern, EdD
William L. White, MA
Editors

*Alcohol Problems in the United States: Twenty Years of Treatment Perspective* has been co-published simultaneously as *Alcoholism Treatment Quarterly*, Volume 20, Numbers 3/4 2002.

The Haworth Press, Inc.
New York • London • Oxford

*Alcohol Problems in the United States: Twenty Years of Treatment Perspective* has been co-published simultaneously as *Alcoholism Treatment Quarterly*, Volume 20, Numbers 3/4 2002.

The Haworth Press, Inc., 10 Alice Street, Binghamton, 13904-1580 USA

Cover design by Jennifer M. Gaska

**Library of Congress Cataloging-in-Publication Data**

Alcohol problems in the United States: Twenty years of treatment perspective/ Thomas F. McGovern, William L. White, editors.
    p.; cm.– (Alcoholism treatment quarterly; v. 20, no. 3/4)
    Includes bibliographical references and index.
    ISBN 0-7890-2048-3 (hard : alk. paper) – ISBN 0-7890-2049-1 (pbk. : alk. paper)
    1. Alcoholism–treatment–United States–History–20th century.
    [DNLM: 1. Alcoholism–therapy–United States. 2. History of Medicine, 20th cent.–United States.
    3. Substance Abuse Treatment Centers–history–United States. WM 274 A352578 2002]
    I. McGovern,Thomas F. II. White, William L., 1947- III. Series.
RC565.7.A43 2002
616.86´106–dc21

2002155542

# Indexing, Abstracting & Website/Internet Coverage

This section provides you with a list of major indexing & abstracting services. That is to say, each service began covering this periodical during the year noted in the right column. Most Websites which are listed below have indicated that they will either post, disseminate, compile, archive, cite or alert their own Website users with research-based content from this work. (This list is as current as the copyright date of this publication.)

Abstracting, Website/Indexing Coverage . . . . . . . . . Year When Coverage Began

- *Abstracts in Anthropology* . . . . . . . . . . . . . . . . . . . . . . . . . . . . . . . . . . **1991**

- *Academic Abstracts/CD-ROM* . . . . . . . . . . . . . . . . . . . . . . . . . . . . . . **1995**

- *Academic Search Elite (EBSCO)* . . . . . . . . . . . . . . . . . . . . . . . . . . . . **1995**

- *Addiction Abstracts <www.tandf.co.uk/addiction-abs>* . . . . . . . . . . . **1995**

- *CNPIEC Reference Guide: Chinese National Directory
    of Foreign Periodicals* . . . . . . . . . . . . . . . . . . . . . . . . . . . . . . . . . . . . **1995**

- *Criminal Justice Abstracts* . . . . . . . . . . . . . . . . . . . . . . . . . . . . . . . . . **1984**

- *EAP Abstracts Plus* . . . . . . . . . . . . . . . . . . . . . . . . . . . . . . . . . . . . . . . **1995**

- *EMBASE/Excerpta Medica Secondary Publishing Division
    <http://www.elsevier.nl>* . . . . . . . . . . . . . . . . . . . . . . . . . . . . . . . . . . **1998**

- *e-psyche, LLC <www.e-psyche.net>* . . . . . . . . . . . . . . . . . . . . . . . . . . **2001**

(continued)

(continued)

*Special Bibliographic Notes related to special journal issues (separates) and indexing/abstracting:*

- indexing/abstracting services in this list will also cover material in any "separate" that is co-published simultaneously with Haworth's special thematic journal issue or DocuSerial. Indexing/abstracting usually covers material at the article/chapter level.
- monographic co-editions are intended for either non-subscribers or libraries which intend to purchase a second copy for their circulating collections.
- monographic co-editions are reported to all jobbers/wholesalers/approval plans. The source journal is listed as the "series" to assist the prevention of duplicate purchasing in the same manner utilized for books-in-series.
- to facilitate user/access services all indexing/abstracting services are encouraged to utilize the co-indexing entry note indicated at the bottom of the first page of each article/chapter/contribution.
- this is intended to assist a library user of any reference tool (whether print, electronic, online, or CD-ROM) to locate the monographic version if the library has purchased this version but not a subscription to the source journal.
- individual articles/chapters in any Haworth publication are also available through the Haworth Document Delivery Service (HDDS).

# Alcohol Problems in the United States: Twenty Years of Treatment Perspective

## CONTENTS

A VIEW FROM THE FIELD

PERSONAL PERSPECTIVES

# ABOUT THE EDITORS

**Thomas F. McGovern, EdD,** is Professor in the Department of Neuropsychiatry, Texas Tech University Health Sciences Center, Lubbock, Texas. He also directs the program on Health Care Ethics and Humanities for the School of Medicine. He has been actively involved in the treatment of alcohol and other drug problems, as clinician, educator and researcher for 25 years. He served on the committee which authored the Institute of Medicine Study, Broadening the Base of Treatment for Alcohol Problems (1990). He has served as the Editor of *Alcoholism Treatment Quarterly* for 15 years.

**William L. White, MA,** is Senior Research Consultant at Chestnut Health Systems, Bloomington, Illinois. He has more than 30 years of experience in the addictions field as a clinician, clinical director, researcher and trainer. He has authored more than 100 articles and monographs, and seven books, including *Slaying the Dragon–The History of Addiction Treatment and Recovery in America.*

# Introduction

Thomas F. McGovern, EdD
William L. White, MA

An overview of trends in the treatment of alcohol problems in the United States marks the publication of this volume. The authors in this collection, combining their many years of experience, address patterns of treatment from the vantage points of broader treatment perspectives, experienced views of the diversity of treatment from the field, and, finally, of personal reflections on treatment issues over the past twenty years. The entire work maintains a historical yet personal perspective as it seeks to capture authentic glimpses of the lived story of treatment in the closing decades of the twentieth century.

This volume is organized into three sections:

Section One: Broader Treatment Perspectives
Section Two: A View from the Field
Section Three: Personal Perspectives

A brief word on content of each of the sections, together with an introduction of the authors follows.

The first section (Broader Treatment Perspectives) looks at some of the major themes which have informed the treatment field over the past twenty years and beyond. Ernest Kurtz, the most respected voice in the significance of Alcoholics Anonymous (AA) and in the Spiritual Dimensions of Recovery, examines the relationship between AA and the disease concept of alcoholism. With remarkable clarity and historical insight, he highlights the contribution of AA to our appreciation of the spiritual aspects of alcohol problems. Paula L. Wilbourne and William R. Miller, drawing on Miller's unique appreciation of

---

[Haworth co-indexing entry note]: "Introduction." McGovern, Thomas F., and William L. White. Co-published simultaneously in *Alcoholism Treatment Quarterly* (The Haworth Press, Inc.) Vol. 20, No. 3/4, 2002, pp. 1-3; and: *Alcohol Problems in the United States: Twenty Years of Treatment Perspective* (ed: Thomas F. McGovern, and William L. White) The Haworth Press, Inc., 2002, pp. 1-3. Single or multiple copies of this article are available for a fee from The Haworth Document Delivery Service [1-800-HAWORTH, 9:00 a.m. - 5:00 p.m. (EST). E-mail address: getinfo@haworthpressinc.com].

the major influences in treatment initiatives over the years, provide an excellent historical analysis and context for the period. Oliver J. Morgan, widely acclaimed for his expertise in describing the spiritual dimensions of treatment, skillfully traces the story of research efforts to describe and quantify the role of spirituality. Stephen K. Valle and Dennis Humphrey, respected pioneers in advocating and providing meaningful treatment for persons in our correctional system, examine the potential of prisons to become treatment centers. In the final piece of this section, William L. White, Michael Boyle and David Loveland combine their many years of expertise and understanding of treatment initiatives to provide a model of treatment which addresses alcoholism and other forms of addiction as chronic illness.

The second section (A View from the Field) presents a varied pattern woven from diverse threads drawn from the rich weave of the human experience of alcohol problems over the past twenty years. Jerome R. Koch and Jean A. Lewis present a thoughtful and revealing sociological analysis of the articles published in *Alcoholism Treatment Quarterly* (ATQ) since its inception. Gail Gleason Milgram, a respected educator and authority on prevention, details the extent of alcohol problems among youthful drinkers in an illuminating fashion. Jane M. Nakken, a long-time advocate of the special treatment needs of women, argues in an eloquent and convincing fashion for a deeper appreciation of women's issues in treatment. Don Coyhis and William L. White, writing from their deep commitment and from their equally convincing appreciation of the challenges faced by Native Americans, advocate changing paradigms and clinical practices in addressing alcohol problems among native peoples. Mark Sanders offers an enlightening national perspective on community responses to alcohol and other drug problems in African-American communities. His emphasis on the importance of spiritual consideration is reechoed by J. B. Kingree and Bryce F. Sullivan, who examine, in an insightful and helpful fashion, the participation of African-Americans in AA. The importance of harnessing the strengths of ethnic communities into any comprehensive approach to alcohol problems is eloquently presented by Melvin Delgado in his thoughtful and meaningful analysis of response to alcohol problems in Latino communities.

The third section (Personal Perspectives) tells the story of treatment from the perspective of authors who have been intimately involved in the field for many years. Their collective memory and wisdom embrace 20 years of dedicated service. Thomas F. McGovern summarizes the reflections and comments of the Editorial Board of ATQ as they identify patterns and trends in treatment over the past two decades. The remembrances and thoughts of Bruce Carruth, the Founding Editor of ATQ, are given special prominence. Jerome F. X. Carroll, a revered leader and pioneer in the innovation of therapeutic communities for the treatment of persons with multiple problems in the addiction field, embraces the challenges of treating our most disadvantaged citizens with candor, honesty and compelling insight.

Edgar P. Nace and Robert M. Morse, respected physicians leaders in the treatment field at many levels for over 30 years, expand Carroll's narrative in addressing the rise and fall of inpatient treatment at Timberlawn Hospital, Dallas and at the Mayo Clinic, Rochester, Minnesota. They trace the many forces, including the economic influences of managed care, which account for the profound changes over the past decades in a thoughtful and even fashion. Robert D. Sparks, writing from the vantage point of a lifetime of distinguished public service in medicine, recalls his role as chair of the committee which authored the highly respected Institute of Medicine Study, Broadening the Base of Treatment for Alcohol Problems (1990). He suggests that the study has influenced treatment initiatives at many levels, clinical, research, public policy, community involvement, and others, and that ongoing use of the study can benefit the treatment field as it meets the challenges of the present and future. William L. White and Thomas F. McGovern, as co-editors of this volume, assume the role of prophets in predicting future trends as our society addresses the many challenges associated with alcohol problems. What fate awaits them, in their role of prophets, remains to be seen. We hope, however, that the voices in this volume, which tell part of the story of where we have been, may illuminate the present and possibly provide vision for the future.

# BROADER TREATMENT PERSPECTIVES

# Alcoholics Anonymous
# and the Disease Concept of Alcoholism

## Ernest Kurtz, PhD

**SUMMARY.** Although the idea of "illness" helped many early and later members of Alcoholics Anonymous (A.A.) to understand their alcoholism, Alcoholics Anonymous neither originated nor promulgated the disease concept of alcoholism. The main contribution of A.A. in this area was the broadening of the extant concept to one of "threefold" malady, with an emphasis on "the spiritual." Examining the political and medical contexts of the time as well as A.A. literature shed light on the culture's chang-

Ernest Kurtz has authored numerous articles, book chapters and monograms on the treatment of alcohol problems, with particular emphasis on the significance of Alcoholics Anonymous and on the spiritual dimensions of recovery. His books include *Not-God: A History of Alcoholics Anonymous* (1978) and *The Spirituality of Imperfection* (1992), co-authored with Kathleen Ketcham. A collection of his articles have been published in *The Collected Ernie Kurtz* (1999).

The writing of this article was subsidized by a grant from the Behavioral Health Recovery Management project, a partnership of Fayette Companies and Chestnut Health Systems funded by the Illinois Department of Human Services Office of Alcoholism and Substance Abuse.

This article was discussed at the Works in Progress Seminar, Brown University, Providence, RI, June 13-15, 2002.

An earlier version of this article appears on the Web site of Behavioral Health Recovery Management: http://www.bhrm.org/papers/addpapers.htm

[Haworth co-indexing entry note]: "Alcoholics Anonymous and the Disease Concept of Alcoholism." Kurtz, Ernest. Co-published simultaneously in *Alcoholism Treatment Quarterly* (The Haworth Press, Inc.) Vol. 20, No. 3/4, 2002, pp. 5-40; and: *Alcohol Problems in the United States: Twenty Years of Treatment Perspective* (ed: Thomas F. McGovern, and William L. White) The Haworth Press, Inc., 2002, pp. 5-40. Single or multiple copies of this article are available for a fee from The Haworth Document Delivery Service [1-800-HAWORTH, 9:00 a.m. - 5:00 p.m. (EST). E-mail address: getinfo@haworthpressinc.com].

5

ing understanding of alcoholism in the second half of the twentieth century. *[Article copies available for a fee from The Haworth Document Delivery Service: 1-800-HAWORTH. E-mail address: <getinfo@haworthpressinc.com> Website: <http://www.HaworthPress.com> © 2002 by The Haworth Press, Inc. All rights reserved.]*

**KEYWORDS.** Alcoholics Anonymous and the disease concept, alcoholism, spirituality

Given the issues and prejudices involved, it is unlikely that the question of the historical relationship between Alcoholics Anonymous and the disease concept of alcoholism will ever be definitively resolved. But this does not mean that study of the topic is useless. We can discover, organize, and evaluate presently available information with aspirations to increased clarity even if not to perfect pellucidity, hoping to approach ever greater accuracy even if–until time-travel be perfected by omniscient observers–we are barred from the Rankin paradise of *we es eigentlich gewesen sei.*

On the basic question, the data are clear: Contrary to common opinion, Alcoholics Anonymous neither originated nor promulgated what has come to be called the disease concept of alcoholism. Yet its members did have a large role in spreading and popularizing that understanding. *How* and *Why* and *So What* are the burden of this paper as a whole.

As is often stated in introductions but too rarely recognized in analyses, Alcoholics Anonymous *is* its members. That membership tries to live their program's Twelve Steps, guided by their fellowship's Twelve Traditions. The Tenth of those Traditions reads: "Alcoholics Anonymous has no opinion on outside issues; hence the A.A. name ought never be drawn into public controversy." (A.A. World Services, 1953). The nature of alcoholism is an "outside issue." Thus, Alcoholics Anonymous *as* Alcoholics Anonymous has no opinion on it, as most members will tell anyone who asks.

But anyone who passes any time with members of Alcoholics Anonymous soon becomes aware of two other realities. First, most members of Alcoholics Anonymous do speak of their alcoholism in terms of disease: the vocabulary of disease was from the beginning and still remains for most of them the best available for understanding and explaining their own experience. But the use of that vocabulary no more implies deep commitment to the tenet that alcoholism is a disease in some technical medical sense than speaking of sunrise or sunset implies disbelief in a Copernican solar system. Second, most members, in the year 2002 no less than in 1939, will also tell an inquirer that their alcoholism has physical, mental, emotional, and spiritual dimensions. This advertence to complexity, and especially the emphasis on "the spiritual," is A.A.'s largest contribution: it is the necessary framework within which any discussion of A.A.'s relationship to the disease concept of alcoholism must be located.

The closest the book *Alcoholics Anonymous* (A.A. World Services, 2001) comes to a definition of alcoholism appears on p. 44, at the conclusion of the first paragraph of the "We Agnostics" chapter, where we are told that alcoholism "is an illness which only a spiritual experience will conquer." Alcoholics Anonymous also has a literature, some of which enjoys a kind of "official" status because it is approved, published and distributed by the General Service Office of Alcoholics Anonymous. Most important among this literature, based on member usage, are the A.A. "Big Book," *Alcoholics Anonymous*, the essays written by longer-lived co-founder and "Big Book" author William Griffith Wilson published as *Twelve Steps and Twelve Traditions* (A.A. World Services, 1953), and the telling of A.A.'s history primarily by Wilson in *Alcoholics Anonymous Comes of Age* (A.A. World Services, 1957).

Among A.A.'s less official literature are *The A.A. Grapevine*, an officially "unofficial" monthly published continuously since June 1944, and other publications and statements of co-founder Wilson. These latter, though also officially unofficial, derive a degree of authority from their acceptance and repetition by members of Alcoholics Anonymous over the years. Their authority derives less from "Bill said" than from the practical reality that many members' experience attests that what Bill said on some topics merits credence.

Among these statements is a reply Wilson gave when specifically asked about alcoholism as a disease after he had addressed the annual meeting of the National Catholic Clergy Conference on Alcoholism in 1960:

> We have never called alcoholism a disease because, technically speaking, it is not a disease entity. For example, there is no such thing as heart disease. Instead there are many separate heart ailments, or combinations of them. It is something like that with alcoholism. Therefore we did not wish to get in wrong with the medical profession by pronouncing alcoholism a disease entity. Therefore we always called it an illness, or a malady–a far safer term for us to use. (N.C.C.A. Blue Book, 1960, 199)

As the parallel with "heart ailments" as well as the proffered synonyms suggest, Wilson is here hardly denying an understanding that includes a medico/physiological element in alcoholism.

Given his expressed hesitancies, why? And why do so many members of Alcoholics Anonymous speak of their alcoholism in the vocabulary of disease? The answer is both simple and complex: simple because Alcoholics

Anonymous, like any reality, reflects the context of its time; complex because A.A. has existed long enough that its context has changed . . . and, indeed, changed more than once.

All realities are shaped by their context. Some entities also make contributions, significantly shaping later contexts. So it is with Alcoholics Anonymous and the culture's understanding of alcoholism. For diverse reasons, circumstances of origin tend to be the most important, to have the most pervasive and lasting effects. Thus we will begin at the beginning–not at the beginning of the disease concept of alcoholism, a far larger and more complex topic, but at the beginnings of Alcoholics Anonymous (for the history of the disease concept of alcoholism, see White, 1998).

Alcoholics Anonymous came into being in the mid- to late 1930s. In that era of the Great Depression, the recent end of the Prohibition controversy by the 21st Amendment's repeal of the 18th Amendment to the Constitution of the United States of America left most people bored with the topic of alcohol–they were tired of hearing about it. Some members of the cultural elite, philanthropists such as John D. Rockefeller and scientists such as those who in 1937 formed the Research Council on Problems of Alcohol, were concerned about the possible societal effects of Repeal (Johnson, 1973; Roizen, 1991; 1996), but even among the social workers who knew that Prohibition had not been a "failure" (Clark, 1976; Lubove, 1965), the drinking of alcohol was not a subject of frequent discussion.

The earliest A.A. candidates, of course, were not bored by the topic of alcohol. If their own drinking did not trouble them, their apparent inability to stop getting drunk was for most a real concern. And for many who "got" A.A., who sobered up and stayed sober in Alcoholics Anonymous after their many other efforts had failed, *why* A.A. worked became a question of interest. As do most people, they turned for answers to the common professional or scientific understanding of the matter. One version of that understanding was mediated to them by Dr. William Duncan Silkworth in the introductory pages of the book, *Alcoholics Anonymous* (A.A. World Services, 2001). Yet even this is not precisely accurate, for what Dr. Silkworth offered was not some theoretical explanation of "alcoholism" but a potent description of the *alcoholic*. "What alcoholism is" was not among the chief worries of the earliest A.A. members. In fact, "what alcoholism is" has never been among the main concerns of later members of Alcoholics Anonymous. Consistently over time, members of Alcoholics Anonymous, especially *as* members of Alcoholics Anonymous, have been interested not in alcoholism but in alcoholics–in people rather than in things.

At the time of the birth and youth of Alcoholics Anonymous, from 1934 through its self-proclaimed "Coming of Age" in 1955, the understandings that "the alcoholic" was a person who "had alcoholism" and that alcoholism was a disease were commonplace in the professional literature. As a report of the Scientific Committee of the Research Council on Problems of Alcohol put it in 1938: "An alcoholic should be regarded as a sick person, just as one who is suffering from tuberculosis, cancer, heart disease, or other serious chronic disorder" (Johnson, 1973, p. 244). Those doubting that "disease" was the orthodoxy before Alcoholics Anonymous came onto the scene should read Genevieve Parkhurst's (1937) "Drinking and Alcoholism" in *Harpers Magazine*. From the mid-1940s on, at first from a base within Yale University's Center of Alcohol Studies, the National Committee on Education on Alcoholism–later the National Council on Alcoholism–actively pushed this understanding under the guiding hand of Mrs. Marty Mann (Roizen, 2001). Few in that era questioned the terminology or its assumptions: Alcoholism-understood-as-disease "worked" and thus passed the pragmatic criterion of truth that ruled the age of World War II and its immediate aftermath. What it "worked" at doing, as Dwight Anderson had set forth even before Ms. Mann arrived on the scene, was to elicit the kind of attention and concern that led to help for the alcoholic (Anderson 1942).

But the setting of the RCPA and Howard Haggard's early Yale efforts were only background, and in fact a context to which A.A. almost from its beginnings contributed. For as co-founder Bill Wilson's personal history and the opening of the book *Alcoholics Anonymous* attest, A.A.'s early understanding of alcoholism came to it directly from Dr. William Duncan Silkworth, who viewed alcoholism as a manifestation of allergy. As set forth in "The Doctor's Opinion" introduction to *Alcoholics Anonymous* (2001), what A.A. learned from Dr. Silkworth was that:

> . . . the body of the alcoholic is quite as abnormal as his mind. It does not satisfy us to be told that we cannot control our drinking just because we were maladjusted to life, that we were in full flight from reality, or were outright mental defectives. These things were true to some extent, in fact, to a considerable extent with some of us. But we are sure that our bodies were sickened as well. In our belief, any picture of the alcoholic which leaves out this physical factor is incomplete.
>
> The doctor's theory that we have a kind of allergy to alcohol interests us. As laymen, our opinion as to its soundness may, of course, mean little. But as ex-alcoholics, we can say that his explanation makes good sense. It explains many things for which we cannot otherwise account. (A.A. World Services, 2001, p. xxvi)

As centrally important as Silkworth's "allergy" and "obsession" ideas were to prove in the continuing understanding that members of Alcoholics Anonymous had of themselves, there is an even deeper significance and contribution tucked away in his "Doctor's Opinion" letter in the A.A. Big Book, where he also noted that: "We doctors have realized for a long time that some form of moral psychology was of urgent importance to alcoholics. . . ." (A.A. World Services, 2001, p. xxvii). Therein lie both the problem and the promise of any investigation of Alcoholics Anonymous and the disease concept of alcoholism. For *disease* in its many names has also long served as metaphor (Sontag, 1978; Kurtz, 1979), and "moral psychology" hints of a realm beyond the physical. Our study of Alcoholics Anonymous and the disease concept of alcoholism, then, will necessarily involve more than the obvious, first-level, physical-science aspect of that question. Again, recall that p. 44 "definition" of alcoholism as "an illness which only a spiritual experience will conquer" (A.A. World Services, 2001).

A supplementary note on the meaning of *disease* in early Alcoholics Anonymous, at least to its most medically educated member: In 1938, while preparing the manuscript of the A.A. Big Book, Bill Wilson asked Dr. Bob Smith (a proctologist) about the accuracy of referring to alcoholism as disease or one of its synonyms. Bob's reply, scribbled in a large hand on a small sheet of his letterhead, read: "Have to use disease–sick–only way to get across *hopelessness,*" the final word doubly underlined and written in even larger letters (Smith [Akron] to Wilson, 15 June 1938).

Reading through the Big Book stories that mention Dr. Smith, one finds consistent emphasis on the thematic reminder that an alcoholic cannot safely drink alcohol ever again. (See for example the almost paradigmatic story of Bill D., "Alcoholics Anonymous Number Three," p. 187 of the second edition.) A.A. may be a "day at a time program," but the admission of powerlessness over alcohol, the surrender to hopelessness, could not be a retractable event, and if the way to get this across was to talk in terms of "disease" or "allergy," then thus would A.A.s carry their message. Certainly Dr. Bob, who had his own "slip" after his first meeting with Bill Wilson, had no doubt about the importance of remembering this facet of his own alcoholism.

As has long been recognized by scholars, any study of Alcoholics Anonymous presents unique difficulties (Bebbington, 1976; Miller & Kurtz, 1994). Not only the anonymity of the fellowship but the emphasis on "spirituality" in its program and its utterly anarchical structure render all generalizations problematic. Especially in recent years also, since the burgeoning of so-called "Twelve-Step Programs," the common popularity of Alcoholics Anonymous has led to much misinformation (Kurtz, 1996). Nor, indeed, is all the error "misinformation": *Varieties* have become the keynote of the contemporary Alcoholics Anonymous experience. Virtually the only valid generalization about Alcoholics Anonymous is that there is none, save that its members have "the desire to stop drinking," the listed membership requirement–and even that has been recently challenged by some non-alcoholic drug addicts who wish to attend closed (members only) A.A. meetings.

But we need not wrestle with these later complexities, for our topic is first an historical one. Our first question, then, is what members of Alcoholics Anonymous thought and taught in the years when the disease concept of alcoholism attained prominence and became, for most, the usual way of understanding the phenomenon of alcoholic drinking–a term then understood to be characterized by a lack of control over one's drinking (Keller, 1960; 1972; 1976; 1982). And our first research question becomes what sources are to be used in our study. No A.A. member sober before 1942 is still alive. Some of that first generation recorded their memories in later years, and those recollections are useful, although the accuracy of many of those narrations is open to question. At times, interviewers patently led their subjects into their own agenda; in other cases, the "high-event" setting of a special occasion evoked ritual remembrance rather than actual memories.

Where, then, do we turn? Members of Alcoholics Anonymous have been and are those who say that they are members of Alcoholics Anonymous; those who say they are members of Alcoholics Anonymous are those who are self-defined members of Alcoholics Anonymous. The main source of such self-descriptions–"stories [that] disclose in a general way what we used to be like, what happened, and what we are like now" (A.A. World Services, 2001, p. 58), in the hallowed words of the A.A. Big Book–are, of course, the stories told by members of Alcoholics Anonymous. We find these stories in especially two places: the book *Alcoholics Anonymous* and the monthly publication *The A.A. Grapevine*. Both sources have flow: *The A.A. Grapevine* by its periodical nature, and the A.A. Big Book by virtue of its successive editions. Originally published in 1939, the second edition of *Alcoholics Anonymous* appeared in 1955, the third in 1976, and the fourth in 2001.

The model stories, of course, are those contained in the book *Alcoholics Anonymous*, and not least "Bill's Story," with which that book opens, and the story of Dr. Bob Smith that begins its "Personal Stories" section. Key to both founding stories is the principle reflected in A.A.'s Fifth Tradition: "Each [A.A.] group has but one primary purpose–to carry its message to the alcoholic who still suffers." Alcoholics Anonymous began because Bill Wilson carried his message to Dr. Bob Smith, and A.A. began to grow because they both went to carry their message to "A.A. Number Three," Bill D. The message, of course, is that recovery is possible. And that message is conveyed by the presence of someone who *has* recovered from alcoholism telling the story of that recovery.

In order to understand the relationship of Alcoholics Anonymous to the disease concept of alcoholism–indeed, in order to understand *anything* about Alcoholics Anonymous–it is necessary to get inside the minds of its first generation, those drinkers who turned to the fellowship and its program out of desperation and then went on, as part of their recovery, to carry the message of their recovery to other alcoholics. This is not an easy task in an age when the popularization of alcoholism treatment and various forms of legal and/or moral coercion incline most to think that they "know about" alcoholism. Even the word *desperation* may cause pause: with so many and so varied helps available for those whose lives are disrupted by their drinking of alcohol, why should anyone in such a situation feel desperate?

But such were not the realities when Alcoholics Anonymous came into being. And understanding the story of A.A.'s relationship with the disease concept of alcoholism requires an imaginative leap into that history, a stripping away of what we think we know about alcoholism, a forgetting of all the supposed gains of the modern alcoholism movement, an ignoring of what the National Council on Alcoholism and Drug Dependence in its various incarnations and other agencies, governmental and private, have propagandized for well over the past half century.

The stories in the first edition of the book *Alcoholics Anonymous* help ease that leap. What was it like to be an alcoholic in the 1940s? The term *alcoholic* may trouble some, but we need not get into distinctions between alcohol abuse and alcohol dependence, problem drinking or chronic alcoholism. The designation *alcoholic* was used at the time, and it meant simply the description offered in the A.A. Big Book of "alcoholics like us"–drinkers who can stop drinking but who apparently cannot stay stopped. They want to stop getting drunk. They mean to stop getting drunk. They resolve to stop getting drunk. But their experience tells them, time and time and time again, that they *cannot* stop getting drunk. We are not looking here for scientific precision: our goal is rather human experience as expressed and understood in that era (see Peabody, 1931; Strecker & Chambers, 1938).

And the main thing that the human experience of the alcoholic tells him–certainly in the 1940s but likely also in the 2000s–is that he, or she, does not understand, cannot grasp, what is going on. To an extent probably inconceivable to most who glibly converse about alcoholism, the alcoholic at what A.A. calls "bottom" is terrified. We are taught to value control. To be civilized, to be human, is to be in control, certainly in control of oneself. And we do control much. In fact, the successful drinking alcoholic who remains employed is a wizard of control. To devote most of one's energy to appearing to be successfully in control but to know within oneself that one is out of control–this is terror.

The terror resides in "What is *wrong* with me?!" Just stop there, with those words, with that word. Don't gloss the phrase or ask, "Why?" Just realize that something is terribly, horribly *wrong* with you, and you do not have any idea what it is. Of course, other people do. Others are all too willing to tell you what is wrong with you. We need not rehearse their diagnostic explanations, which range from the religious to the psychological to the physical to the volitional and back again. What we do need to understand, if we would grasp the origins of Alcoholics Anonymous and its earliest members' understanding of alcoholism, is the dark pit of confused despair on the brink of which every alcoholic teetered back in the enlightened decades of the 1930s and 1940s.[1]

Let me reiterate the point for the sake of accurate emphasis: the chief characteristic of those whose lives were disrupted by the drinking of alcohol sufficient to move them to look into Alcoholics Anonymous, however cursorily, was that they did not understand what was going on within themselves.

For whatever reasons of compassionate listening or experience-based theoretical insight, Dr. William Duncan Silkworth captured what this experience of alcoholism felt like to the early members of Alcoholics Anonymous in his famed "The Doctor's Opinion" Preface to the A.A. Big Book. Recall again the words of the earliest A.A. members: "The doctor's theory . . . interests us. As laymen, our opinion as to its soundness may, of course, mean little. But as ex-alcoholics [later changed to "ex-problem drinkers"], we can say that his explanation makes good sense. *It explains many things for which we cannot otherwise account* (A.A. World Services, 2001, p. xxvi, emphasis added).

A chief point of this paper is that at least into the mid-1970s, most individuals who approached Alcoholics Anonymous were confused to the point of being terrified because they did not understand what was happening to them. Some, many, reached out desperately to any explanation that came along, from oral fixation to "momism" to latent homosexuality–at least it afforded "an answer." But continuing experience soon taught the thinness of those answers.

What Alcoholics Anonymous did, generally by using the words and ideas of Dr. Silkworth, was to suggest an understanding, an explanation, that "fit"–that *explained many things for which we could not otherwise account* . . . that meshed with the actual, lived experience of these alcoholics. The question for these individuals was not "moral or medical": most were individuals of high ideals all too ready to recognize and acknowledge their moral or behavioral deficiencies. They also knew that they were not "Skid Row bums," though many feared that they might end up as such. Most also knew, despite the rhetorical flourishes of Marty Mann and a few others, that they were not evil people, moral reprobates. As their stories make consistently and abundantly clear, they were *idealists*, and recognized themselves as such even as they struggled with the pain of their constant falling short (see especially the second edition: A.A. World Services, 1955).

But there is a larger point in Dr. Silkworth's words: "We doctors have realized for a long time that some form of moral psychology was of urgent importance to alcoholics. . . ." (A.A. World Services, 2001, p. xxvii). We no longer speak of "moral psychology"; but Alcoholics Anonymous has been a large force in accustoming us to speak of *spirituality* (Kurtz, 1996).

For what the earliest members of Alcoholics Anonymous did was not so much to embrace the already extant disease concept of alcoholism as to expand it. In the text of the book *Alcoholics Anonymous* itself, the word *disease* appears only once–in the term *spiritual disease*. And nearby, also on page 64, we read, ". . . we have been not only physically and mentally ill, we have been spiritually sick." The contribution of Alcoholics Anonymous is not the idea of *disease* but of *threefold* disease–the realization that the alcoholic had problems in the physical, the mental, and the spiritual realms, the clear understanding that alcoholism is "an illness which only a spiritual experience will conquer."[2]

Two things characterize the stories in the first edition of the book *Alcoholics Anonymous*, and neither of them is mention of disease, illness, or even "sick." The first is sheer amazement at the discovery that someone else had thoughts and feelings about their drinking of alcohol similar if not identical to their own. The "secret" of Alcoholics Anonymous, the thing that makes A.A. work, is *identification*. As Marty Mann is reputed to have said to her fellow sanitarium inmate on returning to Blythwood from her visit to the Wilson home in Brooklyn Heights for her first A.A. meeting: "Grennie, we aren't alone any more" (A.A. World Services, 1953, p. 18).

The second striking characteristic of the stories in the first edition of the A.A. Big Book is a not dissimilar amazement over the centrality of "the spiritual." Most of the stories in the first edition of the book *Alcoholics Anonymous* came from the nascent fellowship's Akron members: there were twice as many sober in Akron as in New York, and even as the book-writing process unfolded, the Akronites also revealed a steadier sobriety, less tendency to relapse. A constant theme in Akron, soon echoed and expanded by those who visited there from Cleveland, Chicago, Detroit and other midwestern points in order to be hospitalized and have their detoxification supervised by Dr. Smith, concerned the impact made on them by the simple fact that this M.D., this physician, when he spoke with them about their drinking, spoke mainly if not only about "the spiritual." Explicit emphasis on the spiritual evidences itself differently in the stories of the New Yorkers, most of whom had been proudly agnostic when they first encountered Alcoholics Anonymous (A.A. World Services, 1955).

The centrality of spiritual change as essential to its program was recognized by the first scholars who examined Alcoholics Anonymous, though as good scientists they did not let the word "spiritual" escape their pens. Bowman and Jellinek in their 1941 *Quarterly Journal of Studies on Alcohol* article, "Alcohol Addiction and Its Treatment," after citing the A.A. Big Book as well as Silkworth's (1939) two articles mentioning A.A. (and his two 1937 pieces on "allergy"), observed: "Religious conversion without the aid of 'preaching' and of the 'holier-than-thou' attitude is the fundamental idea of the Fellowship of AA. Although they insist that alcohol addiction is also a physical disease, probably of an allergic nature, they consider the main cause to be emotional maladjustment" (Np.). As we shall see, the vocabulary of "emotional maladjustment" will consistently reappear in professional studies of Alcoholics Anonymous. It may clothe the idea of "disease," but its underlying import will always be that which A.A. members view as healed–made whole–by "the spiritual."

### THE A.A. GRAPEVINE

The book *Alcoholics Anonymous*, then, except for "The Doctor's Opinion," says little about disease and certainly attests that Alcoholics Anonymous did not originate the disease concept of alcoholism. The point is important not least because readers of the earliest issues of *The A.A. Grapevine* could be forgiven for thinking otherwise.

Especially in its early years, the *AAGV* seemed dedicated to spreading the disease concept of alcoholism. The very first article of the very first issue headlined: "Two Yale Savants Stress Alcoholism a True Disease," and the piece went on with a detailed description of the then-new Yale Plan Clinics.[3] Similar articles follow in succeeding months, and early Grapevine news stories describe mainly members of Alcoholics Anonymous setting up or aiding hospital programs for alcoholics. Indeed, most mentions of "sick" and "disease" appear in the context of seeking necessary medical and hospital care for the physically deteriorated drunks whom A.A. members were more and more seeking out.[4] Mann stated her point most clearly in a 1948 article on "The Alcoholic in the General Hospital" that appeared in *Southern Hospitals*: "It is our belief that the general hospital is the proper place for alcoholics in the acute stage of their illness. Hospitalization need not be of long duration–in most cases five days is found to be sufficient. Hospitalization for acute alcoholism is in no sense the same as the treatment of alcoholism itself, which may be, and usually is, a protracted affair" (Mann, 1948, p. 28).

There is, however, not that large a difference between the A.A. Big Book and *The A.A. Grapevine* on the question of *disease* if we take their very different contexts into account. In the first place, among the "six ink-stained wretches" who began the *AAGV* were Marty Mann and three of her women friends. Mann apparently saw this venture as another way of spreading the ideas that led her to form the National Committee for Education on Alcoholism, which is given much prominence in early *AAGV* stories. But Mann's involvement with the *AAGV* diminished as her NCEA activities expanded, and the publication's emphasis on the physical aspect of the physical-mental-spiritual triad decreased as time went on, though the pattern of attending to NCEA (and later NCA) interests endured.

Second, the mid-1940s were medically a very different time than the late 1930s. The Great Depression had ended and the "medical miracles" of the World War II years had sensitized people to the benefits of intensive medical care. Before the war, hospitalization had been regarded as unusual, a last resort. Now, sulfa drugs, penicillin and the advances in surgery that wars invariably bring began the long process of making medical treatment in hospitals the rule rather than the exception. Hospitals were where the very sick were treated, and many of their long-drinking friends to whom members of Alcoholics Anonymous carried their message were very sick with the physical manifestations of their decades of alcoholic drinking.

Third and perhaps most importantly, the *AAGV* began as a newsletter–at first as a local New York organ intended to serve as such other local A.A. publications as Cleveland's *Central Bulletin* and *The Eye-Opener* of Los Angeles, later as an effort to maintain a kind of unity at least by awareness of what was going on elsewhere, a task that became increasingly important with the ever-accelerating geographic spread of Alcoholics Anonymous in the post-World War II years. The concern for what would soon be codified as A.A.'s second legacy, *unity*, remained as "unofficial" as everything else about the *AAGV*, but its centrality is evident in both the journal's content and its internal documents.

Only later and only slowly did *The A.A. Grapevine* become what its current cover proclaims "Our meeting in print." Early issues contained no explicit stories. Those that began to sneak in appeared because another purpose of the *AAGV* was to keep A.A. members in the military services in some way connected with the fellowship. Quite a few of those military members wrote letters, that great infantry war pastime. Every issue from the first featured a "Mail Call for All A.A.'s in the Armed Forces." In briefest outline, these letters detailed some problem that had arisen, told of a circumstance or happening that led to its resolution, and then reflected on the gift of a life now enriched by having gone through that experience as well as by the sobriety that made it possible. Not exactly "what we used to be like, what happened, and what we are like now," but close enough to that outline to cement the relationship among "experience, strength, and hope." After the war, in the September 1945 issue, this became "Mail Call for All A.A.s at Home or Abroad," and the pattern continued for a time, until overtaken by the desire of members to discuss how they conducted meetings or initiated newcomers in their areas.

But "Mail Call" was not the only source of letters to the *AAGV*. Under the early heading "Points of View," the journal published comments about some of its articles. Early lead articles by non-A.A. members Philip (*Generation of Vipers*) Wylie and humorist S. J. Perelman invited comments, and features such as "The Children Say What A.A. Means to Them" kept up the flow. The April 1945 issue supplemented "Letters to The Grapevine" with "Tall, But True, Tales: As Told in A.A." It did not last under that title, but the next several issues each feature a fairly long letter telling the kind of story described in the A.A. Big Book–tales of "what we used to be like, what happened, and what we are like now" as they are told at A.A. meetings. Shortly after, in September 1945, there begin to appear "Vino Vignettes: Thumbnail A.A. Biographies," which more closely followed the pattern set forth in the Big Book's Chapter Five outline.

This lengthy excursion into the early *AAGV* is important because, despite the obvious NCEA-inclined bias of the journal as revealed in many of its news stories, there is rarely a mention of "disease" or "illness" or even "sick" in the more story-formatted selections. The topics were life-change, living through difficulties without taking a drink, handling "emotional extremes," what to do when a fellow member friend "slips," home-care of a detoxifying drunk, the dangers of some medications, and other subjects that had to do with "living sober."

Before continuing our exploration of the stories of members of Alcoholics Anonymous in *The A.A. Grapevine* and succeeding editions of the A.A. Big Book, chronology requires noting other events that bear on our topic of Alcoholics Anonymous and the disease concept of alcoholism. Invited, under the auspices of Dr. Harry Tiebout (A.A. World Services, 1957, pp. 2-3), to present a paper at the Annual Meeting of the Medical Society of the State of New York on May 9, 1944, co-founder Bill Wilson responded with the article published as "Basic Concepts of Alcoholics Anonymous" (Wilson, 1944). The piece delineates A.A.'s debts to both medicine (at times, "psychiatry") and religion, opening, after a brief, one-paragraph description of Alcoholics Anonymous, with the words: "Alcoholics Anonymous, or 'A.A.,' popularly so-called, has but one purpose–one objective only–'To help other alcoholics to recover from their illness' " (Wilson, 1944, p. 1805). Wilson then continues in a way that foreshadows what will soon become the significant A.A. central emphasis on the *threefold* nature of the alcoholic malady:

It is from you gentlemen we learn that alcoholism is a complex malady; that abnormal drinking is but a symptom of personal maladjustment to life; that, as a class, we alcoholics are apt to be sensitive, emotionally immature, grandiose in our demands on ourselves and others; that we have usually "gone broke" on some dream ideal of perfection; that, failing to realize the dream, we sensitive folk escape cold reality by taking to the bottle; that this habit of escape finally turns into an obsession, or, as you gentlemen put it, a compulsion to drink so subtly powerful that no disaster, however great, even near death or insanity, can, in most cases, seem to break it; that we are the victims of the age-old alcoholic dilemma: our obsession guarantees that we shall go on drinking, but our increasing physical sensitivity guarantees that we shall go insane or die if we do.

When these facts, coming from the mouths of you gentlemen of science, are poured by an A.A. member into the person of another alcoholic they strike deep–the effect is shattering. (Wilson, 1944, pp. 1807-1808)

Four years later, invited (again under the auspices of Dr. Tiebout) to present a paper at the 105th annual meeting of the American Psychiatric Association, held in Montreal, PQ, Canada, Wilson again reiterated and made clear whence Alcoholics Anonymous had derived its understanding of alcoholism not only as complex but as sickness–from the physicians themselves. After describing his own initial lack of success in attempting to work with alcoholics, Bill continued:

... religious practice [Bill's shorthand description of his own "spiritual experience"] would not touch the alcoholic until his underlying situation was made ready. Fortunately all the tools were at hand. You doctors supplied them.

The emphasis was straightway shifted from "sin" to "sickness"–the "*fatal malady,*" alcoholism [italics in original]. We quoted doctors that alcoholism was more lethal than cancer; that it consisted of an obsession of the mind coupled to increasing body sensitivity. These were our Twin Ogres of Madness and Death. (Wilson, 1949, p. 260)

Years later, describing his Montreal talk, Wilson recalled how after his presentation a past-president of the A.P.A. had noted to him that "outside of the few A.A.s in the room, and myself, I do not think a single one of my colleagues believed a word of your explanation." Bill expressed surprise, for he had been warmly applauded. ". . . the old man replied, 'Well, Mr. Wilson, you A.A.s have a hundred thousand recoveries and we in the psychiatric profession have only a few. They were applauding the results much more than the message' " (Wilson to Dr. John G., 9 October 1967). Another version of this story, retold by a longtime sober A.A. member, ran that Bill had been cautioned about the applause: "Don't take it too seriously: they were not applauding your ideas but your results. You see, they know that they have not had much luck with alcoholics, and they are grateful to A.A. for getting the alcoholics out of their hair."

"Improved" as both these stories may be, each well captures the point at issue here. Especially in the era in question, for physicians *or* psychiatrists, the question of alcoholism as disease involved more than a mere question of human physiology or psychology. The treatment of disease was a function of the science of medicine (Haynes, 1988). But here was a disability, "alcoholism," that had proven singularly unamenable to medical treatments. If physicians or psychiatrists could not cure or even treat it, how could it be disease? One attempted answer, the major psychiatric one, was to suggest that alcoholism was not disease but *symptom*. Yet this hardly solved the problem if even as symptom the phenomenon resisted medical/psychiatric intervention but became amenable to the approach of Alcoholics Anonymous.

In 1941, Bowman and Jellinek had cited the A.A. Big Book in explaining that members of Alcoholics Anonymous, "Although they insist that alcohol addiction is also a physical disease, probably of an allergic nature . . . consider the main cause to be emotional maladjustment" (Bowman & Jellinek, 1941). By the early 1950s, Bowman and Jellinek's "emotional maladjustment" as well as later psychiatric explanations of alcoholism had given way in A.A.'s own understanding to a focus on the *spiritual* dimensions and aspects of the alcoholic disease, malady, illness, sickness, whatever . . . and of recovery from it. Unsurprisingly, the desire arose to codify the emerging understanding–or at least to set it forth in a form available and acceptable to all members. And so Bill Wilson set out to write a book on the heart of the spirituality of both the program and the fellowship of Alcoholics Anonymous: *Twelve Steps and Twelve Traditions*.[5]

## TWELVE STEPS AND TWELVE TRADITIONS

The book *Twelve Steps and Twelve Traditions* (*12&12*) (A.A. World Services, 1953) says little about the disease concept of alcoholism; it offers much on all aspects of the spiritual dimensions of the alcoholic condition. One commentator suggested that this book "was A.A.'s New Testament–bringing to fruition the original revelation of the Big Book, *Alcoholics Anonymous* (Kurtz, 1991, p. 124). A more nuanced observation might suggest that one purpose of this later work was to shift attention from a possible overemphasis on the literal-physical to "the spiritual" aspect in danger of being overshadowed.

This is not the place to explore the many issues discussed in the "*12&12*," as it is usually referred to by members of Alcoholics Anonymous. Important for our purposes are two points: (1) the *12&12* says virtually nothing about alcoholism as physical disease; (2) the *12&12* does, sometimes in the vocabulary of psychology but most often in the language of spirituality, delineate at some length and in greater detail the spiritual aspects of the alcoholic condition, drinking or recovered. Thus, the book's discussion of Step One does mention that "our sponsors pointed out our increasing sensitivity to alcohol–an allergy, they called it" (p. 22). But the emphasis of the essay is on "personal powerlessness" and "complete defeat." Like the vocabulary of "instincts" that Wilson used in discussing the "moral inventory" of Step Four in the *12&12*, the language of disease, wherever it appears in not only in the *12&12* but in Alcoholics Anonymous in general, is more important for what it points to than for the signifier itself–and that to which both point is the spiritual condition of the alcoholic.

Bill began formal work on the articles that became *Twelve Steps and Twelve Traditions* only in 1952. Published first as a series of articles in *The A.A. Grapevine*, the book itself appeared in 1953, just as Wilson set off on two other projects, the examination of which will carry forward our exploration of Alcoholics Anonymous and the disease concept of alcoholism: (1) the revision of the "story section" for the second edition of the book *Alcoholics Anonymous*, published in 1955; and (2) the telling of A.A.'s own story in the book that would be published in 1957 as *Alcoholics Anonymous Comes of Age (AACA)* (1957). Although not a formal or documented history, exhaustive research went into the production of *AACA*, and so what is says about the disease concept of alcoholism merits attention.

In both *Twelve Steps and Twelve Traditions* (1953) and *Alcoholics Anonymous Comes of Age (1957)*, more important than what is there is what is *not* there. Here, in two of the three major texts of Alcoholics Anonymous, there appeared no discussion and bare mention of "disease," much less of the disease concept of alcoholism. This is a not insignificant omission. Yes, many members of Alcoholics Anonymous did speak in terms of their alcoholism as disease. But its paucity of mention in the officially published works of the period suggests that this understanding was hardly central to the thought of Alcoholics Anonymous. The books were self-conscious central statements of the A.A. program and the A.A. fellowship's own story. Each was intended to be as definitive as the context allowed. Such situations do not invite silence about assumptions, no matter how widely assumed to be held. The vocabulary of "disease" was common because it was handy. The reality of disease was a matter of assumption but not necessarily of conviction. If it were as central as some claim, we would hear more about it in these two cornerstone works of what some like to call "the A.A. ideology" (Ogborne & Glaser, 1981; Skinner, 1994).

That context may be even better appreciated if we take a moment to revisit to *The A.A. Grapevine* of the early 1950s. Following its newsletter style, that journal in March 1952 offered an article: "Stethoscope and Periscope: The Doctors Look at Alcohol." Subtitled "A Grapevine Medical Report," the piece noted "[t]hat there is a strong new beat to the pulse of the medical profession's recognition of alcoholism as a disease is indicated by even a casual survey of current medical journals." It went on to offer brief–and accurate–report-summaries of the articles (A.A. World Services, 1952a, Np.).

Two months later, in May 1952, an article titled "AA and GPs: Family Doctors Study the 'Problem Drinker' " listed speakers at the Fourth Annual Scientific Assembly of General Practice. Bill Wilson noted in the piece that "It was a little doctor who loved drunks, the late William Duncan Silkworth, who first told me that alcoholism was a disease, and gave me thereby an indispensable basis for AA's later developed therapy" (A.A. World Services, 1952b, Np.). The listed program on "The Problem Drinker," into which Alcoholics Anonymous had no input, stated: "The alcoholic becomes a problem to the family physician. Alcoholism is now recognized as a form of illness. As such it is medicine's responsibility to study, treat, and attempt preventive measures in this disorder of human behavior" (Np.).

Also first published by the General Service Office (later "Alcoholics Anonymous World Services") in 1952 was the still-in-print-in-2000 A.A. pamphlet, "A.A.–44 Questions." Since some tend to refer to this brochure out of context, here is its complete answer to the question, "What is Alcoholism?"

> *What is Alcoholism?* There are many different ideas about what alcoholism really is. The explanation that seems to make sense to most A.A. members is that alcoholism is an illness, a *progressive* illness, which can never be cured but which, like some other illnesses, *can* be arrested. Going one step further, many A.A.s feel that the illness represents the combination of a physical sensitivity to alcohol and a mental obsession with drinking, which, regardless of consequences, cannot be broken by willpower alone [italics in the original]. (A.A. World Services, 1952c, p. 4)

Note the too-often overlooked qualifications: "many different ideas"; "seems to make sense to most A.A. members"; "many A.A.s feel." Such is not the vocabulary of doctrine. Did A.A.s use the disease concept of alcoholism? Yes. Did A.A.s or A.A. originate or rediscover or dogmatically push the disease concept of alcoholism? Clearly, no.

## THE SECOND EDITION OF ALCOHOLICS ANONYMOUS

The main difference in the "new and revised" second edition of the book *Alcoholics Anonymous* was its expanded section of "Personal Stories." The first 164 pages of the text, as is well-known, remained unchanged with a few exceptions: the second printing's reduction of the first printing's old-style capitalizations remained, as did the eleventh printing's change from "ex-alcoholics" to "ex-problem drinkers." Silkworth's "The Doctor's Opinion" was now paginated in Roman numerals, with the intended result that the book proper now began on page one with "Bill's Story."

The stated main purpose of the expanded story section was to broaden the bases for identification. With one exception, the first edition's storytellers had been middle-class, middle-aged white males whose alcoholic drinking had cost or at least seriously jeopardized comfortably stable employment. By the early 1950s there were women in A.A.–about one in five members were female. And there were Blacks in A.A.–in fact, there was "a Negro Group" in three separate cities. But most importantly, since the mid-1940s, "high-bottom" drunks had appeared in A.A.–those who, in the heading over their stories–"stopped in time" (Kurtz, 1979, p. 132; A.A. World Services, 1957, p. 199). The fellowship was especially interested in attracting more of these, mainly for the altruistic reason of saving others from the horrors they themselves had undergone. Despite the genuineness of this effort, only three of the stories that appeared in the second edition recount "high bottom" experiences (Kurtz, 1979, p. 132).

But more to our purposes, of the thirty-seven stories in the second edition, twenty-one make absolutely no mention of disease, illness, malady, or even "sick." Of those that do mention "disease," all but two emphasize the *progressive* nature of the alcoholic malady–a clear reflection of the aim to motivate those who had not yet reached absolute bottom. This edition did offer Marty Mann's story, "Women Suffer Too": if anything, its strident emphasis on "disease" makes the absence of that advertence in most of the other stories all the more striking (A.A. World Services, 1955). The other heavy "disease" story presents a similar problem. The author of "A Flower of the South," which appears in the "They Stopped in Time" section, tells how she was given the Jack Alexander (1941) *Saturday Evening Post* article on A.A.

> I could see that horrible picture of the awful drunk on the first page; he couldn't get the drink to his mouth, he had a towel around his hand and he needed a shave. But, from the very first paragraph on, something happened to me. I realized that there were other people in this world who behaved and acted as I did, and that I was a sick person, that I was suffering

from an actual disease. It had a name and symptoms, just like diabetes or T.B. I wasn't entirely immoral; I wasn't bad; I wasn't vicious. It was such a feeling of relief that I wanted to know more about it and with that, I think for the first time, came the realization that there was something horribly, horribly wrong with me. Up to that time, I was so completely baffled by my behavior that I had never really stopped to think at all. (A.A. World Services, 1955, p. 351; see also Roizen, 2001)

One wonders whence that realization came, since there is no mention of "disease" or "illness" or "malady" or even "sick," not to mention of "immoral" or "vicious" in the Jack Alexander article (Alexander, 1941, pp. 89-90).

As with many of the first edition stories, Dr. Bob's personal spirituality was emphasized by all who mention him (A.A. World Services, 1955, pp. 217-219). When illness or disease are mentioned, it is almost in passing, never even nearly as central as in the stories of Mann and "A Flower of the South." Sometimes, the topic entered as humor:

My sister heard about this [his wife leaving], and she came running over to the house and says to my wife, "Now wait a minute, before you do a tragic thing like this and leave my brother! Do you realize he is a sick man?" Boy, I thought that I was out of this world–such kind words as "a sick man"! You ought to hear what my family called me before that! (A.A. World Services, 1955, p. 446)

## ALCOHOLICS ANONYMOUS COMES OF AGE

Published in 1957 but based largely on oral presentations given at A.A.'s "Coming of Age" Twentieth Anniversary Convention held in St. Louis in 1955, *Alcoholics Anonymous Comes of Age* is A.A.'s first telling of its own story. History, the accurate history of the A.A. Fellowship, was important to Bill Wilson. For one thing, he had abandoned his exploration of Christian Science as a possible cure for his drinking problem when he found, so he thought, that the organization had falsified its history (Thomsen, 1975). More importantly and practically, as Alcoholics Anonymous spread and grew, different local "origin stories" sprang up in some locales, and occasional arguments over historical points seemed in places to threaten the Fellowship's unity.

And so Wilson set out, beginning in 1954, to record his own recollections and those of as many old-timers as he could arrange to interview. Drawing on the General Service Office's files of inquiry correspondence, he also sent countless letters to those who had started or attempted to start groups, especially in new places, asking for information on the early groups that had begun . . .

or failed. Bill presented the tentative results in his talks at St. Louis in 1955. The book *Alcoholics Anonymous Comes of Age* consists mainly of those presentations, but changes and additions were made in response to conflicting or simply diverse memories elicited by Wilson's St. Louis talks and his distribution of a preliminary draft of the manuscript.

But historiography is not the point here. What is significant is that, given the often assumed centrality of the disease concept of alcoholism to Alcoholics Anonymous, one would expect prominent mention if not explicit discussion of so central an idea. If it were really so central, one would no doubt find it. At the very least, if "disease" had substantive importance, someone in the vast correspondence over the draft would surely have remarked on the absence of its mention. But such is not the case: the dog does not bark. Wilson describes his interaction with Dr. Silkworth in familiar Big Book terms, but with no glosses or added evidence. In the book's eagerness to recognize both "medicine and religion" as sources of Alcoholics Anonymous, presentations by the Rev. Samuel Shoemaker and Father Edward Dowling balance those of American Medical Association President Dr. W. W. Bauer and Dr. Harry M. Tiebout. The book offers much on the acceptance of A.A. by the medical profession; it offers nothing on "disease" beyond the familiar Silkworth ideas of obsession and allergy.

A significant mention does turn up in Wilson's retelling of his first meeting with Dr. Bob Smith. In both Big Book tellings of Dr. Bob's story—"A Vision for You" and "Dr. Bob's Nightmare"—the details of Bill's presentation at their first meeting are sparse. In St. Louis, however, Wilson offered a new detail, one relevant to our larger topic:

> In our first conversation I bore down heavily on the medical hopelessness of Dr. Bob's case, freely using Dr. Silkworth's words describing the alcoholic's dilemma, the "obsession plus allergy" theme. Though Bob was a doctor, this was news to him, bad news. Always better versed in spiritual matters than I, he had paid little attention to that aspect of my story. Even though he could not make them work, he already knew what the spiritual answers were. What really did hit him hard was the medical business, the verdict of inevitable annihilation. And the fact that I was an alcoholic and knew what I was talking about from personal experience made the blow a shattering one. (A.A. World Services, 1957, pp. 69-70)

As noted, this is a significant mention. What seems more significant is that so far as I am aware, no one in or out of Alcoholics Anonymous has ever picked up on this passing mention to make anything of it concerning A.A. and the disease concept of alcoholism.

Perhaps that was because the main mention of "disease" at the 1955 convention and in the 1957 book came from Dr. W. W. Bauer, who offered the first of two presentations on "Medicine Looks at Alcoholics Anonymous." Bauer represented the American Medical Association. Unlike Dr. Harry Tiebout, who followed him to the platform, Bauer was not a psychiatrist. He might as well have been, for his theme was that the alcoholic is "a sick person," someone afflicted by "emotional illness." Concluding, he again reminded his audience "how important it is that people realize what alcoholism really is: a devastating emotional illness that must be treated according to psychosomatic principles" (A.A. World Services, 1957, pp. 237-244). If members of Alcoholics Anonymous came away from St. Louis in 1955 convinced that they suffered a "real disease," it was not by other A.A. members that understanding had been reinforced.

### A JOSTLING FROM OUTSIDE: THE COURTS, THE SUPREME COURT, AND THE CONGRESS OF THE U.S.A.

The disease concept of alcoholism became a legal issue when the social changes of the 1960s moved attention from alcoholism itself to public drunkenness. As an issue connected with broader understandings of addiction, it ranges far beyond the borders of our focused inquiry on Alcoholics Anonymous and the disease concept of alcoholism. We must nevertheless touch on it, for the role of the many A.A. members in the National Council on Alcoholism and the testimony of A.A. co-founder Bill W. before a Senate subcommittee preparing what become known as "The Hughes Act" are a part of our story.

For a surprisingly long period after its "Coming of Age" in 1955, Alcoholics Anonymous grew peacefully, with little direct attention to its understanding and presentation of alcoholism. The fellowship weathered its trustee-ratio change and the first attacks launched on it in the national press. At Toronto in 1965, it adopted its "Declaration": "I Am Responsible. When anyone, anywhere, reaches out for help, I want the hand of A.A. always to be there. And for that: I am responsible." There were a few who wished to see that sense of responsibility extended even further, but true to A.A. tradition on "outside issues," most in the fellowship were happy to leave the "politics of disease" front to the National Council on Alcoholism and its redoubtable director, Mrs. Marty Mann. One claim imputed to Marty was that "N.C.A. will do the things A.A. cannot do." Some, but not even nearly all, members of N.C.A. were also members of A.A.; most members of A.A. were not members of and had little interest in N.C.A. (Kurtz, 1979, Ch. 6).

The issue of the era, by the late 1960s, had become public intoxication or drunkenness as crime. Could someone be arrested and jailed simply because they were drunk in public? Most jurisdictions had statutes against public drunkenness, but there now evolved what Carolyn Wiener has well described as "building an arena around a social problem" (Wiener, 1981).

Largely because of the presence of the National Council on Alcoholism and its passion to make alcoholics, if not alcoholism, respectable, Alcoholics Anonymous could remain uninvolved in this arena and the significant court decisions that issued from the struggles in it–the Easter, Driver, and Powell cases. For those forgetful of the details, in 1965 and 1966, in the cases of DeWitt Easter and Joe Driver, respectively, the United States Court of Appeals for the District of Columbia and the United States Court of Appeals for the Fourth District both unanimously reversed earlier convictions for public intoxication. The DC court held that because Easter "was a chronic alcoholic," he could not be convicted for behavior that was an involuntary product of his disease (Johnson, 1973, pp. 114, 142). The Fourth Circuit Court of Appeals stated in its decision: "The addiction–chronic alcoholism–is now almost universally accepted medically as a disease" (Johnson, pp. 115, 142).

In 1968, after much maneuvering by attorney Peter Barton Hutt and the American Civil Liberties Union (but not the N.C.A.), the case of Leroy Powell was accepted by the United States Supreme Court. The court, in a 5 to 4 decision, upheld Powell's conviction for public drunkenness by the State of Texas on the grounds that he did have access to a residence and so did not have to be intoxicated in a public place. Key to the Texas decision had been three "findings of fact" made by the trial judge in the original county court:

1. "That chronic alcoholism is a disease which destroys the afflicted person's will power to resist the constant, excessive consumption of alcohol.
2. That a chronic alcoholic does not appear in public by his own volition but under a compulsion symptomatic of the disease of chronic alcoholism.
3. That Leroy Powell, defendant herein, is a chronic alcoholic who is afflicted with the disease of chronic alcoholism."

Four Supreme Court Justices (Fortas, Brennan, Douglas and Stewart) agreed with those findings and sought to bring Powell under the protection of the Court's 1962 reversal in Robinson v. State of California, in which it stated that the criminal justice system could punish acts, but not a "status" (Powell v. State of Texas, 1968, retrieved from *http://wings.buffalo.edu/law/bclc/web/powell.htm*) and (Robinson v. State of California, 1962, retrieved from *http://wings.buffalo.edu/law/bclc/web/robinson.htm*).

The lead decision, however, written by Justice Marshall and concurred in by Chief Justice Warren and Justices Black and Harlan, strongly repudiated that attempt to extend Robinson and stated in what became, with Justice White's partial concurrence, the official decision that (1) that the Texas court's " 'findings of fact' are not 'findings of fact' in any recognizable, traditional sense in which that term has been used in a court of law; they are the premises of a syllogism. . . ." and (2) that "the inescapable fact is that there is no agreement among members of the medical profession about what it means to say that 'alcoholism' is a 'disease,' " citing E. M. Jellinek (1960) on the topic as its authority. Justice White's opinion, in concurring with Justices Black's and Harlan's concurrence with the opinion of Justice Marshall, implied acceptance of alcoholism as a disease but focused on "public" aspect of the charge against Powell and the fact that he did have access to a residence.

Argument still flourishes about both the interpretation of the Court's opinions and the role of the National Council on Alcoholism in this outcome. For in the Powell case, somewhat shifting its previous stand, the N.C.A. less than wholeheartedly joined the list of *amicus curiae* when the case went to the Supreme Court, apparently because of its concern with the image of the alcoholic in the eyes of the American people. Leroy Powell was literally a Skid Row bum. But throughout N.C.A.'s history, Marty Mann, Ruth Fox, Yev Gardner, and others had worked to portray the "typical alcoholic" as an industrious and conscientious person who was the unfortunate victim of a disease. Supporting Powell, it was feared, could reinforce the down-and-out stereotype. A more active stance by N.C.A., some argue, would have brought Justice White into the explicitly "disease" column headed by Justice Fortas. According to Nancy Olson, Professional Staff Associate on matters dealing with alcoholism for the Hughes Subcommittee, "Hutt [later told me] that Marty told him, after the Hughes Act had created the National Institute on Alcohol Abuse and Alcoholism, that she had been wrong" (Personal communications of April 7 & 8, 2001). Five-to-four decisions, of course, often continue to be argued among interested parties. An independent observer, historian Bruce Holley Johnson, in his 1973 dissertation on *The Alcohol Movement in America: A Study in Cultural Innovation*, held that "The Supreme Court of the United States, in other words, remained unconvinced that habitual drunkenness is, in fact, a disease" (Johnson, 1973, p. 373).

Whether medical "truth" can be decided by Court judgment seems best left to the discussions of social constructionists and their adversaries. For our purposes here, the main social and cultural result of the Powell decision is that it provided the proximate context for Senator Harold Hughes's involvement in alcoholism legislation. In mid-1969, the National Institute on Mental Health was planning to start funding alcoholism service grants under the Community Mental Health Centers Act of 1963. The newly-elected Senator Hughes, former three-term Governor of Iowa who had publically identified himself as "a recovered alcoholic," had just become chairman of the Special Subcommittee on Alcoholism and Narcotics (later named the Subcommittee on Alcoholism and Drug Abuse) of the Senate Labor and Public Welfare Committee (as it was then named). In Iowa, Governor Hughes had established an alcoholism treatment program, presenting it as an "alternative to the state mental hospitals" and an attempt to "reach alcoholics before they reach rock bottom" (Remembering Harold Hughes, Nd., Para 13). Now in the Senate, Hughes introduced the "Comprehensive Alcohol Abuse and Alcoholism Prevention, Treatment and Rehabilitation Act." This bill, after appropriate hearings, passed both Houses of Congress and was signed into law by President Richard M. Nixon on December 31, 1970, as Public Law 91-616. From the beginning, it was popularly known as the "Hughes Act" (Remembering Harold Hughes, Nd., Para. 2).

The provisions of the Hughes Act, especially its establishment of grant programs in support of treatment, would profoundly change everything concerning alcoholism and its treatment in the culture of the United States. Before turning to examine the effects this had on the relationship between Alcoholics Anonymous and the disease concept of alcoholism, it is useful to glance at the testimony of "Bill W., Cofounder of Alcoholics Anonymous," before the Hughes Committee on July 24, 1969.

Wilson followed Marty Mann to the microphone that morning. His presentation had two parts: (1) a recital of current statistics on Alcoholics Anonymous ("15,000 A.A. groups throughout the world and an active membership of 285,000"); and (2) the by now familiar retelling of his own story, beginning with Rowland H.'s efforts with Dr. Karl [*sic*] Jung, through his own "spiritual experience," to his May 1935 meeting with Dr. Bob Smith, to the publication of the A.A. Big Book, concluding with the "final suggestion, that the resources of Alcoholics Anonymous for mass society have hardly been touched." The main problem A.A. faced, Wilson testified, was the "mass capacity of the alcoholic to rationalize himself out of his predicament." The answer? "It is a process of education, but what kind of education we simply do not know. Another part of the resistance to Alcoholics Anonymous stems from the fact that it has a spiritual content and a great many of our professional friends are apt to believe that Alcoholics Anonymous is for the religiously susceptible only" (U.S. Government Printing Office, 1969).

Not a mention, nor even a hint, then, of "disease" or "illness" or even "sick." And given the linking by proximity of the final two ideas quoted, a case could be made that Wilson's largest concern was the "education" of "our professional friends." But Senator Hughes chose not to hear that and instead reframed a point Bill had made to connect it with his own interest in *treatment*:

I take it from your testimony that as a cofounder of A.A. you certainly believe that in any program this committee and this Congress might develop, that there would be a place and a willingness for A.A. members to work in recovery, education, and counseling of the ailing alcoholics and prevention also?

Possibly wondering whether that was all Hughes understood as "the resources of Alcoholics Anonymous for mass society," Wilson replied: "I should think so. Of course, this is the pleasure of our friends." Presciently he added: "I don't like to see outside agencies just loaded up with A.A." The topics of the rationale for treatment or A.A.'s or Bill's own ideas on alcoholism-as-disease did not arise, perhaps because of Senator Hughes's own respect for A.A.'s co-founder and its Twelve Traditions.

But led by the N.C.A. and pushed on by Brinkley Smithers, the momentum for passage had been achieved, and those committed first and foremost to "treatment" triumphed as "The Hughes Act" was signed into law. The multifarious details and ultimate ramifications of Public Law 91-616 thankfully need not detain us here. Our interest remains Alcoholics Anonymous and the disease concept of alcoholism. Whether the Hughes Act gave federal government blessing to the disease concept, it was certainly thought to do so at the time–though this is a question less of research than of exegesis.

As Wilson's 1969 testimony hinted, enthusiasm for the Hughes Act was not universal within Alcoholics Anonymous. Certainly many members beyond Hughes, Mann and Smithers welcomed the promise of greater help for alcoholics without seeing the dangers inherent in the doors it opened to the exploitation of alcoholics–and ultimately others–by a new generation of unscrupulous health care entrepreneurs. Apparently caught up in the excitement of the moment, the October 1970 *AAGV* printed an "adapted" version of an article originally published as "For Beginners" in the August 1958 *AAGV*: "Alcoholism is a Disease: The Essence of AA" (A.A. World Services, 1958). The piece opened: "Alcoholism is a disease. AA was the first to give me this bit of information" (p. 13). The writer did go on to note that "alcoholism is a disease with physical, mental and spiritual dimensions," referring to it as a "serious, insidious, progressive disease" that becomes a "disease of despair and fear" (p. 15), but the emphasis clearly was on "the physical."

The reprinting of this article has been interpreted as marking "the movement of the disease concept from the periphery of A.A. thought to its center" (White, 2001, p. 5). I would suggest that, more accurately, it reflects the complexity of the impact of treatment programs on A.A. as that impact intensified. This led, in time, to a narrowing of what had been a far different reality that had been present in the fellowship since 1935: the "Varieties of the Alcoholics Anonymous Experience."

We will return to that facet of this article and its significances below. But here, first, it is useful to consider the article's proximate context. Note that it was an "adapted" reprint. Three articles preceded it in the October 1970 *AAGV*, and each of them sheds useful light on wider A.A. opinions of the possibilities about to be opened up by the pending expansion of alcoholism treatment. The issue's lead article, by John L. Norris, M.D., Nonalcoholic Chairman of the A.A. General Service Board, addressed "The Hazards of AAs' Counseling for Pay" (pp. 2-3). The second article was by an A.A. member recently recruited from the factory floor to be a "rehabilitation counselor." "We're Chipping Away at the Stigma" ran its title, but there was no mention of "disease" (pp. 4-5). Finally the pp. 6-8 article, "Me, Expert?," gently mocked an effort to get the author member of Alcoholics Anonymous "to teach what he knows" in an academic setting. If humor triumphs, as it usually does, this was the most telling *AAGV* commentary on the potential of the programs to be enabled by Public Law 91-616.

Two months previously, in August 1970, non-A.A. physician G. E. Deering, M.D. had tackled the question, "Doctor, Why Can't I Stop Drinking?" Deering replied under the heading "Psychiatry and Alcoholism," in terms of "mental health" and relationships. There was no mention of disease.

Meanwhile, outside of Alcoholics Anonymous, perhaps because of greater awareness of the dangers looming in rampant medicalization, scholars accelerated a reexamination of the disease concept of alcoholism. Classic among these efforts is David Robinson's "The Alcohologist's Addiction: Some Implications of Having Lost Control Over the Disease Concept of Alcoholism," which noted that since Jellinek's 1960 expansion of his original 1952 definition: "An ever-increasing range of conditions and behaviors may be conceptualized as related to stages in a disease process" (Robinson, 1972). In a world where the medical profession was increasingly considered to have competence in an ever-widening sphere of life, the term *alcoholism* had become so vague that it has lost its meaning (Cahalan, Cisin & Crossley, 1969).

There were other such articles, but the disease traditionalists also battled back (Keller, 1972; 1982). In 1972, the Criteria Committee of the N.C.A. published its "Criteria for the Diagnosis of Alcoholism" in both *American Journal of Psychiatry* and *Annals of Internal Medicine* (Criteria Committee, National Council on Alcoholism, 1972; 1973; Seixas, 1972).

In 1973, Dr. Stanley Gitlow observed: "The American Medical Association, American Psychiatric Association, American Public Health Association, American Hospital Association, National Association of Social Workers, World Health Organization, and the American College of Physicians have now each and all pronounced alcoholism a disease. The rest of us can do no less" (Gitlow 1973, Np.).

But both the controversy and the research continued. Alcoholics Anonymous, meanwhile, after the death of co-founder Bill Wilson in January 1971, for a brief time seemed hesitant to publish any further literature. When A.A. did issue its first post-Wilson book, *Living Sober*, in 1975, the content accented the spiritual. There is little mention of disease or illness, but a more subtle change adumbrated the future. In discussing the all-important topic of sponsorship, anonymous author Barry L. introduced the subject by in-passing mention that "Often, the sponsor is the first person to call on a problem drinker who wants help . . . or the A.A. member volunteering to 'sponsor' an alcoholic about to be released from a detox or rehab unit, a hospital, or a correctional facility"(A.A. World Services, 1975, p. 23). A "rehab unit": "treatment," as it soon would be called, had attained sufficient presence to merit distinct mention.

By the next year, some A.A.s, at least, had other things on their minds. 1976 saw the publication of the long-awaited third edition of the Big Book, *Alcoholics Anonymous* (1976). Even more than had been the case in 1955, many members eagerly hoped that the new edition's "Personal Stories" section would better reflect the diversity of A.A. membership. A.A. members employed in the still-aborning treatment system especially emphasized the urgency of that broadening. Our concern here is whether those new personal stories attested to greater or broader commitment to the disease concept of alcoholism.

## THE THIRD EDITION OF ALCOHOLICS ANONYMOUS

Many things in what had become "the alcoholism field" had changed by 1976. More would change in the next two decades. Already in 1974, Senator Harold Hughes himself had warned about "a new civilian army that has now become institutionalized," observing that "The alcohol and drug industrial complex is not as powerful as its military-industrial counterpart, but nonetheless, there are some striking similarities. . . ." (Hughes, 1974). Hughes probably did not have "the treatment industry" in mind, but he might well have. In 1966, there had been fewer than 200 alcoholism treatment programs in the U.S.; by 1977, there were 2,400; by 1987, there would be 6,800 (Schmidt & Weisner, 1993). Unsurprisingly, as A.A.'s own surveys would increasingly confirm, more and more people would come to Alcoholics Anonymous not at the suggestion of a physician or clergyperson but by way of a treatment program (McIntyre, 2000).

However people who needed A.A. got to A.A., they were of course welcomed. But treatment programs had two problems that in places led to a rethinking of that welcome. In the first place, after detoxification and education (which usually emphasized alcoholism-as-disease), what? Experience suggested that the only way most alcoholics could attain lasting recovery was by following the program of Alcoholics Anonymous. But A.A. could not be packaged, much less sold, and the fellowship's members were fiercely protective of the independence guaranteed by their Twelve Traditions. We shall examine more directly some of these tensions between Alcoholics Anonymous and treatment below, when we examine the later 1980s and 1990s.

Treatment's second problem involved its financing. Although popular celebrity alcoholics were lessening stigma by making the headlines–the late 1970s saw Betty Ford, Mary Tyler Moore, and Jason Robards publically in treatment, and N.C.A. continued to sponsor periodic celebrity "comings-out"–most people did not have such financial resources. Nor did they have health insurance that covered the costs of alcoholism treatment. Changing that became the top agenda item of the treaters, and bringing about that change involved convincing medical and insurance and especially public authorities as well as the public at large that alcoholism was a genuine disease. The effort was huge, and members of Alcoholics Anonymous, as well as members of Al-Anon and anyone who had any, however tenuous, contact with treatment or alcoholism, alcoholic or not, were mobilized into participating.

Some did, but most did not, join the effort: As the later failure of S.O.A.R.–"The Society of Americans for Recovery"–demonstrated, most alcoholics "in recovery" mainly want to get on with their lives (Remembering Harold Hughes, Nd., Para. 30). Bill Wilson himself had set this pattern, often lamenting that of all the early members of Alcoholics Anonymous, he alone had been unable to return to his previous profession–a goal he did finally at least partially achieve in the final years of his life. Robert Thomsen's *Bill W.* (1975) and Ernest Kurtz's *Not-God* (1979) brought this home to readers at just this time. It was also true that, certainly as the 1980s unfolded and the concept of addiction broadened to include relationships and processes, most A.A. members did not want to do anything that might include them in the *I'm Dysfunctional, You're Dysfunctional* world so effectively skewered by Wendy Kaminer (1992).

It was within this evolving context that the third edition of *Alcoholics Anonymous* appeared in 1976. The new volume contained fifteen new stories, again divided into the "They Stopped in Time" and "They Lost Nearly All" sections. None of these stories reflected the changes just getting underway in the emerging "alcoholism field"–the growth of the treatment industry and the absorption of alcoholism into "addiction" conceptualized as something that could pertain to any process or any person as well as to any substance. Except for the wider variety of individuals depicted–two young people (male and female), a late-life drinker, an inhabitant of India, a Native American talking like a movie Tonto, a five-time felon, an impoverished "Afro-American" woman, etc.–there was little to distinguish these stories from those of the preceding editions, except that most were very short. Two mentioned the importance of learning that their alcoholism was a disease rather than "a weakness" or "a moral issue." The only mention of "alcoholism work" was by the five-time felon, who had become "an alcoholism counselor."

Meanwhile, as the treatment industry grew and helping alcoholics and an ever-increasing number of "addicts" became more and more professionalized, a distinction emerged, one nicely implied by Daniel Yalisove's 1998 title: "The Origins and Evolution of the Disease Concept of Treatment." Although Yalisove does claim too uncritically and generically that "the disease concept is implicit in A.A.," his study appropriately emphasizes the disease concept's history in *treatment*. There was a difference, time had demonstrated, between the disease concept of alcoholism, which helps alcoholics understand their condition, and the disease concept of treatment, which seeks ways to term "disease" anything that might conceivably be labeled an "addiction" for the "curing" of which someone might be persuaded–or coerced–to pay. This may sound harsh, but it is accurate, and it is a necessary point to make if we are to understand some who harshly criticize all aspects of the disease concept of alcoholism (White, 1998, Ch. 28).

## A FINAL GLANCE VIA THE AAGV

The *AAGV*, from 1976 on, tells a somewhat more complicated story, and from the nature of a journal that selects what it publishes, part of that tale concerns what was unpublished. Since the early 1970s, *Grapevine* editors rarely have found themselves short of submissions. Perhaps surprisingly, since entries are published anonymously and without any remuneration, each month sees an inflow of from 150 to 200 articles. The editors' main task is selection. Beginning in the late 1980s, they noted, more and more submissions mentioned treatment–hardly surprising, since more and more people were coming to Alcoholics Anonymous *via* treatment programs. What struck the editors, however, was the increasing number of these submissions that talked the language of treatment rather than that of the Twelve Steps, of "self-esteem," for example, or the "inner child." Many seemed written by people unfamiliar with Alcoholics Anonymous. Of interest here, these same submissions also tended to speak more directly and dogmatically about alcoholism as disease.

But more was going on here. Remember that October 1970 reprinted story, "Alcoholism Is a Disease: The Essence of AA"? In researching the present paper, I conversed with the current editor of the *AAGV* and his immediate predecessor. The first spontaneous observation of the present editor was: "That could never appear in the year 2000." Both went on to comment "how different things have become since the 1980s," agreeing that "that article probably would never have been published after about 1985." "Why?," I queried. They replied, basically, that with the explosion of treatment, many in Alcoholics Anonymous began to feel themselves to be under siege. Many members, as well as their "trusted servants" in Service Offices, saw the frequent confusion of A.A. with treatment as threatening the very essence of the fellowship. They also felt, on the basis of some evidence, that some treatment programs were encouraging that confusion.

The membership of Alcoholics Anonymous seemed divided on the matter of viewing treatment as a boon or a bane. Most at G.S.O., knowing their history, tended to take the more tolerant point of view, looking favorably on treatment. But as they did, members worldwide seemed to become more critical of their Service Offices. The lines were of course muddied by the copyright concerns and lawsuits of the time, but even as a segment of the membership began a "back to basics" movement that at times seemed a direct challenge to the very idea of a General Service Office, many at G.S.O. responded by themselves retreating from new departures. The great implicit fear was "rocking the boat," and anything new and different threatened to do that.

An impression then, but one based on considerable study and experience: So far as the relationship between Alcoholics Anonymous and the disease concept of alcoholism is concerned, the impact of treatment programs led first to an expansion of that acceptance, but then fairly soon to a retreat from it, as A.A. members, *as* A.A. members, became more and more nervous about distinguishing their fellowship and program from some of what some treatment had become.

The published *AAGV* reflects this complex story. Before the mid- to late 1980s there had been occasional letters or comments of complaint over such matters as local treatment centers dropping busloads of their patients at A.A. meetings. Reader opinion was divided on this issue as on most others. But by the late 1980s that began to change. More consistently now, older members observed that newcomers who had been in treatment programs seemed to come to A.A. to teach rather than to learn. And one of the big things about which they wanted to teach was the disease concept of alcoholism, which old-time members realized had very little if anything to do with living A.A.'s Twelve Steps, the heart of its program.

After the middle of the 1980s, criticisms of treatment became more direct and frequent, and more of them made it into print in the *AAGV*. In January of 1986, a contributor questioned whether some detox units and treatment settings might not be acting as enablers. "Perhaps we A.A.s need to take a long, hard look at our Twelfth Step history and current practices. . . . Perhaps we should ask, 'What can I do for this alcoholic?' before asking, 'Where can I put this alcoholic?,' " the author of "A Foot in the Revolving Door" suggested (A.A. World Services, 1986, pp. 22-23).

Late 1989 witnessed lengthy exchanges on the pros and cons of treatment. A kind of climax came in November, when a writer lamented the death of an A.A. friend who had died drunk: "Carl learned at closed meetings that he lacked the necessary knowledge of alcohol and body chemistry that he could only get 'in treatment.' "

The past decade has seen in the *AAGV* a backing away from or at times a very careful balancing of opposite points of view on any topic possibly controversial. Has that balancing accurately reflected the submissions? No answer is yet available, but my sense is that it does not. The net result so far as Alcoholics Anonymous and the disease concept of alcoholism is concerned in the year 2002? My sense is that most knowledgeable A.A. members will acknowledge that while "allergy" is not really accurate, the description that Dr. William Duncan Silkworth offered in "The Doctor's Opinion" does reflect their own experience, and so that is the message they carry to other alcoholics. To most others, they do not bother talking about the subject.

The closest the book *Alcoholics Anonymous* comes to defining alcoholism is "an illness which only a spiritual experience will conquer." That, for most members of Alcoholics Anonymous, says enough about the nature of their "disease." And over time, despite occasional excursions into seemingly more promising understandings, most members of Alcoholics Anonymous seem to come back to their Big Book for their ultimate answers to daily living and especially to understanding themselves.

## NOTES

1.   An excellent contemporary description of this process and this confusion can be found in "The Jack Alexander article"–Alexander (1941)–see especially pp. 89-90, beginning with "Few think anyone is 'born alcoholic' " and continuing to ". . . the alcoholic begins to realize that he does not understand himself."

The passage continues: "If he applies to Alcoholics Anonymous, he is first brought around to admit that alcohol has him whipped that his life has become unmanageable. Having achieved this state of intellectual humility, he is given a dose of religion in its broadest sense. He is asked to believe in a Power that is greater than himself, or at least to keep an open mind on the subject . . . " Note that there is no mention of disease, illness, malady, sickness.

2.    The term *threefold* can pose a problem that becomes evident when one notes that the aspects are sometimes named as "physical, mental, and spiritual," at other times as "physical, emotional, and spiritual," and at still other times as "physical, mental, and emotional." In long years of carefully listening to and observing this reality, I have come to believe that some people conflate "the emotional" and "the spiritual," while others conflate "the mental" and "the emotional." Most academics and professionals fall into the first group, as will be evidenced later in this paper. Most members of Alcoholics Anonymous who speak of "the physical, the mental, and the spiritual," on the other hand, when asked and pressed, will reply that "the emotional" is contained in "the mental," that "the spiritual" is something not reducible to the others, that it is somehow distinct though it does touch all the others.

The idea of "threefold disease" was not original with Alcoholics Anonymous: it can be found explicitly in the literature of the Emmanuel Movement, an early twentieth-century Christian effort that helped alcoholics among others–see Elwood Worcester and Samuel McComb, *Body, Mind and Spirit* (New York, London: C. Scribner's Sons, 1932); Some have claimed it can also be found in the work of psychologist Gustav Fechner, in whose Leipzig laboratory Elwood Worcester, a founder of Emmanuel, studied. Whether there be a line, *on this particular topic*, from Emmanuel *via* the Jacoby Clubs to Alcoholics Anonymous awaits further research. Forthcoming work by Richard Dubiel may cast more light on this question.

The idea of "threefold," of course, goes back to ancient and especially Medieval scholastic thinking.

On "threefold disease" in the A.A. literature, the first printed use and explanation was Dr. Clarence P., "The Medical Approach to Alcoholism," paper presented at the First National and International Meeting of Physicians in Alcoholics Anonymous, held at Cape Vincent, NY, 19-21 August 1949: Conference Record in A.A. archives. The context of its use makes it clear that the physicians present were all familiar with both the term and concept.

3.    Although the Yale Center, especially under the leadership of Selden Bacon, would in later years tend to reject emphasis on physiology if not on the disease concept itself, during the early years, as Johnson (1973) notes (p. 257), emphasis on the medical model of chronic inebriety was crucial to Haggard and Jellinek for four reasons: (1) it was consistent with their effort to debunk traditional moralistic interpretations of issues related to alcohol; (2) it fit their humanistic concern that problem drinkers not be ostracized and condemned; (3) it fit their pragmatism that having the alcoholic view self as a sick person and be accepted as such by society put him in a favorable position to overcome his problem; (4) it complemented their advocacy of moderate or controlled drinking.

4.    For example: the February 1945 *AAGV* announces "Medical Wards" in New York City and features an article, "Hospitalization in Akron Model for AA"; the March 1945 issue leads with the article, "Dr. Sam Parker of Kings County Suggests 'Criteria for AA Work in Hospitals,' " and contains two articles on the "Philadelphia Story on Hospitalization," noting that "This recognition that alcoholism is a disease furnished a tremendous impetus to the [A.A.] movement here," and a story, "Dayton Has Interesting Hospital Record," about getting entree into State Mental Hospital. A year later, February 1946, an article exulted, "AA Ward at Knickerbocker Proves Success." The climax of this drive came in May 1947 with an article "by Bill": "Adequate Hospital-

ization . . . One Great Need" [ellipsis in original] noting that: "Most of us feel that ready access to hospitals and other places of rest and recuperation borders on absolute necessity."

It is noteworthy that Marty Mann, in an article in *Modern Hospital* in January 1946, "Alcoholics Anonymous: A New Partner for Hospitals," makes no mention of "disease," but describes the need for hospitals and how A.A. will cooperate with and work within them.

5.  Over the years, in his correspondence, Wilson mentioned two main reasons for writing the *12&12*: (1) the membership's adamant refusal to let him revise anything in the book *Alcoholics Anonymous*; (2) the need to publicize the then-new Twelve Traditions–Bill indicated in one letter to Fr. Dowling that he wrote the Step chapters in order to motivate members to get the book and so read the Tradition chapters. That this is a bit overstated is indicated by the presentation of the Step essays in the *AAGV* in 1952-1953. The whole context as well as Wilson's later comments make it clear that the co-founder felt he had more to say about sobriety now seventeen years sober than he had four years sober at the time of the Big Book's composition. But the explanatory letters do universally emphasize "the spiritual" and ignore what had been the large "disease" push at the time. *Cf.* also Wilson to Scott B., 4 December 1950, and perhaps most clearly to Charles W., 3 June 1952: "As to changing the Steps themselves, or even the text of the A.A. book, I am assured by many that I could certainly be excommunicated if a word were touched. It is a strange fact of human nature that when a spiritually centered movement starts and finally adopts certain principles, these finally freeze absolutely solid. But what can't be done respecting the Steps themselves–or any part of the A.A. book–I can make a shift by writing these pieces which I hope folks will like."

## REFERENCES

Alcoholics Anonymous World Services. (1952a). Stethoscope and periscope: The doctors look at alcohol. *The AA Grapevine*. New York: Author.

Alcoholics Anonymous World Services. (1952b). The problem drinker. *The AA Grapevine*. New York: Author.

Alcoholics Anonymous World Services. (1952c). *A.A.–44 Questions*. New York: Author.

Alcoholics Anonymous World Services. (1953). *Twelve Steps and Twelve Traditions*. New York: Author.

Alcoholics Anonymous World Services. (1955). *Alcoholics Anonymous* (2nd ed). New York: Author.

Alcoholics Anonymous World Services. (1957). *Alcoholics Anonymous Comes of Age*. New York: Author.

Alcoholics Anonymous World Services. (1958). Alcoholism is a disease: The essence of AA. *The AA Grapevine*. New York: Author.

Alcoholics Anonymous World Services. (1975). *Living Sober*. New York: Author.

Alcoholics Anonymous World Services. (1976). *Alcoholics Anonymous* (3rd ed). New York: Author.

Alcoholics Anonymous World Services. (1986). A foot in the revolving door. *The AA Grapevine*. New York: Author.

Alcoholics Anonymous World Services. (2001). *Alcoholics Anonymous* (4th ed). New York: Author.

Alexander, J. (1941, March 1). Alcoholics Anonymous: Freed slaves of drink, now they free others. *Saturday Evening Post*, 9-11.

Anderson, D. (1942). Alcohol and public opinion. *Quarterly Journal of Studies on Alcohol*, 3(3), 376-92.

Bebbington, P. E. (1976). The efficacy of Alcoholics Anonymous: The elusiveness of hard data. *British Journal of Psychiatry*, 128: 572-80.

Bowman, K. M. & Jellinek, E.M. (1941). Alcohol addiction and its treatment. *Quarterly Journal of Studies on Alcohol*, 2, 98-176.

Brown, J. E. (1980). *The Supreme Court and Alcohol: Case Study of a Shift in Systems of Social Control*. Pittsburgh: University of Pittsburgh Press.

Cahalan, D. Cisin, I.H. & Crossley, H.M. (1969). *American Drinking Practices: A National Study of Drinking Behavior and Attitudes Related to Alcoholic Beverages*. New Brunswick: Rutgers Center of Alcohol Studies.

Clark, N. H. (1976). *Deliver Us From Evil: An Interpretation of American Prohibition*. New York, NY: W.W. Norton and Co., Inc.

Criteria Committee, National Council on Alcoholism. (1972). Criteria for the diagnosis of alcoholism. *American Journal of Psychiatry*, 129, 127-135.

Criteria Committee, National Council on Alcoholism. (1972). Criteria for the diagnosis of alcoholism. *Annals of Internal Medicine*, 77, 249-258.

Criteria Committee, National Council on Alcoholism. (1973). Criteria for the diagnosis of alcoholism. *Journal of the American Osteopathic Association*, 72(5), 502-10.

Durfee, C. H. (1936). Understanding the drinker. *Mental Hygiene* 20(1), 11-29.

Gitlow, S. E. (1973). Alcoholism: A disease. In P. Bourne & R. Fox (Eds.), *Alcoholism: Progress in Research and Treatment* (pp. 1-9). New York: Academic Press.

Haynes, T. L. (1988). The Changing Role of the Physician in the Treatment of Chemical Dependence. Retrieved May 18, 2002, from: *http://www.wemac.com/adm_hist.html*

Hughes, H. (1974, December 13). Address to the North American Congress on Alcohol and Drug Problems, San Francisco, California, in Olson (forthcoming).

Jellinek, E.M. (1960) *The Disease Concept of Alcoholism*. New Haven, CT: Hillhouse Press.

Johnson, B. H. (1973). *The Alcohol Movement in America: A Study in Cultural Innovation*. University of Illinois at Urbana-Champaign.

Kaminer, W. (1992). *I'm Dysfunctional, You're Dysfunctional: The Recovery Movement and Other Self-Help Fashions*. Reading, MA: Addison-Wesley.

Keller, M. (1960). Definition of alcoholism. *Quarterly Journal of Studies on Alcohol* 21, 125-34.

Keller, M. (1972). On the loss-of-control phenomenon in alcoholism. *British Journal of Addiction*, 67, 153-66.

Keller, M. (1976). The disease concept of alcoholism revisited. *Journal of Studies on Alcohol* 37(11), 1694-717.

Keller, M. (1982). On defining alcoholism: With comment on some other relevant words. In E.L. Gomberg, H. R. White & J. A. Carpenter (Eds.), *Alcohol, Science and Society Revisited* (pp. 119-33). Ann Arbor, MI and New Brunswick, NJ: University of Michigan Press and Rutgers Center of Alcohol Studies.

Knight, R. P. (1937). The psychodynamics of chronic alcoholism. *Journal of Nervous and Mental Disease*, 86, 538-48.

Kurtz, E. (1991). *Not-God: A History of Alcoholics Anonymous* (Rev. Ed). Center City, MN: Hazelden Educational Materials, Inc.

Kurtz, E. (1996). Twelve-step programs. In P.H. VanNess (Ed.), *Spirituality and the Secular Quest* (pp. 277-302). World Spirituality: An Encyclopedic History of the Religious Quest, Vol. 22. New York: Crossroad.

Lawrence Robinson, Appellate, v. State of California. (1962). Retrieved from: *http://wings.buffalo.edu/law/bclc/web/robinson.htm*

Leroy Powell, Appellate, v. State of Texas. (1968). Retrieved from: *http://wings.buffalo.edu/law/bclc/web/powell.htm*

Lubove, R. (1965). *The Professional Altruist.* Cambridge, MA: Harvard University Press.

Mann, M. (1948, November). The alcoholic in the general hospital. *Southern Hospitals,* 27-31.

McIntyre, D. (2000). How well does A.A. work?: An analysis of published A.A. surveys (1968-1996) and related analyses/comments. *Alcoholism Treatment Quarterly,* 18(4), 1-18.

Miller, W. R. & Kurtz, E. (1994). Models of alcoholism used in treatment: Contrasting AA and other perspectives with which it is often confused. *Journal of Studies on Alcohol,* 55, 159-66.

National Clergy Council on Alcoholism and Related Drug Problems. (1960). N.C.C.A. Blue Book. Washington, DC.

Ogborne, A. C. & Glaser, F.B. (1981). Characteristics of affiliates of Alcoholics Anonymous: A review of the literature. *Journal of Studies on Alcohol,* 42(7), 661-75.

Olson, N. (forthcoming). *Memoirs of Congressional Aide Years.*

Parkhurst, G. (1937, July). Drinking and alcoholism. *Harpers Magazine,* 158-166.

Peabody, R. R. (1931). *The Common Sense of Drinking.* Boston: Little, Brown, and Company.

Remembering Harold Hughes. (n.d). Retrieved May 14, 2002, from: *http://www.well.com/user/woa/harolde.htm*

Robinson, D. (1972). The alcohologist's addiction: Some implications of having lost control over the disease concept of alcoholism. *Quarterly Journal of Studies on Alcohol,* 33(4A), 1028-42.

Roizen, R. P. (1991). *The American Discovery of Alcoholism, 1933-1939.* Berkeley: University of California.

Roizen, R. P. (1996). Four unsung moments in the genesis of the modern alcoholism movement. Unpublished Manuscript.

Roizen, R. P. (2001). Where did Mrs. Marty Mann learn alcoholism was a disease and why should it matter? Retrieved May 17, 2002, from: *http://www.roizen.com/ron/ranesind.htm*

Schmidt, L. A. & Weisner, C. (1993). Developments in alcoholism treatment. In M. Galanter (Ed.), *Recent Developments in Alcoholism, Volume 11: Ten Years of Progress* (pp. 369-98). New York: Plenum Press.

Seixas, F.A. (1972) Criteria for the diagnosis of alcoholism. *Journal of the American Medical Association,* 222(2), 207-8.

Silkworth, W. D. (1937, March 17). Alcoholism as a manifestation of allergy. *Medical Record.*

Silkworth, W. D. (1937, April 21). The reclamation of the alcoholic. *Medical Record* 145, 322.

Silkworth, W. D. (1939). A new approach to psychotherapy in chronic alcoholism. *The Journal-Lancet* 59(7), 312-314.

Silkworth, W. D. (1939, July 19). Psychological rehabilitation of alcoholics. *Medical Record* 150: np.

Silkworth, W.D. (1941, August 6). A highly successful approach to the alcoholic problem. *Medical Record* 154: np.

Skinner, W. (1994, September). *Spirit(s) in The Postmodern: Recovery as a Retrieval of Self*. Paper presented at the International Conference on Addiction and Mutual Help Movements in a Comparative Perspective, Toronto, Ontario.

Smith (Akron) to Wilson, 15 June 1938; letter in A.A. archives.

Sontag, S. (1978). *Illness as Metaphor*. New York: Farrar, Strauss & Girous.

Strecker, E. A. (1937). Some thoughts concerning the psychology and therapy of alcoholism. *Journal of Nervous and Mental Disease*, 86, 191-205.

Strecker, E. A. & Chambers, F.T., Jr. (1938). *Alcohol: One Man's Meat*. New York: Macmillan.

Thomsen, R. (1975). *Bill W*. New York, New York: Harper & Row.

U.S. Government Printing Office. (1969). The impact of alcoholism: Hearing before the special subcommittee on alcoholism and narcotics of the committee on labor and public welfare, United States Senate, Ninety-First Congress, First Session on Examination of the Impact of Alcoholism, July 23, 24, 25, 1969. Washington, DC: Author.

Wiener, C. (1981). *The Politics of Alcoholism*. New Brunswick, NJ: Transaction Books.

White, W.L. (1998). *Slaying the Dragon: A History of Addiction and Recovery in America*. Bloomington, IL: Chestnut Health Systems.

White, W.L. (Ed.). (2001). The Addiction Disease Chronologies of William White, Ernest Kurtz, and Caroline Acker. Retrieved May 14, 2002, from: *http://www.bhrm.org/papers/addpapers.htm*

Wilson, W. G. (1944). Basic concepts of Alcoholics Anonymous. *New York State Journal of Medicine*, 44, 1805-10.

Wilson, W.G. (1949). The society of Alcoholics Anonymous. *American Journal of Psychiatry*, 106(5), 370-5.

Yalisove, D. (1998). The origins and evolution of the disease concept of treatment, *Journal of Studies on Alcohol*, 59, 469-476.

# Treatment for Alcoholism:
# Older and Wiser?

Paula L. Wilbourne, MS
William R. Miller, PhD

**SUMMARY.** Our understanding of alcoholism and treatments for alcohol problems has developed dramatically in the last 20 years. This review summarizes some key aspects in our understanding of treatment for alcoholism. Few commonalities characterize individuals with alcohol problems or distinguish them from individuals without such problems. Evidence suggests that treatment is effective. Just as individuals vary in their development of alcoholism, they may recover in equally variable ways that include reductions in drinking as well as total abstinence. *[Article copies available for a fee from The Haworth Document Delivery Service: 1-800-HAWORTH. E-mail address: <getinfo@haworthpressinc.com> Website: <http://www.HaworthPress.com> © 2002 by The Haworth Press, Inc. All rights reserved.]*

**KEYWORDS.** Alcohol, alcoholism, treatment, review

Paula L. Wilbourne is a doctoral student, Department of Psychology, The University of New Mexico, Albuquerque, NM. She has a research interest in trends in the treatment of alcohol problems. William R. Miller is affiliated with the Department of Psychology, The University of New Mexico, Albuquerque, NM. He is the author of numerous books, articles and other publications dealing with the treatment of alcohol and other drug problems.

The authors would like to thank Eric Bernart for his assistance in preparing this manuscript.

[Haworth co-indexing entry note]: "Treatment for Alcoholism: Older and Wiser?" Wilbourne, Paula L., and William R. Miller. Co-published simultaneously in *Alcoholism Treatment Quarterly* (The Haworth Press, Inc.) Vol. 20, No. 3/4, 2002, pp. 41-59; and: *Alcohol Problems in the United States: Twenty Years of Treatment Perspective* (ed: Thomas F. McGovern, and William L. White) The Haworth Press, Inc., 2002, pp. 41-59. Single or multiple copies of this article are available for a fee from The Haworth Document Delivery Service [1-800-HAWORTH, 9:00 a.m. - 5:00 p.m. (EST). E-mail address: getinfo@haworthpressinc.com].

Half a century has passed since the first clinical trial of treatment for alcoholism was published by Hoff and McKeown in 1953 (Hoff & McKeown, 1953). During the first 30 years, the development of therapeutic methods was relatively slow (Miller, 1992), but there has been a remarkable acceleration in the evolution of treatment during the past two decades. Over 400 controlled clinical trials of treatment methods for alcoholism have now been published, 72% of which have appeared since 1980 (Miller & Wilbourne, 2002). This review highlights twelve of the most important changes in alcoholism treatment during this period.

## ALCOHOLISM AS A CONTINUUM

In his classic treatise on *The Disease Concept of Alcoholism*, E. M. Jellinek (1960) criticized the idea of alcoholism as a unitary disease. Instead he used "alcoholism" to refer to the full spectrum of alcohol problems, an approach also adopted by the World Health Organization. This is, in fact, what Magnus Huss (1849) meant when he coined the term "alcoholism." Over the past twenty years the American Psychiatric Association (1980) abandoned alcoholism as a diagnostic term, replacing it with the concepts of alcohol *abuse* and *dependence*, both of which can vary along a continuum of severity. This shift was also echoed by the Institute of Medicine (1990) in its landmark report, *Broadening the Base of Treatment for Alcohol Problems*, calling for systems that address the full spectrum of alcohol problems, and not merely the most severely dependent cases. Within the space of two decades, professional opinion changed dramatically, from thinking of alcoholism as a unitary disease that one either has or doesn't have, to a full spectrum of problems related to excessive drinking. Like Huss and Jellinek, that is what we mean when we use the term "alcoholism" in this review.

## TREATMENT WORKS

Alcoholism treatment outcome studies show that the prognosis is bright indeed. If one requires perfection, of course, the percentage of clients who maintain continuous abstinence for a year or more is often low, averaging around 24% in large and well-documented outcome studies (Miller, Walters, & Bennett, 2001). Increasing recognition of the chronicity of alcoholism, however, has prompted a shift away from this perfectionistic standard. Treatment outcomes for substance dependence, for example, compare very favorably with those for other chronic diseases such as diabetes, hypertension, cancer and heart disease

(McLellan, in press). After a single treatment episode, about one in four clients abstain totally, and another one in ten drink moderately and without problems during the subsequent year–together more than one-third total remissions. One-year mortality is under 2%. What often goes unrecognized is that the remaining majority of clients also show, as a group, large improvement. Among those who neither abstain nor drink moderately in the year after treatment, alcohol use decreases by 87% on average. They abstain on three days out of four, and alcohol-related problems diminish by 60% (Miller et al., 2001). Though short of total remission, these outcomes would be regarded as remarkably positive for most chronic diseases (McLellan, in press). Furthermore, the effectiveness of subsequent treatment is not significantly compromised by the number of prior treatment episodes (Miller, Westerberg, Harris, & Tonigan, 1996). In sum, *let your clients know that their chances for beneficial outcomes are excellent.*

## TREATMENTS OF CHOICE

While the overall outcomes of treatment are good, it is surely not the case that all treatment approaches are (equally) effective (Institute of Medicine, 1990). Numerous reviews have asked, "Which treatments work best?" Despite differences in methodology and authors, such reviews have reached relatively similar conclusions. Three comprehensive reviews identified common treatments in their top ten performance rankings: social skills training, community reinforcement approach, self-control training, brief interventions, motivational interviewing, and behavioral marital therapy (Finney & Monahan, 1996; Holder, Longabaugh, Miller, & Rubonis, 1991; Miller, Wilbourne, & Hettema, 2002). Similarly, these reviews found little or no evidence for the effectiveness of some previously popular components of U.S. alcoholism treatment, including educational lectures and films, confrontational interventions, general alcoholism counseling, and milieu therapies.

*Brief Interventions.* It has been known for some time that relatively brief empathic interventions can substantially increase the percentage of problem drinkers who enter treatment (Chafetz, 1963) or return after an initial or missed session (Miller, 1985). It is now also clear from dozens of well-designed studies that even a single session of counseling can significantly decrease alcohol use among heavy and problematic drinkers (Moyer, Finney, Swearingen, & Vergun, 2002). That is, even a little counseling (at least of a certain type) is much better than no counseling. This has led to increased interest in brief "opportunistic" counseling with at-risk or problem drinkers encountered in health care and social service settings (Heather, 1998; Miller & Weisner, in press). Six common components of effective brief intervention have been summarized by the acronym "FRAMES" (Bien et al., 1993). Such interventions have often included personal *Feedback* of current levels of drinking, risk, and impairment, and have acknowledged personal autonomy and *Responsibility* for change. Respectful *Advice* to stop or decrease drinking has typically been offered, along with a *Menu* of alternative methods for doing so. An *Empathic* listening style is used, supporting the person's *Self-efficacy* for change.

How can such brief counseling have any effect on well-established heavy, problematic, or dependent drinking? Interventions of a session or two are unlikely to teach new coping skills, alter cognitive structure, or evoke personality change. Yet the magnitude of change following brief intervention is often similar to that associated with more extended treatment (Bien et al., 1993; Project MATCH Research Group, 1997a). A common explanation is that such interventions primarily enhance motivation for change, triggering clients to draw upon their own knowledge, skills and wisdom to address their drinking problems. The clinical style of *motivational interviewing* was developed specifically for the purpose of mobilizing the client's intrinsic motivation for change, and is well-supported as an alcohol treatment approach (Burke, Arkowitz, & Dunn, 2002). The combination of motivational interviewing with personal feedback of assessment results has been termed *motivational enhancement therapy*, a 4-session form of which was found to yield outcomes similar to those for two 12-session outpatient treatments (Project MATCH Research Group, 1997a).

*Skills Training.* Another treatment approach that has emerged to prominence during the past two decades involves teaching clients practical behavioral skills for avoiding drinking and for leading a rewarding life without alcohol. Several approaches based on skills training now have strong evidence of effectiveness. *Social skills training* typically includes components that are focused on drinking (such as drink refusal skills) as well as more general components that are less specifically tied to drinking, such as communication skills. The *community reinforcement approach* (Meyers & Smith, 1995) incorporates such social skill training, and is more generally designed to make practical changes in the client's lifestyle and environment so that sobriety becomes more rewarding than drinking. This approach typically includes teaching family members or significant others how to reinforce sobriety. *Behavioral self-control training* has also shown success in helping less severe problem drinkers to maintain moderate and problem-free alcohol use (Hester, 1995). The common thread running through these interventions is a focus on practical skills for effective self-management.

*Medications.* Medications have sometimes been regarded as ill-advised in the treatment of substance abuse, in order not to replace one dependence-producing drug with another. It is also the case that until relatively recently, the only medication approved for the treatment of alcoholism was disulfiram (®Antabuse), for which evidence of effectiveness has been mixed at best. This picture has changed significantly over the past two decades. Medications are now widely used to treat concomitant psychological disorders. While they may have little effect on drinking per se, medications such as antipsychotics, antidepressants, and lithium can be invaluable to addressing "dual disorders" (Swift, in press). Also, for the first time in the history of treatment for alcoholism, two medications are found on the list of treatment methods most strongly supported by clinical trials (Miller, Wilbourne, & Hettema, 2002). The first of these is naltrexone (®Revia), which selectively blocks the brain's natural opiate receptors. The second is acamprosate, which has been tested extensively in Europe and, as of this writing, is about to be released for prescription use in the United States. Acomprosate is thought to work by imitating the actions of the neurotransmitter GABA, which has been linked to alcohol consumption. Both medications have been found in large and well-designed studies to be helpful in suppressing alcohol use. Rather than making the client ill if they drink (as disulfiram does), these medications appear to help by reducing the desire for alcohol.

*Addressing the Big Picture.* Another change that has occurred in alcoholism treatment is a broader focus on the client's life and functioning. Whereas once treatment focused almost exclusively on drinking, now it is clear that a client's social environment and support system have a large influence on what happens during and after treatment (Moos, Finney, & Cronkite, 1990; Project MATCH Research Group, 1998a). Perhaps this is why some of the treatment modalities with strongest evidence of effectiveness seem to focus less on alcohol and more on enriching the person's life without alcohol. For example, outcomes of alcoholism treatment are often significantly improved by including a significant other for behavioral marital therapy, or (as discussed above) by teaching skills needed for successful social relationships.

## TREATING CLIENTS WITH MULTIPLE CONCERNS

If ever there was a time when people mostly came to treatment "just with alcohol problems," that time has passed. Polydrug abuse has become normative among treatment-seeking clients, well beyond the traditional combination of alcohol and nicotine. Problems of "dual diagnosis" are now widely recognized, and depending upon the clinical population, between 50% and 80% of those seeking treatment for substance use disorders also have diagnosable psychological disorders (Preuss & Wong, 2000).

*Treating Polydrug Abuse.* Treating multiple substance use problems at the same time was once considered to be a bad idea: it's challenging enough to tackle a drinking problem without attempting to change other addictive behaviors simultaneously. This, too, has changed. Separate "alcohol" and "drug" programs have been replaced by unified substance abuse treatment, now increasingly integrated with health care or mental health service systems. Not only is it safe and reasonable to target multiple substance use simultaneously (Bobo, Schilling, Gilchris, & Schinke, 1986), it has become commonplace and offers certain advantages. In one recent study, adding smoking cessation to an alcohol treatment program actually improved drinking outcomes (Bobo, McIlvain, Walker, & Leed-Kelly, 1998), which makes sense given how closely tied smoking and drinking are as behaviors. Compared to alcohol, tobacco takes a far higher national toll in death, disease, and disability, and smoking is often the largest threat to health among people in recovery from alcoholism.

Polydrug abuse also offers unique challenges to alcoholism counselors, particularly those accustomed to requiring immediate and total abstention. People are often at very different points of readiness to change the various drugs they use. A client may be eager to quit cocaine, willing to consider abstaining from alcohol if it will help (as it often does) in kicking the coke, reluctant to stop smoking tobacco, and unwilling to consider letting go of marijuana. Furthermore, substitution drugs–a widely rejected idea in treating alcoholism, and with good reason–have been quite successful in managing opiate dependence (e.g., methadone, buprenorphine), and helpful in tobacco cessation (e.g., nicotine patch or gum).

*Treating Comorbid Disorders.* Research and clinical experience have demonstrated that alcohol use disorders co-occur with other psychological disorders far more often than would be expected by chance. They co-occur more often in women than in men, in clinical samples than in the general population, and in public clinics than in private ones (Preuss & Wong, 2000). Genetic research generally points to separate risk heritability for most disorders, suggesting that a single, underlying vulnerability explains very few dual diagnoses (Schuckit, Tipp, Bucholz, Nurnberger, Hesselbrock, Crowe, & Kramer, 1997).

The "self-medication" hypothesis has been invoked as one way to explain the co-occurrence of substance use and psychiatric difficulties, but there is little scientific support for it. Drinking tends to exacerbate rather than improve most psychological problems, thus failing to meet the fundamental requirement of a therapeutic medication. Furthermore, alcohol use disorders more often precede than follow psychiatric diagnoses in their onset, making it difficult to implicate the former as motivated by the latter (Preuss & Wong, 2000).

Some practitioners have found it useful to draw distinctions between primary and secondary conditions. An alcohol problem could be considered primary if it preceded the later emergence of a (secondary) psychiatric diagnosis. Similarly, if it preceded appearance of alcohol problems, a psychiatric diagnosis might be considered primary and the alcohol use disorder secondary. Unfortunately, this judgment can be difficult to make reliably, and treatment guidelines thus far do not differ dramatically based on this distinction. Some evidence indicates that with abstinence from alcohol, depression tends to improve or remit without further treatment (Rosenthal & Westreich, 1999), although there seems to be no disadvantage in treating depression concomitantly. Effectively treating only one condition (alcohol use disorder or concomitant psychological disorder) may improve, worsen, or have no effect on the other. Certain chronic conditions, such as schizophrenia or post-traumatic stress disorder, almost always require their own special focus (Preuss & Wong, 2000). Thus far, the treatment(s) of choice for alcohol problems are not different based on the presence or absence of a concomitant disorder. The challenge is to integrate or at least closely coordinate the treatment of dual disorders (Handmaker & Anderson, in press).

*Childhood Abuse.* One clinical issue that has received increased attention in substance abuse treatment over the past 20 years is clients' history of sexual or other physical abuse during childhood. People (particularly women) entering treatment for substance use disorders report a very high rate of such childhood abuse, relative to the general population. Similarly, those who suffered such abuse during childhood (particularly women) are at much higher risk of developing a substance use disorder during adulthood (Simpson & Miller, 2002), although most of them do not. This led to the belief that it may be necessary to address child abuse issues in order to treat addictions successfully. In fact, a recent review of studies on this issue concluded that a history of childhood abuse neither increased nor decreased response to treatment for substance use disorders (Simpson & Miller, 2002). That is, it does not appear to be necessary to open up and resolve childhood abuse issues in order to overcome substance abuse and dependence. Indeed, exploring these issues tends to revivify stressful memories, and can retraumatize clients. Most people with a history of childhood abuse do not currently meet diagnostic criteria for post-traumatic stress disorder (PTSD) (Oddone, Genuis, & Violato, 2001, Foa & Street, 2001). It may be that it is the presence of current, disabling PTSD (rather than childhood history per se) that warrants clinical attention (Simpson, 1999). Even so, it is our opinion that alcoholism counselors should not attempt to treat PTSD unless they have had appropriate clinical training, supervision and experience, because the potential for harm is considerable (Vesper, 1998).

## MOTIVATION FOR CHANGE

Another dramatic change during the past twenty years is in how alcoholism professionals think about and address problems of motivation for change.

Drawing loosely on psychoanalytic concepts, clinicians once attributed clients' reluctance or ambivalence about change to being "in denial," in the belief that overreliance on primitive ego defense mechanisms was a characterologic aspect of alcoholism. In effect, clients were blamed for being unmotivated or for not responding to treatment. Yet, sixty years of research have failed to reveal a common alcoholic or addictive personality (Kerr, 1996), and studies specifically fail to show any systematic pattern of defense mechanisms associated with alcoholism (Miller & Rollnick, 1991).

Ambivalence is now recognized as a normal part of the change process, in part through the rapid growth in popularity of the transtheoretical model of James Prochaska and Carlo DiClemente (1984; Prochaska, DiClemente, & Norcross, 1992). The most familiar aspect of this complex model is its five "stages of change": precontemplation, contemplation, preparation, action, and maintenance. Ambivalence is a defining characteristic of the contemplation stage. Whereas precontemplators see no reason for change, contemplators perceive both pros and cons of their current behavior (and of change). They want to change, and at the same time they don't want to. As the balance of ambivalence tips toward change, the person begins preparing and then taking action to bring about change. In this view, motivation is a process that unfolds over time, rather than a client trait linked to defenses.

If motivation is process, then it may be possible to help the process along. Indeed, enhancing client motivation for change is now understood as part of the counselor's task (Miller, 1999). The question is how best to do so. Ironically, the confrontational strategies once emphasized in addiction treatment turn out to be counter-therapeutic. Voice one side of an ambivalent person's dilemma ("You're an alcoholic and you need to quit drinking"), and the result is predictable: the person defends the other ("No I'm not, and no I don't."). Confrontational counseling *evokes* from clients the very behavior that is then labeled as defensive denial or resistance, which in turn decreases the likelihood that behavior change will occur (Miller & Rollnick, 2002). Despite the past popularity of confontation, every clinical trial has shown either no benefit or a detrimental effect of confrontational approaches in treating alcoholism (Miller & Wilbourne, 2002). The Hazelden Foundation (1985) renounced the use of confrontation two decades ago, and expressed regret that such methods had come to be associated with a "Minnesota model."

Instead, there is now a variety of effective methods for enhancing intrinsic motivation for change in ambivalent or seemingly unmotivated drinkers (Miller, 1999), including the empathic counseling style of *motivational interviewing*, described above (Miller & Rollnick, 2002). The method known as *guided self-change* also makes use of clients' own intrinsic motivation and resources, building on studies of natural change processes among people who overcame drinking problems without professional treatment (Sobell & Sobell, 1999).

## UNILATERAL FAMILY THERAPY

Another effective new tool that has emerged within the past two decades is *unilateral family therapy* (Thomas & Ager, 1993; Thomas et al., 1990). The fundamental approach here is to work constructively through a concerned significant other (CSO) when a problem drinker is initially unmotivated to change or unwilling to seek help. The CSO is empowered, encouraged, and taught specific methods to (1) avoid reinforcing or "enabling" problem drinking, (2) reinforce non-drinking, and (3) encourage help-seeking. Note that this approach is quite different from that encouraged for the CSO in Al-Anon: to accept helplessness to change the drinker, detach lovingly, and stop trying to alter the loved one's drinking. It also should not be confused with the intervention promoted by the Johnson Institute (1993), which builds toward a confrontational family meeting designed to have the drinker admitted to treatment.

A unilateral family therapy based on the community reinforcement approach was first described by Sisson and Azrin (1986), and has since been developed and tested by Robert Meyers and his colleagues (1999; Meyers & Miller, 2001; Meyers & Smith, 1995). This *community reinforcement and family training (CRAFT)* approach has been compared directly with Al-Anon and Johnson Institute methods for engaging unmotivated drinkers in treatment. When the concerned family member was given CRAFT, 64% of their loved ones entered alcoholism treatment, typically within 1-2 months of CRAFT counseling. Both the Al-Anon (13%) and Johnson Institute (30%) approaches were significantly less effective in engaging unmotivated problem drinkers in treatment (Miller, Meyers, & Tonigan, 1999). A principal obstacle to success with the Johnson Institute method was the unwillingness of a majority of families to complete the family confrontation meeting (cf. Liepman, 1993). Meyers found similar success with CRAFT in counseling concerned significant others with loved ones who were abusing illicit drugs themselves (Meyers et al., 1999).

A parenthetical note is warranted here regarding the once popular concept of "codependence." No consensus definition or diagnostic criteria for codependence ever emerged, but anecdotal writings on the subject generally cast it as a pernicious personality disorder related to living with a family member's alcoholism. It represented, in a way, a reversion to 1950s psychodynamic speculation about personality abnormalities of "the alcoholic wife," a view long rejected for pathologizing the victim. The concept of codependence has also been criticized as being vague and ill-defined, without scientific basis, and even misogynistic (Stafford, 2001). The broad panoply of symptoms allegedly linked to codependence do not differentiate people with versus without a family history of addictive disorders (Cullen & Carr, 1999). This is not at all to minimize the suffering of the family members of people with substance use disorders, or to diminish the importance of addressing relationships when treating addiction. As noted above, there is good evidence for the efficacy of behavioral marital therapy in the treatment of alcoholism. In contrast, therapies prescribed to treat "codependence" remain speculative and untested.

## DIFFERENCES AMONG COUNSELORS

A fascinating finding over the past two decades is that the "same" treatment can have very different outcomes depending upon the person who delivers it (Najavits & Weiss, 1994). Even when randomly assigned to their therapists, clients of some counselors fare far better (or worse) than those in other counselors' caseloads within the same program or treatment approach (Miller, Taylor, & West, 1980; Luborsky, Crits-Christoph, McLellan, Woody, Piper, Liberman, Imber, & Pilkonis, 1986; Project MATCH Research Group, 1998b).

What is it that distinguishes more effective counselors? It was once believed that having a personal history of recovery increased a counselor's effectiveness, but it is now clear from many studies that being in recovery neither increases nor decreases a counselor's success in treating clients with substance use disorders (Culbreth, 2000; McLellan, Woody, Luborsky, & Goehl, 1988; Project MATCH Research Group, 1998b). Neither are age, gender, and years of education or experience good predictors of counselor effectiveness.

What does seem to be consistently linked to higher rates of success in alcoholism treatment is therapeutic *empathy*–not an identification with one's clients by virtue of common experience, but rather the skill of reflective listening (accurate empathy) as described by Carl Rogers and his students (Truax & Carkhuff, 1971). In one study, counselors' empathic skill was rated independently by three supervisors as they treated problem drinkers who had been randomly assigned to their caseloads (Miller et al., 1980). Rates of successful client outcomes at 6 months ranged from 25% for the lowest-empathy counselor, to 100% for the highest-empathy counselor. Even two years later, therapist empathy still predicted drinking outcomes (Miller & Baca, 1983). In another study with random assignment of clients to counselors, those being treated by high-empathy counselors had a significantly lower rate of relapse, as compared with much higher rates of relapse for clients in the caseloads of lower-empathy counselors (Valle, 1981).

## COERCED TREATMENT

The past two decades have also seen increased rates of clients being mandated to treatment by the courts, probation, employers, and licensure boards. (Of course it is also the case that many "voluntary" clients also come to treatment under varying degrees of pressure from others.) Does coercion undermine the effectiveness of treatment? The available evidence now indicates that source of referral, including coerced versus voluntary status–is not significantly related to treatment outcomes. That is, clients who enter treatment under overt coercion seem to fare just as well as those not reporting such coercion (Miller & Flaherty, 2000; Polcin, 2001). What may be more important for both mandated and voluntary clients is the *kind* of treatment they receive, the counselor who delivers it, and their network of social support for sobriety after treatment.

## WHEN CLIENTS REFUSE ABSTINENCE

Not all clients are willing to accept total abstinence as their initial treatment goal. Younger clients and those with less severe drinking problems are particularly likely to prefer moderation over lifelong abstinence as a goal. What should a counselor do in this case?

There are now well-developed methods for helping clients to pursue a goal of moderation (Hester, in press; Sanchez-Craig, 1993). Even in treatment where the program's goal is total abstinence, roughly one client in ten winds up drinking moderately and without problems (Miller et al., 2001; Project MATCH Research Group, 1997). Rather than evicting a client who refuses cold-turkey abstinence as a goal, there are several "warm turkey" alternatives (Miller & Page, 1991). One is to give moderation a try, with close monitoring and the best professional support you can offer. Such a trial period of moderation was prescribed long ago by Marty Mann (1950) as a challenge to those who doubted their need to abstain, but we now know much more about how to help people achieve it. If the client succeeds, fine. If not, often the experience of failing at (or the difficulty of) moderation is the best convincer of the need for abstinence. Data are even available from which to advise clients about the probability of their succeeding with moderation versus abstinence (Miller, Leckman, Delaney, & Tinkcom, 1992; Miller, Zweben, DiClemente, & Rychtarik, 1992). A second approach with those reluctant to abstain is "sobriety sampling" (Meyers & Smith, 1995), in which the client is encouraged to give abstinence a try for a limited amount of time, without making a long-term commitment teetotaling. (The extreme form of this, of course, is "one day at a time.") Like a trial at moderate drinking, sobriety sampling allows the client time to warm up to the idea of longer-term changes. It can give clients a chance to experience some of the positive aspects of sobriety, perhaps for the first time in a long while. Third is the option of gradually tapering down to abstinence. This is an approach used with some success in smoking cessation, cutting down step by step the number and nicotine content of cigarettes, perhaps by half, to reduce dependence level in preparation for a quit attempt.

## ALCOHOLICS ANONYMOUS (AA)

AA is not new, of course, having been founded in 1935. What has been new during the past 20 years is increased interest in the scientific study of AA processes and outcomes (McCrady & Miller, 1993). Several reviews and meta-analyses have summarized the now large body of research on AA (Emrick, Tonigan, Montgomery, & Little, 1993; Humpreys, Moos, & Finney, 1996; Tonigan, Toscova, & Miller, 1996), and a few common conclusions can be drawn. First, voluntary AA attendance or involvement during and after (but not before) treatment is modestly associated with more positive outcomes, particularly higher rates of abstinence. Thus, there is reason to encourage clients to try AA. Contrary to speculation by some writers, research reflects no detrimental effects of voluntary AA attendance, even for those who identify themselves as agnostic or atheistic in belief (Tonigan, Miller, & Schermer, in press). At the same time, several controlled trials now show no benefit of *mandated* AA attendance, whether coerced by courts or employee assistance programs (Kownacki & Shadish, 1999). This is consonant with the core literature of AA itself, in that AA was always intended to be a voluntary organization that works by attraction, not compulsion. In sum, we concur with Glaser (1993) that all clients should be encouraged to sample AA, but that no one should be required to attend. Very little is known about the benefits of attending any of the other alcoholism mutual-help groups currently available in the United States.

## MATCHING CLIENTS TO TREATMENTS

The largest controlled trial ever conducted for alcoholism treatment methods is Project MATCH (1997), which was conducted during the final decade of the 20th century. The central purpose of the trial was to test the common-sense clinical belief that clients will fare better if we match them to the treatment method most appropriate for them. The MATCH trial evaluated, with 1,726 clients at nine sites, virtually every client-treatment matching hypothesis for which supporting evidence had been previously reported, testing methods for matching clients to Twelve Step Facilitation therapy (TSF; Nowinski, Baker, & Carroll, 1992), Motivational Enhancement Therapy (MET; Miller et al., 1992), and Cognitive-Behavioral Skills Training (CBT; Kadden, Carrol, Donovan, Cooney, Monti, & Abrams, 1992). All three treatments yielded excellent outcomes, with a slight overall advantage for the Twelve Step treatment when the outcome criterion was complete abstinence (Project MATCH Research Group, 1997a, 1997b, 1998a, 1998b). Surprisingly few of the previously reported matches held up under scrutiny. Angry clients consistently fared better in MET, which is designed to minimize client resistance and resolve ambivalence about change (Miller & Rollnick, 2002). In the long run (3 years after treatment), clients whose social support systems favored continued drinking were helped most by the TSF treatment (Project MATCH Research Group, 1998a), which engaged them in a new social support system that favors sobriety. Outpatients with less severe psychological symptoms fared better in TSF. A full professional report of the MATCH study, with special emphasis on clinically relevant findings, was recently released in book form (Babor & Del Boca, in press).

## *INTENSITY OF TREATMENT*

Clearly with the increasing penetration of managed care in the United States, the treatment of alcoholism has shifted dramatically away from intensive and inpatient services. While this has made it more difficult to find inpatient beds when they are needed, this change in treatment delivery systems was not unwarranted. Randomized trials have rather consistently shown no better outcomes from inpatient than from outpatient treatment, or from longer versus shorter inpatient stays (Institute of Medicine, 1990; Miller & Hester, 1986). As noted above, even studies of larger versus smaller doses of outpatient have not reflected consistent differences. Part of the problem here is that "treatment" has usually been poorly defined in these studies, and there is no reason to expect that larger doses of just any treatment would yield improvement. Rather, it makes sense that larger doses of *effective* treatment methods should improve outcomes. Indeed, studies of undifferentiated "general" or eclectic alcoholism counseling provide little evidence of effectiveness, whereas (consistent with the larger psychotherapy literature) better outcomes are associated with adherence to a coherent treatment approach.

It is noteworthy, however, that better treatment outcomes *are* associated with clients' length of voluntary stay (Cannon, Keefe, & Lark, 1997; Fiorentine, 2001). That is, the longer a client sticks with a treatment, the more treatment sessions attended, the more AA meetings attended, the more prescribed medication taken (even if the pills are placebo), the better that client's outcomes. There is something about *doing something* to get better–taking steps toward change. This suggests that instead of worrying about how to make clients attend and comply with a particular treatment, it makes sense to help them find something that they *will* stick with, even if it is not what we might choose for them. Said more simply, let clients choose from a menu, and match themselves to treatment alternatives. In truth, they already do.

## BRIDGING THE RESEARCH-PRACTICE GAP

The pace of change in alcoholism treatment has accelerated, and more is expected of practitioners in this area than ever before. The good news is that much has been learned during the past two decades that is directly relevant to clinicians in helping their clients change. The bad news is that it often takes a long time for new knowledge and methods to find their way into routine practice–a problem that is by no means unique to the alcoholism field (Rogers, 1995). Clinician-friendly journals such as *Alcoholism Treatment Quarterly* represent one useful method for keeping up with developments. The Center for Substance Abuse Treatment (http://www.samhsa.gov/centers/CSAT2002) has produced a wide range of Treatment Improvement Protocols for clinicians. Evidence-based treatment guidelines for therapists are increasingly available (http://www.nida.nih.gov, Miller & Hester, in press). The gap is also being narrowed by new initiatives to foster direct collaboration between clinical researchers and front-line practitioners, an innovation well represented by the National Institute on Drug Abuse Clinical Trials Network (http://www.nida.nih.gov/CTN/Index.htm) and the CSAT's treatment improvement exchange. Such collaborations are likely to render new and effective treatment methods more readily accessible to practicing clinicians, and also to shape future research to address the practical problems faced by those who commit their daily lives to the treatment of alcoholism.

## REFERENCES

American Psychiatric Association. (1980). *Diagnostic and statistical manual of mental disorders* (3rd ed.). Washington, DC: Author.

Babor, T. F. & Del Boca, F. K. (in press). *Treatment matching in alcoholism.* Cambridge, UK: Cambridge University Press.

Bien, T. H., Miller, W. R., & Tonigan, J. S. (1993). Grief interventions for alcohol problems: A review. *Addiction, 88*(3), 315-335.

Bobo, J. K., McIlvain, H. E., Lando, H. A., Walker, R. D., & Leed-Kelly, A. (1998). Effect of smoking cessation counseling on recovery from alcoholism: Findings from a randomized community intervention trial. *Addiction 93*(6), 877-887.

Bobo, J. K., Shilling, R. F., Gilchrist, L. D., & Schinke, S.P. (1986). The double triumph: Sustained sobriety and successful cigarette smoking cessation. *Journal of Substance Abuse Treatment, 3*(1), 21-25.

Burke, B. L., Arkowitz, H., & Dunn, C. (2002). The efficacy of motivational interviewing and its adaptions: What we know so far. In W. R. Miller and S. Rollnick (Eds.), *Motivational interviewing: Preparing people for change.* (2nd Ed.) (in press). New York: Guilford Publishing.

Cannon, D. S., Keefe, C. K., & Clark, L.A. (1997). Persistence predicts latency to relapse following inpatient treatment for alcohol dependence. *Addictive Behaviors, 22*(4), 535-543.

Chafetz, M. E. & Blane, H. T. (1963). Alcohol-crisis treatment approach and establishment of treatment relations with alcoholics. *Psychological Reports, 12*(3), 862.

Culbreth, J. R. (2000). Substance abuse counselors with and without a personal history of chemical dependency: A review of the literature. *Alcoholism Treatment Quarterly, 18*(2), 67-82.

Cullen, J. & Carr, A. (1999). Codependency: An empirical study from a systemic perspective. *Contemporary Family Therapy, 21*(4), 505-526.

Emmrick, C. D., Tonigan, J. S., Montgomery, H., & Little, L. (1993). Alcoholics Anonymous: What is currently known? In B. S. McCrady & W. R. Miller (Eds.), *Research on Alcoholics Anonymous.* (pp. 41-76), Brunswick, NJ: Rutgers Center of Alcohol Studies.

Emrick, C. (1987). Alcoholics Anonymous: Affiliation processes and effectiveness as treatment. *Alcoholism: Clinical and Experimental Research, 11*(5), 416-423.

Finney, J. W. & Monahan, S. C. (1996). The cost-effectiveness of treatment for alcoholism: A second approximation. *Journal of Studies on Alcohol, May Issue*, 229-243.

Fiorentine, R. (2001). Counseling frequency and the effectiveness of outpatient drug treatment: Revisiting the conclusion that "more is better." *American Journal of Drug and Alcohol Abuse, 27*(4), 617-631.

Foa, E. B. & Street, G. P. (2001). Women and traumatic events. *Journal of Clinical Psychiatry Special Issue: Understanding posttraumatic stress disorder, 62* (Suppl17), 29-34.

Glaser, F. B. (1993). Matchless? Alcoholics Anonymous and the matching hypothesis. In B. S. McCrady & W. R. Miller (Eds.), *Research on Alcoholics Anonymous: Opportunities and alternatives* (pp. 379-395).

Handmaker, N. S., & Anderson, R. E. (submitted for publication). Integrating substance abuse treatment in mental health care. In W. R. Miller & C. Weisner (Eds.), *Changing substance abuse through health and social systems.* New York: Kluwer/Plenum.

Hazelden Foundation (1985). You don't have to tear 'em down to build 'em up. *Hazelden Professional Update, 4*(2), 2.

Heather, N. (1998). Using brief opportunities for change in medical settings. In W. R. Miller & N. Heather (Eds.), *Treating addictive behaviors* (2nd ed.). (pp. 133-147). New York: Plenum.

Hester, R. K. (1995). Behavioral self-control training. In R. K. Hester & W. R. Miller (Eds.), *Handbook of alcoholism treatment approaches: Effective alternatives* (2nd ed.) (pp. 148-159). Needham Heights, MA: Allyn & Bacon.

Hester, R. K. (in press). Behavioral self-control training. In W.R. Miller & R.K. Hester (Eds.), *Handbook of alcoholism treatment approaches*. (3rd ed.) Needham Heights, MA: Allyn & Bacon.

Hester, R. K. & Miller, W. R. (Eds.). (in press). *Handbook of alcoholism treatment approaches: Effective alternatives* (3rd ed.). Boston, MA: Allyn & Bacon.

Hoff, E. C. & McKeown, C. E. (1953). An evaluation of the use of tetraethylthiuram disulfide in the treatment of 560 cases of alcohol addiction. *American Journal of Psychiatry, 109*, 670-673.

Holder, H., Longabaugh, R., Miller, W. R., & Rubonis, A.V. (1991). The cost effectiveness of treatment for alcoholism: A first approximation. *Journal of Studies on Alcohol, 52*(6), 517-540.

Humpreys, K., Moos, R. H., & Finney, J. W. (1996). Life domains, alcoholics anonymous, and role incumbency in the 3-year course of problem drinking. *Journal of Nervous and Mental Disease, 184*(8), 475-481.

Huss, M. (1849). *Alcoholismus chronicus. Chronisk alkoholisjukdom: Ett bidrag till dyskrasiarnas kanndon*. Stockholm: Bonnier/Norstedt.

Institute of Medicine. (1990). *Broadening the base of treatment for alcohol problems*. Washington, DC: National Academy Press.

Jellinek, E. M. (1960). *The disease concept of alcoholism*. New Haven, Conn.: Hillhouse.

Kadden, R., Carroll, K., Donovan, D., Cooney, N., Monti, P., Abrams, D., Litt, M., & Hester, R. (1992). *Cognitive-behavioral coping skills therapy manual: A clinical research guide for therapists treating individuals with alcohol abuse and dependence*. (Volume 3, Project MATCH Monograph Series) Rockville, MD: National Institute on Alcohol Abuse and Alcoholism.

Kerr, J. S. (1996). Two myths of addiction: The addictive personality and the issue of free choice. *Human Psychopharmacology Clinical and Experimental 11* (Suppl 1), S9-S13.

Kownacki, R. J. & Shadish, W. R.(1999). Does Alcoholics Anonymous work? Results from a meta-analysis of controlled experiments. *Substance Use and Misuse, 34*(13), 1897-1916.

Liepman, M. R. (1993). Using family influence to motivate alcoholics to enter treatment: The Johnson Institute intervention approach. In T. J. O'Farrell (Ed.), *Treating alcohol problems: Marital and family interventions* (pp. 54-77). New York: Guilford Press.

Luborsky, L., Crits-Christoph, P., McLellan, A. T., Woody, G., Piper, W., Liberman, B., Imber, S., & Pilkonis, P. (1986). Do therapists vary much in their success? Findings from four outcome studies. *American Journal of Orthropsychiatry, 56*, 501-512.

Mann, M. (1950). *Primer on alcoholism*. New York: Rinehart.

McLellan, A. T. (in press). Questioning the effectiveness of addiction treatments: What is the evidence? In W. R. Miller & C. Weisner (Eds.), *Changing substance abuse through health and social systems*. New York: Kluwer/Plenum.

McLellan, A. T., Woody, G. E., Luborsky, L., & Goehl, L. (1988). Is the counselor an "active ingredient" in substance abuse rehabilitation? An examination of treatment success among four counselors. *Journal of Nervous and Mental Disease, 176*(7), 423-430.

Meyers, R. J., Miller, W. R., Hill, D. E., & Tonigan, J. S. (1999). Community reinforcement and family training (CRAFT): Engaging unmotivated drug users in treatment. *Journal of Substance Abuse, 10*(3), 1-18.

Meyers, R. J. & Smith, J. E. (1995). *Clinical guide to alcohol treatment: The community reinforcement approach*. New York, NY: The Guilford Press.

Meyers, W. R. & Miller, W. R. (Eds.) (2001). *A community reinforcement approach to addiction treatment*. Cambridge, UK: Cambridge University Press.

Miller, N. S. & Flaherty, J. A. (2000). Effectiveness of coerced addiction treatment (alternative consequences): A review of the clinical research. *Journal of Substance Abuse Treatment, 18*(1), 9-16.

Miller, W. R. (1985). Motivation for treatment: A review with special emphasis on alcoholism. *Psychological Bulletin, 98*(1), 84-107.

Miller, W. R. (1992). The evolution of treatment for alcohol problems since 1945. In P. G. Erickson & H. Kalant (Eds.), *Windows on science: 40th anniversary scientific lecture series* (pp. 107-124). Toronto: Addiction Research Foundation.

Miller, W. R. (Ed.) (1999). *Enhancing motivation for change in substance abuse treatment*. Treatment Improvement Protocol (TIP) Series, No. 35. Rockville, MD: Center for Substance Abuse Treatment.

Miller, W. R. & Baca, L. M. (1983). Two-year follow-up of bibliotherapy and therapist directed controlled drinking training for problem drinkers. *Behavior Therapy, 14*(3), 441-448.

Miller, W. R. & Hester, R. K. (1986). Inpatient alcoholism treatment: Who benefits? *American Psychologist, 41*(7), 794-805.

Miller, W. R. & Hester, R. K. (in press). Treating alcohol problems: Towards an informed eclecticism. In W. R. Miller & R. K. Hester (Eds.), *Handbook of alcoholism treatment approaches*. (3rd ed.) Needham Heights, MA: Allyn & Bacon.

Miller, W. R., Leckman, A. L., Delaney, H. D., & Tinkom, M. (1992). Long-term follow-up of behavioral self-control training. *Journal of Studies on Alcohol. 53*(2), 249-261.

Miller, W. R., Meyers, R. J., & Tonigan, J. S. (1999). Engaging the unmotivated in treatment for alcohol problems: A comparison of three strategies for intervention through family members. *Journal of Consulting and Clinical Psychology, 67*, 688-697.

Miller, W. R. & Page, A. C. (1991). Warm turkey: Other routes to abstinence. *Journal of Substance Abuse Treatment, 8*(4), 227-232.

Miller, W. R. & Rollnick, S. (2002). *Motivational interviewing: Preparing people for change* (2nd ed.). New York: Guilford Press.

Miller, W. R., Taylor, C. A., & West, J. C. (1980). Focused versus broad-spectrum behavior therapy for problem drinkers. *Journal of Consulting and Clinical Psychology, 48*(5), 590-601.

Miller, W. R., Walters, S. T., & Bennett, M. E. (2001). How effective is alcoholism treatment in the United States? *Journal of Studies on Alcohol, March Issue*, 211-220.

Miller, W. R. & Weisner, C. (Eds.) (in press). *Changing substance abuse through health and social systems.* New York: Kluwer/Plenum.

Miller, W. R., Westerberg, V. S., Harris, R.J., & Tonigan, J. S. (1996). What predicts relapse? Prospective testing of antecedent models. *Addiction, 91* (Supplement), S155-S171.

Miller, W. R. & Wilbourne, P. L. (2002). Mesa grande: A methodological analysis of clinical trials of treatments for alcohol use disorders. *Addiction, 97,* 265-277.

Miller, W. R., Wilbourne, P. L., & Hetema, J. (2002). What works? A methodological analysis of the alcohol treatment outcome literature. In W. R. Miller & R. K. Hester (Eds.), *Handbook of alcoholism treatment approaches.* (3rd ed.) Needham Heights, MA: Allyn & Bacon.

Miller, W. R., Zweben, A., DiClemente, C. C., & Rychtarik, R. G. (1992). *Motivational enhancement therapy manual: A clinical research guide for therapists treating individuals with alcohol abuse and dependence.* (Volume 2, Project MATCH Monograph Series) Rockville, MD: National Institute on Alcohol Abuse and Alcoholism.

Moos, R. H., Finney, J. W., & Cronkite, R. C. (Eds.). (1990). *Alcoholism treatment: Context, process and outcome.* New York: Oxford University Press.

Moyer, A., Finney, J. W., Swearingen, C. E., & Vergun, P. (2002). Brief interventions for alcohol problems: A meta-analytic review of controlled investigations in treatment-seeking and non-treatment seeking populations. *Addiction, 97,* 279-292.

Najavits, L. M. & Weiss, R. D. (1994). Variations in therapist effectiveness in the treatment of patients with substance use disorders: An empirical review. *Addiction, 89*(6), 679-688.

Nowinski, J., Baker, S., & Carroll, K. (1992). *Twelve step facilitation therapy manual: A clinical research guide for therapists treating individuals with alcohol and dependence.* (Volume 1, Project MATCH Monograph Series) Rockville, MD: National Institute on Alcohol Abuse and Alcoholism.

Oddone P. E., Genuis, M. L., & Violato, C. (2001). A meta-analysis of the published research on the effects of child sexual abuse. *Journal of Psychology, 135,* 1, 17-36.

Polcin, D.L. (2001). Drug and alcohol offenders coerced into treatment: A review of modalities and suggestions for research on social model programs. *Substance Use & Misuse, 36*(5), 589-608.

Preuss, U. W. & Wong, W. M. (2000). Comorbidity. In G. Zernig, S. Alois, M. Kurz, & S. S. O'Malley, *Handbook of alcoholism* (pp. 287-303). Boca Raton, FL: CRC.

Prochaska, J. O. & DiClemente, C. C. (1984). *The transtheoretical approach: Crossing traditional boundaries of therapy.* Homewood, IL: Dow Jones-Irwin.

Prochaska, J. O. & DiClemente, C. C. (1998). Toward a comprehensive, transtheoretical model of change: Stages of change and addictive behaviors. In W. R. Miller & N. Heather (Eds.), *Treating addictive behaviors* (2nd ed.) (pp. 3-24). New York: Plenum.

Prochaska, J. O., DiClemente, C. C., & Norcross, J. C. (1992). In search of how people change: Applications to addictive behaviors. *American Psychologist, 47,* 1102-1114.

Project MATCH Research Group (1997a). Matching alcoholism treatments to client heterogeneity: Project MATCH posttreatment drinking outcomes. *Journal of Studies on Alcohol, 58,* 7-29.

Project MATCH Research Group (1997b). Project MATCH secondary a priori hypotheses. *Addiction, 92*(12), 1671-1698.

Project MATCH Research Group (1998a). Matching alcoholism treatments to client heterogeneity: Project MATCH three-year drinking outcomes. *Alcoholism: Clinical and Experimental Research, 22,* 1300-1311.

Project MATCH Research Group (1998b). Therapist effects in three treatments for alcohol problems. *Psychotherapy Research, 8,* 455-474.

Rogers, E. M. (1995). *Diffusion of innovations.* New York: The Free Press.

Rosenthal, R. N. & Westreich, L. (1999). Treatment of persons with dual diagnoses of substance use disorder and other psychological problems. In B. S. McCrady & E. E. Epstein (Eds.), *Addictions: A comprehensive guidebook.* (pp. 439-476). New York: Oxford Press.

Sanchez-Craig, M. (1993). *Drinkwise: How to quit drinking or cut down.* (2nd Ed.). Toronto, Canada: Addiction Research Foundation.

Schuckit, M. A., Tipp, F. E., Bucholz, K. K., Nurnberger, J. I., Hesselbrock, V. M., Crowe, R. R., & Kramer, J. (1997). The life-time rates of three major mood disorders and four major anxiety disorders in alcoholics and controls. *Addiction, 92*(10), 1289-1304.

Simpson, T. L. (1999). An exploration of the functional roles of alcohol use among women drinkers with and without a history of childhood sexual abuse. *Dissertation Abstracts International, 60*(4-B), 1873.

Simpson, T. L. & Miller, W. R. (2002). Concomitance between childhood sexual and physical abuse and substance abuse: A review. *Clinical Psychology Review, 22,* 27-77.

Sisson, R. W. & Azrin, N. H. (1986). Family-member involvement to initiate and promote treatment of problem drinkers. *Journal of Behavior Therapy and Experimental Psychiatry, 17,* 15-21.

Sobell, M. B. & Sobell, L. C. (2000). Guiding self-change. In W. R. Miller & N. Heather (Eds.), *Treating addictive behaviors* (2nd Ed.). New York: Plenum Press.

Stafford, L. L. (2001). Is codependency a meaningful concept? *Issues in Mental Health Nursing, 22,* 273-286.

Swift, R. M. (in press). Psychotropic medications. In W. R. Miller & R. K. Hester (Eds.), *Handbook of alcoholism treatment approaches* (3rd ed.). Needham Heights, MA: Allyn & Bacon.

Thomas, E. J., Adams, K. B., Yoshioka, M. R., & Ager, R. D. (1990). Unilateral relationship enhancement in the treatment of spouses of uncooperative alcohol abusers. *American Journal of Family Therapy, 18,* 334-344.

Thomas, E. J. & Ager, R. D. (1993). Unilateral family therapy with the spouses of uncooperative alcohol abusers. In T. J. O'Farrell (Ed.), *Treating alcohol problems: Marital and family interventions* (pp. 3-33). New York: Guilford Press.

Tonigan, J. S., Toscova, R., & Miller, W. R. (1996). Meta-analysis of the Alcoholics Anonymous literature: Sample and study characteristics moderate findings. *Journal of Studies on Alcohol, 57,* 65-72.

Tonigan, T. S., Miller, W. R., & Schermer, C. (in press). Atheists, agnostics and Alcoholics Anonymous. *Journal of Substance Abuse.*

Truax, J. A. & Carkhuff, R. R. (1971). *Toward effective counseling and psychotherapy.* Chicago: Aldine.

Valle, S. K. (1981). Interpersonal functioning of alcoholism counselors and treatment outcome. *Journal of Studies on Alcohol, 42,* 783-790.

Vesper, J. H. (1998). Mismanagement of contertransference in posttraumatic stress disorder: Ethical and legal violations. *American Journal of Forensic Psychology, 16*(2), 5-15.

# Spirituality, Alcohol and Other Drug Problems: Where Have We Been? Where Are We Going?

Oliver J. Morgan, PhD, NCC

**SUMMARY.** A brief examination of the history, central figures, and literature of spirituality in addiction studies is followed by a review of central concepts and a look toward the future of spirituality research. Some current initiatives are also examined. *[Article copies available for a fee from The Haworth Document Delivery Service: 1-800-HAWORTH. E-mail address: <getinfo@haworthpressinc.com> Website: <http://www.HaworthPress.com> © 2002 by The Haworth Press, Inc. All rights reserved.]*

**KEYWORDS.** Spirituality, alcohol problems, addiction, research

*At present, it must be acknowledged that our lack of knowledge on these matters far outweighs what is known. There is much to be discovered about spirituality and how it relates to addiction disorders and their treatment.*

–National Institute for Healthcare Research, 1997

Oliver J. Morgan is Professor and Chair, Department of Counseling and Human Services, University of Scranton, Scranton, PA. He is also a National Certified Counselor (NCC).

[Haworth co-indexing entry note]: "Spirituality, Alcohol and Other Drug Problems: Where Have We Been? Where Are We Going?" Morgan, Oliver J. Co-published simultaneously in *Alcoholism Treatment Quarterly* (The Haworth Press, Inc.) Vol. 20, No. 3/4, 2002, pp. 61-82; and: *Alcohol Problems in the United States: Twenty Years of Treatment Perspective* (ed: Thomas F. McGovern, and William L. White) The Haworth Press, Inc., 2002, pp. 61-82. Single or multiple copies of this article are available for a fee from The Haworth Document Delivery Service [1-800-HAWORTH, 9:00 a.m. - 5:00 p.m. (EST). E-mail address: getinfo@haworthpressinc.com].

Hailed as a new "Fifth Force" in the overall development of counseling, psychology, and clinical practice (Stanard, Sandhu, & Painter, 2000), spirituality is currently a "growing edge" topic in the field of addiction studies as well.

Morgan (1999b; in press) has described the development of addiction science and the later emergence of spirituality as an important topic for research and practice. As the "science" (medical, neurochemical, physiological, psychological) of addiction inquiry became ascendant in the early days of the field, other ways of thinking became less prominent. The early promise of a collaborative and integrative model receded into the background (Keller, 1975; Morgan & Jordan, 1999). Many areas of addiction science that are critically important today evolved during this time, including research into the genetics and chemistry of addiction, greater understanding of the neurochemical pathways in the brain, cross-cultural and epidemiological studies, research into the "stages of change" leading to recovery, relapse prevention, and the like.

With the arrival of *family systems* theory and exploration into the family dynamics at work within the lives of addicts, greater understanding developed around the intergenerational patterns, adaptive mechanisms, and familial consequences of addictive behavior (Morgan, 1999b). Various models of treatment–for addicts and for those who love them–became available. This was an important second phase in the evolution of addiction studies. It is worth noting that the work of several specialists from within the family field, such as Gregory Bateson (1972) and David Berenson (1990), helped pave the way for what was to come.

The next phase of development within addiction studies came with renewed interest and attention to the dynamics of *recovery*. The work of Stephanie Brown (1985) was particularly important here. Her work marked a return to (a) scientific interest in the development, progression and dynamics of recovery as a process of its own, separate from the addictive "career," (b) understanding the dynamics of mutual-help groups such as Alcoholics Anonymous, (c) attention to the "lived experience" of addicts and recovering persons themselves, and (d) an understanding of the need for collaboration among all those concerned with fostering recovery, particularly between clinical professionals and the recovery movement as "partners" (Brown, 1985, pp. x-xiii; see also Morgan, 1995, 1999). Brown's work has proven to be fertile ground for many of those studying the dynamics of recovery and the importance of spirituality (Kubicek, 1998; Morgan, 1992; Sommer, 1992; Turner, 1993; Kubicek, Morrison, & Morgan, in press).

The turn to recovery research was a decisive moment in the emergence of a focus on recovery spirituality.

## MID-1980s: A TIME OF FERMENT

However, it must also be noted that other investigators and practitioners within the field of addiction studies were coming to similar conclusions and that their writings fostered a mounting interest in the spiritual dimensions of addiction and recovery (see Table 1).

In 1984 the first volume of *Alcoholism Treatment Quarterly* appeared and signaled its intention to help initiate and contribute to a conversation on the role of spirituality in alcoholism/addiction. That first volume included a three-part series (Volume 1, Numbers 1, 2, and 4) by Charles Whitfield on "Stress Management and Spirituality During Recovery: A Transpersonal Approach," including a copy of Whitfield's 36-item Spirituality Self Assessment Scale. In that same first volume, Rev. Leo Booth published two Clinical Comments, utilizing his experience as Spiritual Director of Chemical Dependency at San Pedro Peninsula Hospital, while a very positive review of *Not-God: A History of Alcoholics Anonymous* by Ernest Kurtz (1979) appeared. It is instructive that Booth forcefully challenges the staff of treatment centers to take spirituality seriously as part of recovery (1984, p. 139), while the reviewer points out Kurtz's insight that "what A.A. has done so well is to make the word 'spiritual' acceptable" (1984, p. 148). These are small indicators of the embryonic "state of the conversation" around spirituality and recovery at that time.

In 1985, along with the publication of Brown's book, *Treating the Alcoholic*, Whitfield published his *Alcoholism, Attachments and Spirituality: A Transpersonal Approach* and began conducting a number of workshops around the country on the dynamics of spirituality and recovery; Booth (1985) published *Spirituality and Recovery*. Rev. James Royce, S.J. (1985a and b) also published two articles on recovery spirituality that same year.

Perhaps not surprisingly, 1985-1986 saw the emergence of a counter-movement against the notion of spirituality, particularly in its connection with recovery through A.A. Albert Ellis (1985) published his influential article, "Why Alcoholics Anonymous Is Probably Doing Itself and Alcoholics More Harm than Good by Its Insistence on a Higher Power," bringing into clearer and more specific focus some of his earlier arguments in *The Case Against Religiosity* (1983), and foreshadowing his more developed views in "Divine Intervention and the Treatment of Chemical Dependency" (1990). Ellis' primary concerns revolve around (a) those who cannot or choose not to enter recovery through Alcoholics Anonymous, in part because of the air of "religiosity" in A.A., and (b) the potential iatrogenic effects of believing in a God or Higher Power as a way to recovery rather than believing in one's self and in one's own resources. It is interesting to note that in the same 1985 first issue of *Employee Assistance Quarterly*, following Ellis' review, there were two brief follow-up

## TABLE 1. Select Spirituality Timeline

### *Founding of Addiction Studies (see White, 1998; Morgan, 1999b)*

| | |
|---|---|
| **1935** | Alcoholics Anonymous founded (A.A.) |
| **1937** | Research Council on Problems of Alcohol (RCPA) |
| **1939** | First Edition of "Big Book," *Alcoholics Anonymous* |
| **1940** | Founding of *Quarterly Journal of Studies on Alcohol* (*QJSA*) |
| **1943** | Yale Center of Alcohol Studies<br>Yale Summer School of Alcohol Studies |
| **1944** | Yale Plan Clinics<br>National Committee for Education of Alcoholism |
| **1942 – 1961** | Harry Tiebout, "1st advocate and friend of A.A. from within psychiatry" (White, 1998, p. 142) publishes seminal articles |

### *Addiction and Spirituality: Early Days*

| | |
|---|---|
| **1951** | Ford, SJ: *Depth psychology, morality and alcoholism* |
| **1954** | Founding of NYC Medical Society on Alcoholism (later, American Society of Addiction Medicine) |
| **1955** | Ford, SJ, *Man takes a drink* (*What about your drinking?*) |
| **1961** | Clinebell, *Understanding and counseling the alcoholic (1st edition)* |
| **1963** | Clinebell, "Philosophical-religious factors in the etiology and treatment of alcoholism." *QJSA, 24*, 473-488. |
| **1966** | Harry Tiebout dies. |
| **1971** | Bateson, "The cybernetics of 'self': A theory of alcoholism." |
| **1979** | Kurtz, *Not-god: A history of Alcoholics Anonymous* |
| **1982** | Kurtz, "Why AA works: The intellectual significance of Alcoholics Anonymous." |
| **1983** | Ellis, *The case against religiosity* |

### *Mid-1980s: A Watershed; Time of Ferment*

| | |
|---|---|
| **1984** | ATQ, Volume 1, Number 1 (Spring). This Journal signals its intention to publish at least some articles in the area of spirituality and alcoholism/addiction with series by Whitfield, Booth and book review of Kurtz's *Not-god* |
| **1985** | Whitfield, *Alcoholism, attachments and spirituality: A transpersonal approach* |
| | S. Brown, *Treating the alcoholic* |
| | Booth, *Spirituality and recovery* |
| | Royce, "What do you mean, spiritual illness?" AND "Sin or solace? Religious views on alcohol and alcoholism" |
| | Ellis, "Why Alcoholics Anonymous is probably doing itself and alcoholics more harm than good by its insistence on a higher power" |
| | Christopher, "Sobriety without superstition" |
| | Rational Recovery (R.R.) founded by Jack Trimpey |

| | |
|---|---|
| **1986** | First meeting of Save Our Selves/Secular Organizations for Sobriety |
| **1987** | Buxton, Smith & Seymour, "Spirituality and other points of resistance to the 12-step recovery process" |
| | Seymour & Smith, *Drugfree: A unique, positive approach to staying off alcohol and other drugs* |
| | Royce, "Spiritual Progression Chart" |
| **1988** | Brown, Peterson and Cunningham, three part series in ATQ volume 5, plus three more articles in 1989, 1990, and 1991 Tom McGovern takes over as Editor of *ATQ*, succeeding Bruce Carruth |
| | May, *Addiction and grace* Christopher, *How to stay sober: Recovery without religion* |
| **1989** | Trimpey, *Rational recovery from alcoholism: The small book* |

### *1990s to Present: Ongoing Development*

| | |
|---|---|
| **1990** | Berenson, "A systemic view of spirituality: God and twelve step programs as resources in family therapy" |
| | Miller, "Spirituality: The silent dimension in addiction research. The 1990 Leonard Ball oration" |
| | Ellis & Schoenfeld, "Divine intervention and the treatment of chemical dependency" |
| **1995** | Howard Brown, Jr. dies |
| **1996** | Mercadante, *Victims & sinners: Spiritual roots of addiction and recovery* |
| **1997** | Miller, "Spiritual aspects of addictions treatment and research" |
| | National Institute on Healthcare Research, *Scientific Research on Spirituality and Health: A consensus report* |
| **1998** | Clinebell, *Understanding and counseling persons with alcohol, drug, and behavioral addictions [revised and enlarged edition]* |
| | Miller, "Researching the spiritual dimensions of alcohol and other drug problems" |
| | White, *Slaying the dragon: The history of addiction treatment and recovery in America* |
| **1999** | Miller & Bennett, *Annotated Online Bibliography – Spirituality and substance use* |
| | Morgan & Jordan, *Addiction and spirituality: A multidisciplinary approach* |
| **2000** | NIAAA & Fetzer RFA [AA-00-002]: "Studying spirituality and alcohol" |

articles by G. Alan Marlatt, a cognitive behavioral psychologist, and Abraham Twerski, psychiatrist and rabbi, both of whom are a bit more sympathetic to A.A. and to the notion of spirituality. These three brief articles in response to the publication of *Alcoholics Anonymous, 3rd edition* indicate once again the vigorous discussion that was occurring around these ideas.

At the same time, James Christopher and Jack Trimpey made their appearance in the field. Each was the founder of a new mutual-help recovery resource.

Trimpey founded Rational Recovery (R.R.) in 1985 and Christopher held the first meeting of Save Our Selves/Secular Organizations for Sobriety (S.O.S.) in 1986. Both groups consciously offer alternatives to A.A. *and* its spiritual approach to recovery. Once again, these very events bring spirituality to the fore.

## CONTINUED DEVELOPMENT

From the mid-1980s until now, as the reader can see in reviewing the Select Spirituality Timeline (Table 1), the topic of spirituality has been the subject of increasing reflection, research, and publication. Several important names and seminal publications have appeared. David Smith, M.D., founder of the Haight-Asbury Clinic, and his collaborators Richard Seymour (1987) and Millicent Buxton (1987) have published several key works that highlight the role of spirituality. James Royce (1987) and Charles Whitfield (1987, 1989) continued to publish in the same area.

Over time new names appeared and made significant contributions. Before the untimely death of Howard Brown, Jr., in 1995 (see Miller, 1996), he and his colleagues published a number of important articles in *Alcoholism Treatment Quarterly* and other journals, exploring a psychospiritual approach to addiction assessment, treatment, aftercare, and scientific understanding (Brown et al., 1988a, b, and c, 1989, 1990a and b, 1991, 1992, 1993). They called their perspective a "behavioral/cognitive spiritual model." Brown's initial work appeared in *ATQ* in 1988, as Tom McGovern took over editing the journal. This was the same year that Gerald May (1988) published the popular *Addiction and Grace*, in which he argued that notions such as "addiction" and "attachment" might be useful for a modern understanding of sin (see Miller, 1998).

The important work of William Miller into the spiritual dimension of addiction and recovery began to appear in 1990 (Miller, 1990, 1995, 1997, 1998). His explorations have led to several important research initiatives, which we will discuss at the end of this article. In 1995 Robert Kus edited a fine volume entitled *Spirituality and Chemical Dependency*, bringing together a number of older and newer writers on the topic. In 1996 Linda Mercadante published *Victims & Sinners: Spiritual Roots of Addiction and Recovery*, a provocative theological exploration of 12-step spirituality, the recovery "movement," and allied issues. It stands as a serious work that must be included in any contemporary reflections on the topic. One of the earliest and most provocative writers on addiction from within the field of pastoral counseling, Howard Clinebell, Jr., resurfaced in 1998 with a revised and enlarged edition of his classic work, *Understanding and Counseling Persons with Alcohol, Drug, and Behavioral Addictions*.

In 1999 William Miller and Melanie Bennett released their online comprehensive bibliography, *Spirituality and Substance Use*, providing a rich resource for addiction scholars and investigators. In that same year Morgan and Jordan published *Addiction and Spirituality: A Multidisciplinary Approach*, gathering both familiar and new voices into the conversation about addiction and spirituality, while pointing a way forward for this field of inquiry.

As the reader can see, this has been a varied and rich history. In what follows we will review some of the developments, important figures, and possible future directions for the ongoing understanding of spirituality as it relates to addiction. We will examine the thinking of several major advocates for inclusion of this theme in a more comprehensive model of understanding. As we will see, some of the literature is more narrative in tone and speculative in nature, while newer literature moves in the direction of standard social science research designs that are more likely to be published in peer-reviewed professional venues and, therefore, may have broader impact (Miller, 1998). Finally, we will examine several recent developments in this area and some potential ways in which research and thinking may fruitfully proceed.

It should be noted that, while spirituality as it relates to addiction may be discussed in other ways and a number of spiritual traditions may be usefully examined in this regard (see, for example, O'Connell & Alexander, 1994), our discussion will focus primarily on the classic writers and literature related to 12-step spirituality and Alcoholics Anonymous. This understanding will help to ground future, and hopefully more diverse, work.

## SPIRITUALITY, RELIGION, AND RECOVERY: WHAT HAVE WE LEARNED?

In "Spirituality and Other Points of Resistance to the 12-Step Recovery Process," Smith and his colleagues (1987) outline a number of the issues that have dogged discussion of 12-step recovery. They discuss the focus on recovery, especially as it occurs through 12-step support, as a starting point for renewed interest in spirituality (p. 279) and then proceed to distinguish between "religion" and "spirituality," as other authors have, before and since (see, for example, Brown et al., 1988a; Chappel, 1993; Kurtz, 1979; Miller, 1998; Tiebout, 1946).

Religion is often seen and defined in the literature as a "social phenomenon," an "organized structure . . . defined by its boundaries–by particular beliefs, practices, and forms of governance and rituals" (Miller, 1998). Sometimes it has been hard to untangle the interwoven threads of religious roots and history in A.A., so that its *spiritual* dynamics might emerge more clearly (Buxton, Smith, & Seymour, 1987). The confusion of religious ante-cedents and themes with spirituality, and the obvious connections of *both* reli-gion and spirituality to A.A., has often made for some of the difficulty and resistance within the scientific community to appreciating the role of spiritual-ity, as well as to the fellowship and program of A.A.

Spirituality, however, has also been difficult to define (and operationalize) in its own right, making it difficult to study in any scientific way (Buxton et al., 1987; Miller, 1998). The standard scientific research into addiction and recov-ery uses methodological assumptions and a quantitative research paradigm that, while valuable for investigating a number of phenomena, may be of lim-ited utility in studying the realm of spiritual experience, at least initially. Kurtz (1986, 1991) has suggested that spirituality is so deeply ingrained in the realm of personal experience that attention to narrative and story–more qualitative dimensions of human living–may be the only way that spiritual dynamics will fully reveal themselves (see also Whitfield, 1985).

## A CRITICAL CROSSROAD

It is at this point that we come to a critical crossroad in our discussion. Much of the literature that exists currently in the field of spirituality and addiction is more reflective and speculative in nature, often rooted in the lived experience of addicts themselves and gathered through clinical, qualitative and narrative research (Morgan, 1999b & c). It is often augmented by the writer's sense of recovery history and cultural context (for example, Kurtz, 1979), philosophy (Kurtz, 1982), theology (Clinebell, 1998), transpersonal psychology (Alexan-der, 1997; Grof, 1993; Small, 1981), and Eastern mysticism (Whitfield, 1985; see Kurtz, 1982 as well). This material describes the "core spiritual experi-ences" of addiction and recovery somewhat densely and theoretically, trying to present the whole of the experience and its deep psychological and philo-sophical roots. This literature is important and foundational.

There is another strain in the literature, however, that attempts to be more directly "empirical" and descriptive as these terms are commonly understood. This body of literature utilizes a more standard social scientific paradigm, gathering data through surveys, research interviews, and psychometric instru-mentation. Less theoretical, it often feels more grounded and practical to the reader. This strain has been used, sometimes alone and sometimes in conjunc-tion with qualitative methods, in several hallmark studies (Brown, 1985; Brown, Peterson, & Cunningham 1988a, b, & c; Project MATCH Research Group, 1993, 1997). Increasingly it is being seen as the "next step" in studying spirituality in addiction science.

Both strains are important to this field of study, but they make for very different reading. We will first present a synthesis of the core spiritual experiences of addiction and recovery, gathered from a number of writers in the speculative camp. As we will see, their assertions, though profound and often acknowledged positively by recovering persons, are also difficult to prove and hard to follow-up with further studies. Next, we will look at how contemporary researchers are beginning to explore the question of spirituality, not so much by speculation spun out of whole cloth but rather through examination of various spiritual changes, beliefs and practices that are acknowledged by a wide range of recovering persons.

### CORE SPIRITUALITY: A TALE OF DEGENERATION, SURRENDER, AND TRANSFORMATION

From the beginnings of the recovery movement and the founding of addiction studies, there have been those professionals (physicians, researchers, pastors, etc.) who, in listening to the lived experience of successfully recovering persons, have underscored the importance of spirituality in the recovery process.

Rev. John C. Ford, S.J. (1902-1989), a confidante to Bill Wilson and other early recovery leaders, was a strong pastoral voice in favor of the young A.A. movement and over the years helped to forge a pastorally-sensitive, ecumenical view of alcoholism and addiction. His work with the Yale Summer School on Alcohol Studies and his relationships both with A.A. and with many early addiction scientists aided in the formation of the early collaborative approach to alcohol and other drug problems (Morgan, 1999a & b).

Ford took seriously A.A.'s "threefold disease" concept–a disease of body, mind, and soul–as the way to understand the nature of alcoholism and addiction. He listened carefully to the testimony of recovering persons and their families, and found agreement with this concept. He listened as well to the evolving scientific views that were coming to the fore. To these perspectives he added his own clear theological voice, seeing the progression of alcoholism as having a "definite degenerative effect" on its sufferers (Morgan, 1999a, 38):

> Alcoholism is not just a disease, and not just a moral problem. It is both. It is a sickness of body, mind, and soul.
> The sickness of the body refers to whatever physiological factors scientists can point out as contributing to the abnormal drinking.
> The sickness of the mind is the compulsive or addictive thinking which sometimes takes possession of the alcoholic with regard to drinking.

> *The sickness of the soul is the moral and spiritual deterioration characteristic of so many alcoholics.* (Ford, 1961, 111; *emphasis mine*)

In Ford's view, over time and with continued use of alcohol to "escape from pain," personal virtues (e.g., honesty, humility) and character begin to deteriorate, the person becomes increasingly more self-centered, "spiritually bankrupt," and "at odds with God, at odds with his [sic] own conscience, and finally deprived of his own self-respect" (1961, p. 110).

This "diagnosis" allowed Ford to attribute the success of A.A. to its understanding or "definition" of addictive illness (see also Siegler, Osmond, & Newell, 1968) through the threefold disease concept as well as its application of spiritual principles ("medicine of the soul") to recovery. He believed that the Twelve Steps were "a program of moral and spiritual regeneration" that counteracted the degenerative effect of addiction as a "sickness of soul" (Ford, 1950, p. 4; 1951, p. 63). Spirituality in this view is related to character, virtue, and one's responsible relationship to the self, to others, and to the world of God's creation (Morgan, 1999a).

Harry Tiebout, MD (1896-1966), sometimes called "A.A.'s psychiatrist," was influential in fostering relationships between A.A. and the world of medicine. He was also one of the first writers to grasp and articulate the need for a spiritual perspective in addiction treatment, something he learned from his work with those in recovery (Tiebout, 1946).

Tiebout began to notice that his difficult patients were recovering from alcoholism through the new A.A. and, what's more, that real character change was occurring as well. His investigations led him to listen keenly, producing some unexpected insights.

> Something had taken place under my very nose which could not be doubted and which could not be explained away as mere coincidence. I found myself facing the question: What had happened? My answer is that the patient had had a religious or spiritual experience. The answer, however, did not prove particularly enlightening and it was not until much later that I began to appreciate the real meaning of the answer. (1944, pp. 468-469)

In a long series of publications, Tiebout describes a deeply transforming process that leads to successful recovery, a "deep shift in the patient's emotional tone" and a "discrete pattern of response" (1961, p. 53). He speaks of "surrender" to a "Power greater" and the reduction of ego that accompanies it, as the crucial elements leading to recovery. Tiebout admits that "surrender" was a new word added to his psychiatric vocabulary. He came to see it as the healthy result of "hitting bottom" which engendered authentic humility.

It is now clear that hitting bottom can produce a surrender and that without surrender an individual can hit bottom a thousand times without anything significant taking place. . . . In A.A. language he has accepted a Power greater than himself. He has quit competing for his place in the ranks of the high and mighty. A.A. members would say that his ego has been reduced. And they are right. . . .

A conversion occurs when the individual hits bottom, surrenders, and thereby has his ego reduced. His salvation lies in keeping that ego reduced, in staying humble. These insights, gained from long study of Alcoholics Anonymous and the process it initiates, appear to give meaning and order to the change which A.A. induces. Conversion is no longer an event "out of the blue" but a logical outgrowth of human responses; hitting bottom and surrender. (Tiebout, 1961, pp. 58, 65)

In Tiebout's view this "change which A.A. induces" is a spiritual process of conversion and surrender with clear psychoemotional, cognitive, and behavioral roots and dynamics. Surrender to a Power greater and acceptance of oneself leads to cognitive and behavioral change, to a transformation of identity, and to a profound difference in terms of lifestyle (Morgan, 1992, 1995).

Others have undertaken the task of exploring and understanding these dynamics in more detail.

## FURTHER ELABORATION OF SPIRITUAL ELEMENTS

*What is the addict's central (spiritual) problem?* The diagnosis of Alcoholics Anonymous is clear on this point. In the Big Book of A.A., the reader is told: "Selfishness–self-centeredness! That, we think, is the root of our troubles . . . the alcoholic is an extreme example of *self-will run riot*, though he usually doesn't think so" (Alcoholics Anonymous, 1976, p. 62; *emphasis mine*). When this insight is combined with another from *Twelve Steps and Twelve Traditions*, we get a clear picture of the alcohol/addict's plight: "The chief activator of our [character] defects has been *self-centered fear*" (Alcoholics Anonymous, 1986, p. 76; *emphasis mine*). Taken together, these insights–"self-will run riot" and "self-centered fear"–allow us to delve into the heart of the spiritual dilemma the addict faces and what s/he needs for full recovery.

In a seminal article published in 1982, Ernest Kurtz attempts to address these issues and, in doing so, provides a perspective for understanding how A.A. works (Kurtz, 1982). His work is similar to the understanding of others trying to unravel the threads of addiction and recovery spirituality. We will try to weave these threads together into a coherent summary below.

"Addictions are attempts to shortcut and outsmart our finitude by the illusion of chemical transcendence," says Howard Clinebell (1998, p. 270). Faced with the truth of essential limitation and finitude as a human person, yet yearning to transcend this truth, the alcoholic/addict experiences existential anxiety. S/he experiences what could be understood as a religious and spiritual "hunger," potentially leading to deep affiliation with God (Clinebell, 1998, p. 267). This hunger is in all of us.

Yet in the addict this hunger is hijacked! In a futile attempt "to satisfy deep inner conflicts and hungers," the alcoholic/addict constructs piece-by-piece a "pseudo-religious solution" (Clinebell, 1963; 1998, p. 121), a "counterfeit" spirituality (van Kaam, 1966), an idolatrous spiritual stance (Miller, 1998; Morgan & Jordan, 1999), claiming "God-like powers" such as absolute control over feelings, the environment and others (Kurtz, 1982), attempting to will "what cannot be willed" (Tiebout in 1954 had described the addict as "His majesty, the baby"), and claiming absolute independence. Because of this resort to power and control in the face of anxiety, the addict experiences alienation, loneliness, isolation, shame, feelings of unloveability, fear, and hopelessness (Kurtz, 1982). Alienation and loneliness arise from the refusal to accept one's essential limitation, the central truth of human life. Alcohol and other drugs become a substitute higher power (Miller, 1998). As Whitfield (1985, p. 1) had said earlier, "We become addicted or attached to the way we think things should be." The addict accepts a host of false and negative beliefs–an "implicitly negative theological script"–about the self, about the world, about others, and about God (Morgan & Jordan, 1999, pp. 256-257).

Alcoholics Anonymous brings two "core insistences" to the task of recovery, namely the acceptance of essential limitation and the need to live in humble mutuality (Kurtz, 1982, p. 39). In the view of some, these two pillars of recovery are exactly what C. G. Jung had suggested to Bill Wilson long ago: *spiritus contra spiritum* (Buxton, Smith, & Seymour, 1987). The acceptance of limitation is seen in the title of Kurtz's book, *Not-God* (1979); in recovery the struggling alcoholic/addict surrenders to the essential limitation of human living and being, and comes to understand that she is "not god" and that no one else is, either. That is, the acceptance of limitation–the relinquishment of power and the myth of control, as well as adopting a stance of "letting be" toward the world and others–leads one to affirm "connectedness" with others who are similarly limited and vulnerable. These two core dynamics, the acceptance of limitation and the affirmation of mutual connectedness, are the heart of what Kurtz sees as "A.A.'s therapeutic dynamic: shared honesty of mutual vulnerability, openly acknowledged" (Kurtz, 1982, p. 42).

Along with the important aspects of addiction related to physiology, biochemistry, brain function, habit, conditioning, personality, and the like, these elements of anxiety, power, control, alienation, distorted beliefs, and acceptance of self are also intimately related to the experience of addiction, as a human drama. They are part of the deep background, the philosophical and theological core, of spirituality (Morgan & Jordan, 1999a).

*What, then, is the central core of recovery?* Harry Tiebout spoke, as the 12 steps and the Big Book of A.A. do (Alcoholics Anonymous, 1976, pp. 569-570), of a "spiritual awakening" that was necessary for true sobriety:

> Characteristic of the so-called typical alcoholic is a narcissistic egocentric core, dominated by feelings of omnipotence. . . . Inwardly the alcoholic brooks no control from man or God. He, the alcoholic, is and must be master of his destiny. He will fight to the end to preserve that position. . . .
>
> . . . a religious or spiritual awakening is the act of giving up one's reliance on one's omnipotence. The defiant individual no longer defies but accepts help, guidance and control from outside. And as the individual relinquishes his negative, aggressive feelings toward himself and toward life, he finds himself overwhelmed by strongly positive ones such as love, friendliness, peacefulness, and pervading contentment, which state is the exact antithesis of the former restlessness and irritability. And the significant fact is that with this new mental state the individual is no longer literally "driven to drink." (Tiebout, 1944, pp. 469-470)

As he says in several places, Tiebout believed that this "giving up" or "surrender" was a *powerful psychological event with spiritual effects,* "leading to a new type of inner response, spiritual in quality" (1946, p. 158; 1949). He describes the effect as a new "frame of mind," characterized by qualities such as peace, calm, contentment, serenity, and the like. And, along with these changes in emotional tone comes a concomitant change in personality, in which an "egocentric hostile pattern" is replaced and "spiritual strengthening" occurs (1946, p. 164). This change of character and approach to life was dramatic, and seen in the way one lived one's life ever after.

The spiritual program of the 12 steps and engagement in fellowship with "fellow sufferers" leads to recovery in this view. Steps 1 through 3 lead to an acceptance of limitation and reality as it is (Kurtz's "not-god"), while the rest of the 12 steps build on this acceptance and branch out into (1) a "therapy of mutuality" through sharing of stories–experience, strength and hope–among fellow sufferers and (2) tools for ongoing sober living. As Whitfield and Kurtz both suggest, the telling of stories in recovery is a powerful recovery tool for "remapping our belief systems into a new way of life that involves a new way of thinking, and the process of identification with the stories of others" (Whitfield, 1985, p. 86; see also Kurtz, 1986). Stories complement other tools such as moral inventories, use of recovery sponsors, confession, and service.

These factors counteract the "self-centeredness" at "the root of our troubles" (Kurtz, 1982, p. 58), and lead to a daily acceptance of life as "mystery" and openness to "miracles" happening (versus control), with characteristic attitudes such as release, gratitude, humility, and tolerance (Kurtz, 1986; Morgan, 1995).

If the experience of addiction leads to a degeneration of spirit, then the experience of recovery may be seen as "regeneration," a gradual transformation of self, rooted in surrender (Clinebell, 1963; Morgan & Jordan, 1999).

## *STUDIES OF RECOVERY SPIRITUALITY*

The spiritual dimension of those "core" experiences, described above in more speculative terms, has been helpfully described and elaborated in studies utilizing both quantitative and qualitative research paradigms.

Brown, Peterson, and Cunningham (1988a, b, & c) identified a "working definition" of spirituality as related to relationship with self, others and God. They then proceeded to "operationalize" this working definition into sets of cognitive and behavioral factors suitable both for research and for inducing change.

Brown and his coworkers labeled their approach a "behavioral/cognitive spiritual mode," phraseology which both emphasizes the value of behavior in effecting spiritual change, and they present spirituality as capable of being operationalized through measurable behaviors and cognitive actions. Their work represents a real step forward in opening possible empirical and quantitative approaches to spirituality and recovery, as well as the potential uses of spirituality in treatment and aftercare; their focus on "spiritual behaviors" and growth in a "spiritual lifestyle" is also important as research moves forward. As we will see, a number of contemporary researchers are building on their work.

In a study of long-term recovering alcoholics, Morgan (1992) found that the founding moment of recovery–surrender, conversion–was understood as a moment of intervention and grace, pulling addicted persons out of the vicious cycle of addiction, degeneration, and loss of self. Those who spoke about this experience also described a felt experience of being cared for, of being the recipient of providential care. Over time in recovery, these persons described a deepening attitude of trust, acceptance, and reliance on providence, attitudes not confined to past experience but involving deep beliefs about the present and future as well. They experience God or their "Higher Power" continuing to intervene and work in and through their lives, along with a sense of guidance and protection in living, a sense of "miracles" happening, and a sense of "benevolent serendipity" operative in living (Morgan, 1992; Morgan & Jordan, 1999, p. 262).

These changes made a difference in the way they lived their lives. Many recovering persons believe in the ongoing care and intervention of their Higher Power. They stake their recoveries, and their lives, on this confidence. This profoundly altered view of self, their relationship to God and to the world lies at the core of recovery spirituality (Brown, 1985; Morgan, 1992). God becomes approachable and prayer becomes meaningful; service to others, particularly to those still caught in the mire of addiction, becomes a vocation. Loved and loveable, these recovering persons experience a kind of mutuality and connectedness that is truly life-changing (Morgan, 1995).

## *WHERE DO WE GO FROM HERE?*

Taken together, the classic literature of spirituality in addiction studies illuminates both the "core experiences" of addiction and recovery spirituality, and the "effects" of those experiences. These effects are behavioral, cognitive, attitudinal, affective, and relational. This distinction has led to "a way forward" in new addiction research.

A number of contemporary researchers, spurred particularly by the work of Miller (1990, 1998), are coming to understand that spirituality can be seen as a "multidimensional" construct, much like health or personality. As such, one can articulate certain dimensions or elements ("effects") of spirituality, such as behavior or beliefs, operationalize them, and then move to study them in the experience of a wide range of addicts and recovering persons (Fetzer Institute, 1999a & b; Miller, 1998; Larson, Swyers, & McCullough, 1997).

Within a multidimensional construct like "spirituality," some aspects or experiences such as "surrender" or a sense of "providential care" and "serendipity" might be difficult to study without narrative tools. Indeed, the deep meaning of some aspects, such as "self-centeredness," or "humility," or "gratitude"–or, indeed, an ongoing relationship with a Higher Power–may not be available for direct study and may only reveal something of itself through story and relationship. This ought not be surprising. However, other aspects of spirituality understood as a multidimensional construct–for example, the cognitive, attitudinal or behavioral "effects" of true surrender or of a relationship with God–may appropriately and productively be studied using more standard social scientific models and instruments. Tiebout (1946) had foreshadowed such an eventuality in his writings. Interestingly, a body of psychometric instruments for the study of spiritual and religious constructs does exist in the literature of psychology and religion (Hill, 1999; Hill & Hood, 1999; Miller, 1998).

## A WAY FORWARD

To that end a number of research initiatives are currently underway that offer great promise for the elaboration of a more nuanced and complete understanding of addiction and spirituality. The Consensus Report on *Scientific Research on Spirituality and Health* (Larson, Swyers, & McCullough, 1997), utilizing the work of many respected professionals in a variety of fields, called for new kinds of research into spirituality. The panel members examining "Addictions: Alcohol/Drug Problems" included many of those scientists and practitioners concerned with the spiritual dimensions of recovery, such as Bill Miller, Stephanie Brown, G. Alan Marlatt, Peter Nathan, John Wallace and others. Their concern about increasing the quality and credibility of research in this area is notable. Their recommendations regarding use of "good science," increased funding, and renewed, honest communication among researchers in the area of addiction and spirituality are important and timely (NIHR, 1997, pp. 77, 79).

The recent RFA on "Spirituality and Alcohol" issued by the National Institute on Alcohol Abuse and Alcoholism in conjunction with the Fetzer Institute (2000), and the subsequent granting of research monies for several quantitative and qualitative projects, is another indicator of expanded interest in the topic and a follow-up to the recommendations of NIHR. The work of Project MATCH, "the largest randomized trial of a spiritually based treatment," is an example of the benefits of such an approach (Miller, 1998). Clearly, sustained scientific study of spirituality and its interrelationships with addictive illness is now understood as a critical endeavor in addiction studies.

The Fetzer Institute's *Multidimensional Measure of Religiousness/Spirituality* and its accompanying materials (1999a & b), adapted from examination of many other useful instruments and scales, will be increasingly used to examine operationalized aspects of spirituality (e.g., Forgiveness, Religious/Spiritual Coping, Religious Support, Commitment) across a range of populations and conditions. It is a work-in-progress but is already being used to good effect in research. Other instruments, old and new, and several structured interview formats are also being used in addiction research (Morgan, in press; Tonigan, Toscova, & Connors, 1999).

The next five to ten years may prove to be an exciting time in the study of spirituality within addiction studies. Now that there is more general acceptance of the need to study this phenomenon, several "next steps" need to be taken.

Study of spirituality will require a willingness on the part of researchers (a) to consider new questions and ways of pursuing them, (b) to include questions of spirituality into more general studies utilizing appropriate instrumentation, and (c) to attempt research efforts with an expanded base of participants, including but moving beyond A.A. recoverers and 12-step programs (Miller, 1997, 1998).

Hopefully, studies of spiritual variables in treatment as well as recovery will be forthcoming, and will utilize rigorous quantitative and qualitative empirical paradigms and methods. Several studies of such variables and recommended interventions are available for further follow-up (Miller, 1997; Project MATCH, 1993, 1997).

Future efforts will require new and sustainable sources of funding, as well as institutional and governmental support, so that high quality investigations can be conducted over time. An area of support that is very much needed will include the training and mentoring of young researchers who are interested in pursuing spiritual questions for understanding (Miller, 1998). At present, only a select cadré of investigators are examining the spiritual dynamics of addiction and recovery, and many standard training programs in psychology, counseling and medicine do not include study of spirituality. Learning from senior researchers and previous literature will be a crucial task for apprentice scholars in this field.

There is still much to learn in the area of spirituality and addiction/recovery. Much has been done recently to inject new life into this intriguing area of study. Further research offers the promise of more complete understanding and greater effectiveness in our approach to addictive illness.

## REFERENCES

Alcoholics Anonymous. (1984). *Pass it on. The story of Bill Wilson and how the AA message reached the world.* New York: Alcoholics Anonymous World Services.

Alcoholics Anonymous. (1976). *Alcoholics Anonymous: The story of how many thousands of men and women have recovered from alcoholism, 3rd edition.* New York: Alcoholics Anonymous World Services.

Alexander, W. (1997). *Cool water: Alcoholism, mindfulness, and ordinary recovery.* Boston: Shambhala.

Bateson, G. (1972). The cybernetics of "self:" A theory of alcoholism. In *Steps to an ecology of mind.* New York: Ballantine. [Original work published in 1971]. *Psychiatry, 34*(1), 1-18.

Berenson, D. (1990). A systemic view of spirituality: God and twelve step programs as resources in family therapy. *Journal of Strategic and Systemic Therapies, 9*(1), 59-70.

Booth, L. (1985). *Spirituality and recovery: Walking on water.* Pompano Beach, FL: Health Communications, Inc.

Booth, L. (1984). The gauntlet of spirituality. *Alcoholism Treatment Quarterly, 1*(1), 139-141.

Booth, L. (1984). Aspects of spirituality in San Pedro Peninsula Hospital. *Alcoholism Treatment Quarterly*, *1*(2), 121-123.

Brown, H.P. (1993). Tools for the logotherapist: A twelve-step spiritual inventory. *The International Forum for Logotherapy*, *16*, 77-88.

Brown, H.P. (1992). Substance abuse and the disorders of the self: Examining the relationship. *Alcoholism Treatment Quarterly*, *9*(2), 1-27.

Brown, H.P. & Peterson, J.H. (1989). Refining the BASIC-IS: A psycho-spiritual approach to the comprehensive outpatient treatment of drug dependency. *Alcoholism Treatment Quarterly*, *6*(3/4), 27-61.

Brown, H. P. & Peterson, J.H. (1990a). Rationale and procedural suggestions for defining and actualizing spiritual values in the treatment of dependency. *Alcoholism Treatment Quarterly*, *7*(3), 17-46.

Brown, H.P. & Peterson, J.H. (1990b). Values and recovery from alcoholism through Alcoholics Anonymous. *Counseling and Values*, *35*, 63-68.

Brown, H.P. & Peterson, J.H. (1991). Assessing spirituality in addiction treatment and follow-up: Development of the Brown-Peterson Recovery Progress Inventory (B-PRPI). *Alcoholism Treatment Quarterly*, *8*(2), 21-50.

Brown, H.P., Peterson, J.H., & Cunningham, O. (1988a). Rationale and theoretical basis for a behavioral/cognitive approach to spirituality. *Alcoholism Treatment Quarterly*, *5*(1/2), 47-59.

Brown, H.P., Peterson, J.H., & Cunningham, O. (1988b). A behavioral/cognitive spiritual model for a chemical dependency aftercare program. *Alcoholism Treatment Quarterly*, *5*(1/2), 153-175.

Brown, H.P., Peterson, J.H., & Cunningham, O. (1988c). An individualized behavioral approach to spiritual development for the recovering alcoholic/addict. *Alcoholism Treatment Quarterly*, *5*(1/2), 177-192.

Brown, S. (1985). *Treating the alcoholic: A developmental model of recovery*. New York: John Wiley.

Buxton, M.E., Smith, D.E., & Seymour, R.B. (1987, July-September). Spirituality and other points of resistance to the 12-step recovery process. *Journal of Psychoactive Drugs*, *19*(3), 275-286.

Chappel, J.N. (1993, March). Long-term recovery from alcoholism. *Psychiatric Clinics of North America*, *16*(1), 177-187.

Clinebell, H. J. (1998). *Understanding and counseling persons with alcohol, drug, and behavioral addictions*. Nashville: Abingdon.

Clinebell, H.J. (1963). Philosophical-religious factors in the etiology and treatment of alcoholism. *Quarterly Journal of Studies on Alcoholism*, *24*, 473-488.

Ellis, A. (1985). Why Alcoholics Anonymous is probably doing itself and alcoholics more harm than good by its insistence on a higher power. [Review of *Alcoholics Anonymous, 3rd ed.*]. *Employee Assistance Quarterly*, *1*(1), 95-97.

Ellis, A. (1983). *The case against religiosity*. New York: Institute for Rational Emotive Therapy.

Ellis, A. & Schoenfeld, E. (1990). Divine intervention and the treatment of chemical dependency. *Journal of Substance Abuse*, *2*, 459-468, 489-494.

Fetzer Institute. (1999a, January). *Multidimensional measurement of religiousness/spirituality for use in health research*. Kalamazoo, MI: Author. [John E. Fetzer Institute].

Fetzer Institute. (1999b, October). *Multidimensional measurement of religiousness/spirituality for use in health research: A report of the Fetzer Institute/National Institute on Aging Working Group with additional psychometric data.* Kalamazoo, MI: Author.

Ford, J.C. (1961). *What about your drinking?* Glen Rock, NJ: Paulist.

Ford, J.C. (1951). *Depth psychology, morality and alcoholism.* Weston, MA: Weston College Press.

Ford, J.C. (1950). Alcohol, alcoholism and moral responsibility: When a skinful is sinful. *Blue Book* [Proceedings of the Second National Clergy Conference on Alcoholism, August 22, 1950. St. Joseph College, Rensselaer, Indiana], *2*, 89-120.

Grof, C. (1993). *The thirst for wholeness: Attachment, addiction, and the spiritual path.* San Francisco: HarperSanFrancisco.

Hill, P.C. (1999, February 1). *An overview of measurement issues and scales in the scientific study of spirituality.* Paper presented at the meeting "Studying Spirituality and Alcohol," co-sponsored by the National Institute on Alcohol Abuse and Alcoholism and the Fetzer Institute. Bethesda, MD.

Hill, P.C. & Hood, R.W., Jr. (Eds.). (1999). *Measures of religiosity.* Birmingham, AL: Religious Education Press.

Keller, M. (1975). Multidisciplinary perspectives on alcoholism and the need for integration: An historical and prospective note. *Journal of Studies on Alcohol, 36*(1), 133-147.

Kubicek, K. (1998). Self-defined attributes of success: A phenomenological study of long-term recovering alcoholics. Ph.D. dissertation, St. Louis University.

Kubicek, K., Morrison, N.C., & Morgan, O.J. (in press). Paths of recovery success: A pilot comparison of spontaneous remitters and members of AA. *Alcoholism Treatment Quarterly.*

Kurtz, E. (1991). The twelve-step approach to spirituality. *The Addiction Letter, 7*(8), 1-2.

Kurtz, E. (1986, June). Origins of A.A. spirituality. *Blue Book, 38*, 35-42.

Kurtz, E. (1982). Why A.A. works: The intellectual significance of Alcoholics Anonymous. *Journal of Studies on Alcohol, 43*(1), 38-80.

Kurtz, E. (1979). *Not-god: A history of Alcoholics Anonymous.* Center City, MN: Hazelden Educational Materials.

Larson, D.B., Swyers, J.P., & McCullough, M.E. (Eds.). (1997). *Scientific research on spirituality and health: A consensus report.* Washington, DC: National Institute for Healthcare Research.

Marlatt, G.A. (1985, Fall). Is reliance upon a higher power incompatible with learning self-management skills? *Employee Assistance Quarterly, 1*(1), 97-99.

May, G. A. (1988). *Addiction and grace: Love and spirituality in the healing of addictions.* San Francisco: Harper Collins.

Mercadante, L. (1996). *Victims and sinners: Spiritual roots of addiction and recovery.* Louisville, KY: Westminster John Knox.

Miller, W.R. (1998). Researching the spiritual dimensions of alcohol and other drug problems. *Addiction, 93*(7), 971-982.

Miller, W.R. (1997). Spiritual aspects of addictions treatment and research. *Mind/Body Medicine, 2*(1), 37-43.

Miller, W.R. (1996). In memoriam: Howard P. Brown, Jr., PhD. *Alcoholism Treatment Quarterly, 14*(3), 3-6.

Miller, W.R. (1995). Toward a biblical view of drug use. *Journal of Ministry in Addiction and Recovery, 2,* 77-86.

Miller, W.R. (1990). Spirituality: The silent dimension in addiction research. The 1990 Leonard Ball oration. *Drug and Alcohol Review, 9,* 259-266.

Miller, W.R. & Bennett, M. (1999). *Spirituality and substance use* [On-line Annotated Bibliography]. University of New Mexico. Available online at the following address: *http://casaa-0031.unm.edu/bib/fetzer.html.*

Morgan, O.J. (in press). Alcohol problems, alcoholism and spirituality: An overview of measurement and scales. *Alcoholism Treatment Quarterly.*

Morgan, O.J. (1999a) "Chemical comforting" and the theology of John C. Ford, S.J.: Classic answers to a contemporary problem. *Journal of Ministry in Addiction & Recovery, 6*(1), 29-66.

Morgan, O. (1999b). Addiction and spirituality in context. In O. Morgan and M. Jordan, (Eds.), *Addiction and spirituality: A multidisciplinary approach* (pp. 3-30). St. Louis: Chalice.

Morgan, O. (1999c). Qualitative studies in addiction and spirituality: Rationale and recent examples. In *Conference summary: Studying spirituality and alcohol* (pp. 20-22). National Institute on Alcohol Abuse and Alcoholism, National Institutes of Health, and The Fetzer Institute. Bethesda, MD. February 1-2, 1999.

Morgan, O.J. (1995). Extended length of sobriety: The missing variable. *Alcoholism Treatment Quarterly, 12*(1), 59-71.

Morgan, O.J. (1992). *In a sober voice: A psychological study of long-term alcoholic recovery with attention to spiritual dimensions. Dissertation Abstracts International, 52*(11), 6069-B. [University Microfilms No. 92-10480].

Morgan, O. & Jordan, M. (1999a). Addiction and spirituality: A clinical-theological reflection. In O. Morgan and M. Jordan (Eds.), *Addiction and spirituality: A multidisciplinary approach* (pp. 251-267). St. Louis: Chalice.

Morgan, O.J. & Jordan, M. (1999b). *Addiction and spirituality: A multidisciplinary approach.* St. Louis, MO: Chalice Press.

National Institute on Alcohol Abuse and Alcoholism [NIAAA]. (2000, February 7). *Studying spirituality and alcohol.* RFA: AA-00-002. Washington, DC: Author. Co-sponsored with The Fetzer Institute.

O'Connell, D.F. & Alexander, C.N. (1994). *Self-recovery: Treating addictions using transcendental meditation and Maharishi Ayur-Veda.* New York: Haworth [Special Issue of *Alcoholism Treatment Quarterly, 11*(1-4)].

Project MATCH Research Group. (1997). Matching alcoholism treatments to client heterogeneity: Project MATCH post-treatment drinking outcomes. *Journal of Studies on Alcohol, 58,* 7-29.

Project MATCH Research Group. (1993). Project MATCH: Rationale and methods for a multisite clinical trial matching patients to alcoholism treatment. *Alcoholism: Clinical and Experimental Research, 17,* 1130-1145.

Royce, J.E. (1987). *The spiritual progression chart.* Center City, MN: Hazelden Educational Materials.

Royce, J.E. (1985a, Winter). Sin or solace? Religious views on alcohol and alcoholism. *Journal of Drug Issues, 15*(1), 51-62.

Royce, J.E. (1985b, January-February). What do you mean spiritual illness? *Alcoholism, 5*, 28.

Seymour, R.B. & Smith, D.E. (1987). *Drugfree: A unique, positive approach to staying off alcohol and other drugs*. New York: Facts on File Publications.

Siegler, M., Osmond, H., & Newell, S. (1968). Models of alcoholism. *Quarterly Journal of Studies on Alcohol, 29*, 571-591.

Small, J. (1981). *Becoming naturally therapeutic*. Austin, TX: Eupsychian Press.

Sommer, S.M. (1992). *A way of life: Long-term recovery in Alcoholics Anonymous. Dissertation Abstracts International, 53*(7), 3795B. [University Microfilms No. 9236722].

Stanard, R.P., Sandhu, D.S., & Painter, L.C. (2000). Assessment of spirituality in counseling. *Journal of Counseling and Development, 78*, 204-210.

Tiebout, H.M. (1961). Alcoholics Anonymous–An experiment of nature. *Quarterly Journal of Studies on Alcohol, 22*, 52-68.

Tiebout, H.M. (1954). *The ego factors in surrender in alcoholism*. Center City, MN: Hazelden Educational Materials (Reprinted from *Quarterly Journal of Studies on Alcohol, 15*, 610-621).

Tiebout, H.M. (1949). The act of surrender in the therapeutic process with special reference to alcoholism. *Quarterly Journal of Studies on Alcohol, 10*, 48-58.

Tiebout, H.M. (1946). Psychological factors operating in Alcoholics Anonymous. In B. Glueck (Ed.), *Current therapies of personality disorders* (pp. 154-165). New York: Grune & Stratton.

Tiebout, H.M. (1944). Therapeutic mechanisms of Alcoholics Anonymous. *American Journal of Psychiatry, 100*, 468-473.

Tonigan, J.S., Toscova, R.T., & Connors, G.J. (1999). Spirituality and the 12-step programs: A guide for clinicians. In W.R. Miller (Ed.), *Integrating spirituality into treatment: Resources for practitioners* (pp. 111-131). Washington, DC: American Psychological Association.

Turner, C. (1993). *Spiritual experiences of recovering alcoholics. Dissertation Abstracts International, 56*(3), 1128A. [University Microfilms No. 9521866].

Twerski, A.J. (1985, Fall). Go to the patients; not to a book. *Employee Assistance Quarterly, 1*(1), 99-100.

Van Kaam, A. (1966). "Addiction: Counterfeit of religious presence." In Van Kaam, *Personality fulfillment in the spiritual life* (pp. 123-153). Wilkes-Barre, PA: Dimension.

White, W.L. (1998). *Slaying the dragon: The history of addiction treatment and recovery in America*. Bloomington, IL: Lighthouse Institute (Chestnut Health Systems).

Whitfield, C.L. (1989). Co-dependence: Our most common addiction–Some physical, mental, emotional and spiritual perspectives. *Alcoholism Treatment Quarterly, 6*(1), 19-36.

Whitfield, C.L. (1987). *Healing the child within: Discovery and recovery for adult children of dysfunctional families*. Pompano Beach, FL: Health Communications, Inc.

Whitfield, C.L. (1985). *Alcoholism, attachments and spirituality: A transpersonal approach*. East Rutherford, NJ: Thomas W. Perrin.

Whitfield, C.L. (1984). Stress management and spirituality during recovery: A transpersonal approach: Part 1: Becoming. *Alcoholism Treatment Quarterly, 1*(1), 3-54.

Whitfield, C.L. (1984). Stress management and spirituality during recovery: A transpersonal approach: Part II: Being. *Alcoholism Treatment Quarterly, 1*(2), 1-50.

Whitfield, C.L. (1984). Stress management and spirituality during recovery: A transpersonal approach: Part III: Transforming. *Alcoholism Treatment Quarterly, 1*(4), 1-54.

Zinberg, N.E. & Bean, M.H. (1981). Introduction: Alcohol use, alcoholism, and the problems of treatment. In M.H. Bean and N.E. Zinberg (Eds.), Dynamic approaches to the understanding and treatment of alcoholism (pp. 1-35). New York: Free Press.

# American Prisons as Alcohol and Drug Treatment Centers: A Twenty-Year Reflection, 1980 to 2000

Stephen K. Valle, ScD, MBA
Dennis Humphrey, EdD

**SUMMARY.** Treatment of the alcohol and drug offender in the criminal justice system has undergone substantial changes over the past several decades. While initially a reluctant stepchild to jail/prison-based program services, substance abuse treatment programs for offenders with alcohol and drug problems now occupy a major place in the development

---

Over the past twenty-five years, Stephen K. Valle has held the positions of counselor, program director, and senior executive of several health and corrections-based service companies. In 1993, he was nominated by Senator Harold E. Hughes to be the administrator of the Federal Substance Abuse and Mental Health Services Administration (SAMHSA). He is the creator of the Accountability Training treatment model and founder of Grace House, a spiritually-based self-supporting and self-governing sober house located in Lynn, Massachusetts. He is currently President and Chief Executive Officer of AdCare Criminal Justice Services (ACJS), Worcester, MA.

Dennis Humphrey is a career corrections professional who pioneered the development of corrections-based treatment programs in Massachusetts. As Associate Commissioner for Treatment Programs for the Massachusetts Department of Correction, Executive Director of the Massachusetts Committee on Criminal Justice, and Deputy Superintendent of the Suffolk County (Boston) Sheriff's Department, he has overseen the implementation of alcohol, drug abuse, mental health and education services for several correctional agencies. He is currently a corrections consultant to AdCare Criminal Justice Services and adjunct faculty at Boston University, University of Massachusetts, and Emerson College.

[Haworth co-indexing entry note]: "American Prisons as Alcohol and Drug Treatment Centers: A Twenty-Year Reflection, 1980 to 2000." Valle, Stephen K., and Dennis Humphrey. Co-published simultaneously in *Alcoholism Treatment Quarterly* (The Haworth Press, Inc.) Vol. 20, No. 3/4, 2002, pp. 83-106; and: *Alcohol Problems in the United States: Twenty Years of Treatment Perspective* (ed: Thomas F. McGovern, and William L. White) The Haworth Press, Inc., 2002, pp. 83-106. Single or multiple copies of this article are available for a fee from The Haworth Document Delivery Service [1-800-HAWORTH, 9:00 a.m. - 5:00 p.m. (EST). E-mail address: getinfo@haworthpressinc.com].

*83*

of correctional policy, planning, and delivery of services in our nation's correctional facilities.

This article will highlight the significant developments in offender treatment from the perspective of two career correctional and treatment professionals who, combined, represent more than fifty years of hands-on experience in the development and management of alcohol and drug treatment services for offenders housed in jail and prison correctional facilities. This article will provide a brief overview of the literature on the treatment of the alcohol and drug offender as a backdrop for presenting some of the issues and models for effective jail/prison alcohol and drug treatment programs. *[Article copies available for a fee from The Haworth Document Delivery Service: 1-800-HAWORTH. E-mail address: <getinfo@haworthpressinc.com> Website: <http://www.HaworthPress.com> © 2002 by The Haworth Press, Inc. All rights reserved.]*

**KEYWORDS.** Substance abuse treatment, prison/jail treatment

## *INTRODUCTION*

From the beginning, the American prison has espoused a philosophical belief in the ability of the individual to change. For the first 150 years of its history, the notion that offenders could be "cured" prevailed. The emergence of the "penitentiary," a place where offenders could reflect on their misdeeds, repent, and prepare for life as crime-free citizens, was the principal structural innovation (Rothman, 1971).

For much of the first 150 years of its existence, faith in the prison's curative powers endured. Although the conditions in which inmates were housed during this period were frequently harsh, and by today's standards probably a violation of the 8th Amendment, the mission of the prison as a carefully planned social institution went unchallenged. By the end of the 1970s, however, this consensus on the purpose of imprisonment had shattered and the notion of prisons as punishment became prevalent. This reversal of sentiment was based, in part at least, on evaluation studies that showed that correctional treatment programs did not work.

## *THE "NOTHING WORKS" ERA*

It is not possible to identify the single year during which one era ends and another begins, but the conservative critique of the liberal crime-control policies of the 1960s began to find its voice during the early 1970s. The mantra that "nothing works" emerged from an article published in 1974 in *The Public Interest*, "What Works?–Questions and Answers About Prison Reform" (Martinson). This cynical notion emerged from a larger co-authored research report (Lipton, Martinson, and Wilks, 1975), in which an assessment of 231 evaluation studies of treatment programs conducted between 1945 and 1967 was summarized. Concurrent with Martinson's work, questions were raised about the dangers posed by repeat offenders being placed on bail, the prosecution of habitual criminals, lengths of prison sentences, and the whole notion of reducing crime through social reform.

The election of Ronald Reagan in 1980, more than any other single event, heralded the beginning of a national shift in criminal justice policy, especially at the federal level, from rehabilitation to crime control through incapacitation. As president, Reagan set the conservative tone that would prevail for the next two decades and would result in the doubling of the nation's prison population. Paradoxically, the get tough on crime policy of this era also marked the shift back toward rehabilitation and the beginning of the era of drug and alcohol treatment as the cornerstone of prison programming.

Because longer and more certain sentences have led to increases in prison populations, because significantly more attention has been paid to the "drug problem," and because court orders on conditions of confinement have limited overcrowding, more prisons have been built and taxpayers have become increasingly more concerned about the efficacy of the war on drugs. At the end of the Reagan presidency, the proportion of drug users in the incarcerated population increased to one-third of those sent to state prison–the highest proportion in history. The current reemphasis on providing drug abuse treatment in prisons and jails appears to be driven by the need to do something about the large numbers of substance abusers who are incarcerated. The reemphasis is also driven by recent research findings, which will be presented in some detail in the following sections, which demonstrate the effectiveness of drug abuse treatment.

## THE ALCOHOL-INVOLVED OFFENDER

Offenders with alcohol problems have always been present in the correctional system, and in the last two decades it has been widely recognized that there is a direct association between alcohol and crime. Nearly 4 in 10 violent victimizations involve alcohol, about 4 in 10 fatal motor vehicle accidents are alcohol related, and about 4 in 10 offenders self-report that they were using alcohol at the time of the offense. Among the 5.3 million convicted offenders under the jurisdiction of corrections agencies in 1996, nearly 2 million (36%)

were estimated to have been drinking at the time of the offense (U.S. Department of Justice, 1998). [It is important to note, however, that while a relationship exists between alcohol and crime, most alcohol consumption does not result in crime–the vast majority of people who consume alcohol do not engage in criminal behavior (U.S. Department of Justice, 1998).]

Driving under the influence of alcohol (DUI), and driving while intoxicated (DWI) represent the largest category of arrests by police. In 1996 DUI/DWI accounted for 1 in 10 of arrests for all crimes nationwide–an estimated 1,467,300 arrests.

Drunk driving arrests peaked in 1983 where nearly two million DUI arrests occurred–one for every 80 licensed drivers. In 1996, there were nearly 1.5 million arrests for DUI, representing a rate of 1 arrest for every 122 licensed drivers–a decline of 34%. In 1986 there were about 1 intoxicated driver in a fatal accident for every 10,500 licensed drivers. By 1996, this rate was one for every 17,200. In 1986 highway alcohol-related fatalities represented 52% of all traffic fatalities, while in 1996 it had declined to 40.9%. Over this ten-year span, the number of alcohol related traffic fatalities decreased from 24,045 to 17,126, representing a 29% reduction (U.S. Department of Justice, 1998). While this decrease in arrests and fatal accidents can be attributed to a variety of legal, social, and law enforcement initiatives, the emphasis on providing intensive corrections-based treatment for the hard-core drunk driving offender was clearly one of the significant factors.

## TREATMENT OF THE ALCOHOL-INVOLVED OFFENDER

There are a number of problems related to the treatment of alcohol abusers, both in the general society and in prison. Traditionally, Americans have viewed the social use of alcohol as recreational behavior rather than deviance. Consistent with this point of view, treatment programs are frequently designed to focus on breaking through the individual's denial in order to move them to recognize the nature of his or her own problems with alcohol, and to accept their problem drinking/alcoholism as a chronic disease process. By admitting their "powerlessness" over this disease process as a first step, they then are responsible for taking further "steps" to stop the progression of this chronic disease. In the disease model approach that dominated the "free world" treatment programs, there is no known cure for this addictive disease process. While one can arrest it, and recover from its effects by first abstaining from any alcohol or drugs, and then practicing "the steps," it cannot be cured. The 12-step AA (Alcoholics Anonymous) model, which has been so successful in the "free world" treatment arena, incorporates this philosophy and it was assumed that its success would automatically carry over to offenders in prison or jail.

The AA model's usefulness to criminal offenders has often been hindered due to the inherent limitations of a correctional facility, and the nature of the AA programs itself. Crucial for allowing the AA program to realize its maximum benefit is the individual's voluntary recognition of a problem and the self-motivation to embark on a program of behavior modification. These characteristics are inconsistent with the coercive nature of treatment in corrections, which may require attendance in AA as a condition of a desired classification status or a favorable parole recommendation. The inmate's voluntary participation in the program, then, is often viewed with suspicion by corrections managers and the likelihood that he/she will continue to participate upon release in community-based AA groups is doubtful. Yet, for years, AA was the only source of help available in prisons and for some it was an invaluable resource. But ultimately it was the poor fit between AA's voluntary peer-group structure and the involuntariness of corrections that provided the impetus for the creation of the accountability-based treatment programs that are commonly found in correctional settings today. Most of these programs include involvement in AA/NA or other forms of self-help, but only as one component of a more comprehensive range of treatment services.

With the advent of the "get tough" laws of the early 1980s aimed toward getting drunk drivers off the highways and into either treatment programs or jails, the profile of incarcerated offenders began to change. In 1980, for example, more than 13% of the locally incarcerated population had a Driving Under the Influence as a governing offense as compared to less than 6% in 1979. To some extent, at least, the seemingly ambivalent attitudes of most Americans toward alcohol use–it being seen as recreational behavior rather than deviance–had begun to change. Consequently, a need for treatment programs that emphasized personal accountability, coercion for recalcitrant offenders and confinement in the interest of public safety became apparent.

Prior to 1980, treatment of the alcohol-abusing offender and, as we will see later, the drug addicted offender, was not a correctional priority. As a sub-group, the populations were small and were serving relatively short-term sentences. From a prison management perspective, they did not present significant behavioral problems nor were they viewed as habitual criminals, but rather as habitual drunks or regular guys who drank a little too much. The ambivalent societal attitude toward alcohol use is mirrored in the correctional attitude of that period. In many county-based correctional facilities and local jails, for example, the problem drinker was often a regular guest who was well known to the staff, someone who may have become a little disruptive because they couldn't hold their liquor, but not a criminal in the traditional sense of the word.

Given the lack of serious attention paid to the alcohol abuser by the criminal justice system prior to 1980, it is not surprising to note the lack of substantive, comprehensive programming in most correctional facilities of this period. These sub-populations mostly received token attempts at addressing their chronic alcoholism–usually limited to basic alcohol education groups and Alcoholics Anonymous meetings staffed entirely by volunteers who had to contend with a frequently hostile environment. In retrospect, it could be argued that the prison attitude of indifference to the needs of the alcoholic offender was not so much a denial of the need for treatment but rather the lack of recognition of a problem. Furthermore, since the general societal attitude toward alcohol use at that time was one of ambivalence, why would we expect our prisons to have different values?

## THE EMERGENCE OF THE CORRECTIONAL-BASED ALCOHOL TREATMENT PROGRAMS

Prior to the 1980s, most sentenced alcohol offenders were mixed in with the general prison population of offenders which included alcoholics who committed criminal acts while under the influence of alcohol; alcoholics who committed frequent, though mostly nonviolent crimes; the chronically alcoholic homeless population that was civilly committed to county jails and prison-based addiction centers; and the alcoholic who was incarcerated for repeat drunk driving offenses. Corrections professionals generally regarded the repeat drunk driving offender as a different sub-culture of offenders and attempted to find more effective means to address this population. Incarcerated drunk driving offenders tended to be better educated, had more stable employment records, were more likely to be married, were older and posed less of a security problem than the rest of the correctional population (Fair, 1986; Williams, 1984). The prevailing thought among corrections officials was that the hard-core drunk driving offender had a less severe criminal history, with their criminality typically limited to traffic or alcohol-related offenses. The fact that the offense itself stemmed from an alcohol problem led to the prevailing thought that the repeat drunk driving offender could better be handled through treatment. Recognizing that lower security was the most appropriate placement for the repeat and hard-core drunk driving offender, and acknowledging that this behavior was not likely to change without intensive treatment, corrections officials began to implement specialized treatment programs for the drunk driving offender that were separate from the main population. With the creation of specialized facilities for the treatment of the alcoholic offender, faith in the curative powers of prison emerged.

### THE LONGWOOD TREATMENT CENTER–A MODEL PROGRAM FOR THE INCARCERATED DRUNK DRIVING OFFENDER

Beginning in the mid 1980s and continuing until the early 1990s when the emphasis of treatment shifted from alcohol, to drugs and alcohol, there were several model correctional drunk driving treatment programs established throughout the country. Of particular note are the Baltimore and Prince George's County programs in Maryland, Suffolk County in New York, Pima County in Arizona and the Longwood Treatment Program created by the Massachusetts Department of Correction. Because the authors were the principal architects of the Longwood Treatment Facility in Massachusetts, an internationally recognized model program, and one the authors of this article has continued to be involved with it over the last twenty years, we will use it to illustrate what we consider to be the essential components of an effective treatment program.

Recognizing that 25% of commitments to local Houses of Corrections in Massachusetts were multiple D.U.I. offenders, the Massachusetts Department of Corrections, in cooperation with the Governor's office and the Division of Alcoholism, established a separate minimum security facility to provide comprehensive treatment for the multiple drunk driver offender. The Longwood Treatment Center was established in 1984 as a 125-bed minimum-security facility.

Corrections staff determine appropriateness for placement in the facility by conducting an initial screening assessment. Sentences vary from three months to one year. Programs are individualized for inmates depending upon the length of the inmate's sentence and their progress in attaining the treatment goals and objectives established in their individualized treatment plan.

The three-phase program begins with an orientation phase where the emphasis is on assessment and development of the initial treatment plan. A classification board consisting of corrections and clinical staff meets regularly to coordinate each inmate's treatment plan. Following the orientation and assessment phase, inmates participate in a series of didactic lectures, structured small group counseling sessions and individual counseling, when necessary. Typically, inmates attend a didactic lecture and two group sessions daily as well as AA/NA meetings. Inmates enter the second phase only when they have successfully completed all of the treatment expectations identified in their initial treatment plan. Phase II is a much less structured program than Phase I and is designed to foster self-reliance and dependence on one's self rather than the treatment team. There are mandatory journal writing, directed study assignments, and additional lectures and group therapy sessions. Participation in victim impact awareness groups and participation in sessions put on by Mothers Against Drunk Driving (MADD) are integrated into the program during this phase. Upon completion of the benchmarks determined by the treatment team for this phase, the inmate enters the third phase of treatment.

In Phase III, the inmate is eligible for work release status and becomes eligible to work outside of the facility. Phase III inmates are reclassified from minimum security to pre-release. They continue to attend daily groups and program activities at the facility, but also must attend three AA/NA meetings outside the institution. The emphasis of this phase is on relapse prevention and reintegration back into the community. Upon release, all inmates agree to participate in weekly aftercare support meetings that are held at various locations throughout the state.

Among its many recognitions, the Longwood program was the first correctional facility in the nation to receive both ACA and CARF accreditation, thus forming one of the earliest bridges for the corrections and treatment fields to demonstrate that partnership and collaboration are critical for effective correctional treatment interventions. It was also the first correctional drunk driving treatment program to publish results of outcome studies on the effectiveness of corrections treatment for the hard-core drunk driver. These studies have consistently demonstrated some of the lowest recidivism rates of corrections-based treatment interventions (LeClair, 1987; LeClair and Guarino-Ghezzi, 1997; Valle, 1986).

The Longwood Treatment Facility has undergone several minor changes over the almost two decades of its existence. The core of the program–intense structured programming, close collaboration among corrections and treatment staff in the design and delivery of services, active involvement of AA/NA, and an emphasis on reintegration and follow-up services–remain cornerstones of this model program (Valle, Kerns, and Gaskell, 1986). As of this writing, the Longwood program has graduated more than 6,000 offenders and the recidivism rate continues to be less than 8%.

## THE DRUG OFFENDER IN CORRECTIONS

The demographics of the general correctional population changed significantly from the late 1970s through the mid 1980s. Concurrent with the increase in the alcohol offender population, many of whom were convicted under newly created legislation specifically targeted to the repeat drunk driver, there was a dramatic increase in the drug offender population. The more conservative criminal justice philosophy that was the cornerstone of the Reagan Justice Department was evidenced in the plethora of mandatory sentencing legislation that was enacted during this period at both the federal and state levels. The rush to criminalize and incapacitate the drug dealers and users doubled the prison population and brought into the system a population with which correctional officials had had relatively little experience.

In contrast to the drunken driving offender, the drug offender represented a serious dilemma for corrections. By definition their behavior was compulsive and likely to be repeated, but the mere act of abuse of drugs was not considered a serious offense as compared to other offenders. The lack of effective treatment programs for this population put corrections in a further bind: the punishments imposed by mandatory, lengthy sentences seemed to outweigh the seriousness of the acts being punished. On the other hand, repeated criminality by addicts, coupled with the "war on drugs," often made the criminal justice system appear inordinately lenient and ineffectual. From these seemingly conflicting goals–punishment vs. treatment–the view that the prison could meet the treatment needs of this population, while simultaneously satisfying the larger mandate of public safety, was once again affirmed.

Correction managers had begun to see some evidence that some treatment professionals could work effectively within the structure and chain of command authority of the correctional environment, without compromising security. As inmates responded to the strict structure of programs where an inmate is accounted for all the time by his participation in program services, corrections professionals experienced an unexpected benefit of treatment–better inmate management. Inmates who participated in treatment services consistently had lower disciplinary reports, decreased incidences of fighting, and were more cooperative, all resulting in an improvement in safety and inmate management. Thus, treatment programs in jails/prisons became another tool for effective inmate management as treatment professionals became part of the corrections management team.

## DRUG OFFENDERS AND PRISON OVERCROWDING

Current concern about substance abuse presents one of the major political, social, and economic issues in our country. The loss in human potential and associated social, health, and criminal justice costs are staggering (Chavaria, 1992). Available indicators of drug use among arrestees are at epidemic levels, resulting in significant overcrowding in the prison population (Lipton et al., 1992). Rates have fluctuated over the years but since the early Drug Use Forecasting (DUF) data to the current Arrestee Drug Abuse Monitoring (ADAM) research, a significant proportion of all arrestees have, and continue to, test positive for some drug. At least 45 percent, and in some cities up to 80 percent, of arrestees charged with violent crimes or income generating crimes tested positive for drugs (National Institute of Justice, 1989). Their drug use includes the use of various chemicals, mostly in combination with alcohol, to the extent that it pervades their lifestyle and preoccupies their daily hours (Lipton et al., 1992).

In terms of the number of arrests reported by the Federal Bureau of Investigation (FBI), there has been a persistently upward trend in the number of arrests for drug offenses. For example, in 1980, drug offenses accounted for 5.6% (580,900) of all arrests. In 1997, this number had increased to 10.4% (1,559,100), and in 1999 there were 1,532,200 drug arrests, which accounted for 10.9% of all arrests (Federal Bureau of Investigation, U.S. Department of Justice, 2000).

Clearly, one of the driving forces for the relationship between drugs and crime is the need to get money to buy drugs to support the addictive lifestyle. More specifically, the Bureau of Justice Statistics reports that a significant number of jail, federal and state inmates have committed their offense to get money for drugs. For example, in 1996 16% of jail inmates had committed crimes to get money for drugs, and in 1997 16% of federal inmates and 19% of state prisoners had committed their current offense to obtain money for drugs (Bureau of Justice Statistics, 1999). It is important to note that this data is based on self-reports, which are likely conservative estimates. Studies have demonstrated that arrestees' self-reports underestimated drug use detected by urinalysis by 40 to 60 percent (Lu, Taylor, and Riley, 2001; Johnson, Taylor, Golub, and Eterno, 2001). Thus, the actual rates are likely to be considerably higher than that reported by inmates.

Drug and alcohol abuse and addiction are implicated in the incarceration of up to 83% of the 1.7 million men and women behind bars (ONDCP, 2001; CASA, 1998). In 1999, approximately 6.3 million adults–3.1% of the nation's adult population were under some form of correctional supervision. Drug offenders accounted for 21% (236,800) of the state prison population in 1998, up from 6% in 1980 (Bureau of Justice Statistics, U.S. Department of Justice, 2000; 1995), and 59% (55,984) of the federal prison population in 1998, up from 25% in 1980 (Federal Bureau of Prisons, U.S. Department of Justice, 2000). Furthermore, 26% (152,000) of all inmates under the jurisdiction of a local jail or House of Correction were incarcerated for drug offenses (Bureau of Justice Statistics, U.S. Department of Justice, 2000).

Clearly, it has been demonstrated through solid research that the extraordinary increase in prison populations is directly related to a single source–the significant increase in serious drug involvement among offenders. Thus, there is an inextricable relationship between drug use and crime (Ball et al., 1981,

1982, 1983; Chaiken and Chaiken, 1983, 1982; Chaiken, 1985, 1986; Wexler et al., 1991). This increasing need for prison beds is not likely to change in the near future. Many states are under some form of court order or consent decree to relieve prison overcrowding directly due to the increase in drug-related arrests and sentencing practices regarding drug offenders (NIDA, 1992). Mandatory sentences, longer sentences, increased incarceration rates for first time felons, and overcrowding have resulted in the need to develop more effective interventions to reduce the recidivism rates and reduce the higher profile criminogenic issues of chronic substance abusers. By the year 2053, if we continue at our present rate of prison population increase, more than half of America will be in prison (Bronstein, 1990)!

## DRUG TREATMENT IN JAIL/PRISONS

Given that an enormous amount of crime is committed by a proportionately small number of drug abusers (Wexler, Blackmore, and Lipton, 1991), sound correctional policy would appear to dictate strategies that address the treatment needs of offenders. State officials estimate that 70 to 85% of inmates need some level of substance abuse treatment. But in 1996, only 15% of state inmates were in any treatment. Approximately 840,000 state and federal inmates were in need of treatment; however, only about 150,000 inmates actually received treatment, and much of that treatment was inadequate (CASA: Behind Bars–Substance Abuse and America's Prison Population, 1998). In 1997, 1 in 10 state prisoners reported being treated for drug abuse since admission and only 9% of federal prisoners reported receiving treatment since admission. In 1997, 20% of both federal and state prisoners reported being enrolled in less intensive services as self-help, peer groups, or drug education classes (Bureau of Justice Statistics, 1999).

The history of prison-based drug treatment in the United States can be traced back to 1939 when the first "narcotic farms" were established for the incarceration and treatment of heroin addicts (Walters et al., 1992). More treatment programs appeared in the 1960s (Nevada State Penitentiary, 1962, Fort Grant, Arizona, 1969), and by 1980, there were about 160 prison treatment programs serving about four percent of the prison population (Tims, 1981). By 1987, it was estimated that 11.1 percent of the inmates in the fifty states were in some form of drug treatment program (Chaiken and Johnson, 1989), and by 1992, approximately 15 percent of the federal and state inmate populations were estimated to be receiving treatment (ABA, 1993). The most recent study (CASA, 1998) found only 15% of state inmates were in any type of treatment.

Although scarce in comparison to need, drug treatment programs were held in fairly positive regard through the 1960s and early 1970s. By the end of the 1970s, however, this consensus was shattered when Martinson (1974) published his results of over 200 evaluation studies of treatment programs reported in the literature between 1945 and 1967. His conclusion that "with few and isolated exceptions, the rehabilitative efforts . . . have led to no appreciable effect on recidivism" gave great impetus to what has become known as the "nothing works" phenomenon. The "nothing works" cliché had enormous influence on both popular and professional thinking throughout the 1980s, resulting in a shifting of priorities from rehabilitation to that of control and punishment. This occurred despite the fact that Martinson, in a 1979 article reviewing the more recent evaluation studies of treatment programs, stated that based upon a further review of studies "new evidence leads me to reject my original conclusion" (Martinson, 1979).

Subsequent research on the effectiveness of treatment clearly revealed that treatment programs in correctional settings do produce positive results in terms of reduced drug use and criminality following release (Des Jarlais and Wexler, 1979). In five separate reviews of the literature on drug treatment programs covering the period from 1973-1987 and several hundred reports, the authors concluded that treatment participants had greater reductions of law violating behavior of between 10% to 30%, with reduced rates in the 50% to 80% range (Gendreau and Ross, 1979, 1981, 1987; Ross and Gendreau, 1980; Ross and Fabiano, 1985).

In an analysis of the outcome data from the first three years of a prison-based substance abuse treatment program, researchers found that participants had lower parole revocation rates, significantly fewer revocations and lower reincarceration rates (Wexler, Falkin, and Lipton, 1988). The Bureau of Justice Statistics (1994) reports that the rate of recidivism from inmates completing treatment programs range from 7% to 28%–compared to well over 40-60% for inmates not receiving treatment.

As mentioned earlier, the results of comprehensive treatment for the hardcore drunk driving offender has demonstrated to produce positive outcomes. Evaluation studies on the effectiveness of the Longwood and Baltimore County programs have indicated a recidivism rate of between 6-8% (LeClair, 1987; LeClair and Guarino-Ghezzi, 1997; Valle, 1986, 1996). In both programs the majority of inmates also reported having other drug problems.

The Federal Bureau of Prisons conducted a survey of drug treatment outcomes among inmates who completed the residential drug abuse treatment program. The survey found that only 3.3% were likely to be rearrested in the first 6 months after release, compared with 12.1% of inmates who did not receive treatment. Among those who received treatment, 20.5% were likely to use drugs in the first six months after release. In the group without treatment, 36.7% used drugs after release (Federal Bureau of Prisons, 1998).

Evaluations of therapeutic community type programs have generally found positive results (Lipton, 1995, 1998) and are recommended as a "what works" approach in a review by MacKenzie and Hickman (1998). A successful Therapeutic Community, according to Lipton et al. (1992), includes *such factors as:*

1. Adequate staffing
2. Administrative support
3. Programming in an isolated area
4. Client selection
5. Financial security
6. Positive/accepting interaction between treatment and custodial staff
7. Autonomy

Inciardi et al. (1997, 1999) identified the above factors as critical to the therapeutic community's success and added aftercare provisions as the critical eighth factor.

## THE PRINCIPLES FOR EFFECTIVE CORRECTIONS DRUG TREATMENT PROGRAMS AND COGNITIVE-BEHAVIORAL TREATMENT

A growing number of scholars and practitioners support the position that "the effectiveness of correctional treatment is dependent upon what is delivered to whom in a particular setting" (Andrews, 1980, 1983, 1989; Basta and Davidson, 1988; Ross and Fabiano, 1985; Gendreau and Ross, 1987). This model empirically supports the position that services address the three criminogenic principles: risk, need, and responsivity.

The risk position articulates that higher levels of intervention are best focused on higher risk inmates and lower risk inmates are best served by low levels of services.

Andrews identifies the need factor as static or dynamic in nature. Static risk factors may include environmental, familial, and systemic influences of individuals. Dynamic risk factors include mainly intra-psychic issues of antisocial attitudes, peer association, self-indulgence and chemical use.

Responsivity deals with the identification/selection of services that are most effective in influencing intermediate targets (based on individual issues) and which appropriately match learning styles of inmates with modes of treatment. Translating individual and group learning styles and preferences into programming is based on the position that each inmate has established learning styles. In a group format, facilitators must be able to present activities/tasks that access visual, auditory, and neuro-motor preference styles.

The cognitive-behavioral treatment philosophy is founded on the principle that a person's emotional and behavioral reaction is determined by their concept of reality and their thinking (Beck, 1970; Beck et al., 1993). Abuse of drugs and alcohol, according to this model, is associated with a multidimensional defect in thinking that constricts reality in a rigid, self-defeating polarized fashion. "An intensive program, utilizing cognitive theory and techniques, can offer a powerful mechanism for change. Intervention in the cognitive realism is relatively easy to do, non-threatening and conducive to short-term demonstrable results" (Wormer, 1988, p. 31).

Cognitive distortions, maladaption, dysfunctional beliefs, and behavioral patterns receive considerable attention in cognitive-behavioral treatment programs. Alcoholics Anonymous (AA) uses the term "stinking thinking" to characterize the type of irrational, dysfunctional mind set which is frequently cited as a precursor for drinking and drugging.

Distortion may occur when a person is under the influence of drugs, alcohol, stress, states of fatigue, diminished states of consciousness or in a heightened state of arousal. Maladaptive thinking/thought is applied in ideation (beliefs) that interferes with the ability to cope with life experiences. In a habitual state, these are known as automatic thoughts, which frequently lead to self-defeating behavior (Beck, 1970; Beck et al., 1993; Ellis, 1975).

Research on the thinking styles, modes, and process of substance abuse indicates that dysfunctional thinking patterns precedes the use of mood alternating substances (Begleiter et al., 1984; Deykins et al., 1987; Gorenstein et al., 1987; Wormer, 1988). As a dynamic intervention, controlling one's thinking process is viewed as the basis for shaping emotions and behavior. Specific techniques as positive self-talk, cognitive restructuring, reframing, and matching current behaviors to positive, healthy thinking patterns, are primary vehicles of change.

The cognitive behavior-based change process is formulated in the following behavioral sequence:

1. Propose a specific project/task to the client;
2. Elicit their reasons for opposing the proposal;
3. Ask the individual to weigh the validity of their "reasons";
4. Indicate why those reasons are self-defeating;
5. Stimulate interest in attempting to perform the assignment;
6. Set up the task in such a way that the individual must test the validity of their belief/thoughts;
7. After completion, indicate why the individual's thoughts/beliefs were self-defeating;

8. Review, with the individual, the constructive attitudes/beliefs; repeat as necessary.

In summary, most recent empirical evidence indicates that substance abuse treatment and services in a correctional setting should be based on the principles of *risk analysis, basic need identification, and responsivity* (selection of style and modes of services that match inmates' learning-functioning styles (Andrews et al., 1990). Learning modes/styles are based on neuro-linguistic principles that support the most effective learning techniques utilizing strengths of the individual (visual, auditory and kinesthetic).

The "risk principle" analysis indicates targeting of higher risk cases with higher levels of service, and lower risk levels with lower levels of service. The "needs factor" principle targets support and focuses interactions on dynamic needs to reduce criminal conduct. Static needs, which are less promising for change, include more environmental, systemic, and familial issues beyond the primary targets of interventions (Wormith, 1984).

## THERAPEUTIC COMMUNITY (TC) TREATMENT PROGRAMS IN CORRECTIONS

In 1994 the Crime Control Act authorized Residential Substance Abuse Treatment (RSAT) block grants to expand the TC treatment programs that were 6-12 months in duration, had separate living facilities and provided treatment toward the end of the inmate's stay in prison/jail (Lipton, 1995). Many of the RSAT process evaluation reports available from NCJRS[1] (2001) merely describe the populations served and some of the reasons implementation had been delayed. Where evaluations were actually completed the results supported the factors identified by Lipton (1995, 1998) and Inciardi (1997) as important. In particular:

- *Staffing*–highlighted in the report of the Delaware KEY Experience and Ozark Correctional Center report.
- *Administrative Support*–Ozark Correctional Center (MO), Michigan Department of Corrections RSAT Program.
- *Client Selection*–Barnstable House of Correction (MA), Barret Juvenile Corrections Center (VA), Delaware KEY Experience, Michigan RSAT.
- *Financial Considerations*–Pennsylvania Program for Drug-Involved Parole Violators.
- *Treatment/Custodial Staff Interaction*–Minnesota RSAT, Pennsylvania Program for Drug-Involved Parole Violators.

- *Autonomy*–Delaware Key Experience, Michigan Department of Corrections RSAT Program.
- *Aftercare*–Delaware Key Experience, Michigan Department of Corrections RSAT Program.

The term Therapeutic Community (TC) has come to represent a distinct approach that can be applied in almost any setting with almost any population. In recent years, TC models have been increasingly adapted for incarcerated substance abusers in prison settings. Overcrowded prisons, the influx of drug offenders, and the documented success of TC prison models in reducing recidivism and relapse have fostered this development. Modifications of the traditional TC model are shaped by the unique features of the individual correctional institution and the prison culture itself (De Leon, 1998). The prison/jail modified TC is an intense resocialization model most appropriate for the hard- core criminally involved addict who has not succeeded, or who is not appropriate for placement, in other forms of treatment The most effective modified TCs in jails or prisons are at least six months in length with the best results obtained in programs lasting 9-12 months in duration.

In the prison/jail modified therapeutic community (TC), the operation of the community itself is the task of the offenders working together under staff supervision. Work assignments, or job functions, are arranged in a hierarchy according to seniority, individual progress, and productivity. The new offender enters a social order of upward mobility based upon sequential completion of job assignments. Job assignments begin with the most menial tasks (e.g., floor mopping) and lead vertically to levels of coordination and management. This social organization reflects the fundamental aspects of the TC approach: mutual self-help, work as education and therapy, peers as role models, and staff as rational authorities.

Each therapeutic community is a self-governing unit operating under the direct supervision of staff who function as the rational authority. The offender population within each community is organized hierarchically, with each offender accepting various responsibilities and owing certain duties to the group as a whole. Security staff and program staff function as role models and facilitators to ensure that the modified therapeutic community functions in accordance with the guidelines and objectives of the program, as well as the rules and regulations of the agency and facility.

The modified TC in prison is designed to teach offenders basic life skills, to use more effective communication techniques, to develop coping mechanisms, to make rational responses in dealing with daily conflicts and to live an alcohol/drug-free lifestyle. Peer group members reinforce the program objectives by encouraging individual community members to confront their personal problems. They do so through a system of "rules and tools" that are incorporated within the therapeutic community structure. The rules of the community allow for a safe environment for growth and positive risk taking. Program rules include cardinal rules, major rules, and group house rules. The "tools" of the program coincide with a graded system of privileges and sanctions that reinforce positive behaviors and call attention to negative behaviors–always within the current security system and rules of the corrections department. Some of these tools include the use of verbal pull-ups, written pull-ups, haircuts, learning experiences, confrontation groups, general meeting, prospect chair, tight house, or disciplinary hearings. Although therapeutic communities have been demonstrated to be effective in reducing both drug use and recidivism, they also typically have a very high treatment dropout rate (Austin, 1998). This is a critical variable as success has been directly related to the amount of time spent in treatment (Lipton, 1995, 1998). Most recently, TC programs have placed greater emphasis on selecting the type of inmate who is better matched for the intense resocialization aspects of a therapeutic community and developing strategies to improve inmate retention and completion of treatment. Some, Austin (1998) in particular, question whether therapeutic communities within the prison system are being "over sold" and argue that the focus should be on community-based drug treatment programs for offenders. The evidence, however, suggests that this should not be an either or proposition, but rather that treatment should begin in prison and continue into the community.

### TOWARD DEVELOPMENT OF A PREFERRED MODE OF TREATMENT FOR OFFENDERS– ACCOUNTABILITY TRAINING: A PUBLIC SAFETY TREATMENT MODEL

By the mid 1980s the need for a new treatment model for substance abuse offenders emerged, as it became evident that traditional mental health and public health models were largely ineffective with the substance abuse offender population.

As a result of the success in developing correctional treatment programs for the drunk driving offender, it became apparent that the approaches and modalities used in healthcare settings for treatment of alcohol and drug problems needed to be modified if treatment was to be successful for the incarcerated offender. The characteristics of the incarcerated client and the setting in which treatment took place were very different. At times, the approaches and techniques applied by the clinician in a healthcare setting were incongruent, and sometimes, in direct conflict with the corrections culture. It became apparent that clinicians needed a new model to guide them in the application of treatment approaches when working with alcohol/drug offenders, particularly in programs that were located in secure facilities. Also, in healthcare settings, the primary goal is rehabilitation, whereas in working with the offender, habilitation is the more realistic goal. From these beginnings, Dr. Steve Valle and associates adapted and reframed certain elements of the above-mentioned theoretical positions that seem better matched to the substance abuse offender population, and then integrated them with concepts learned from treating substance abuse offenders in various criminal justice settings in Massachusetts. The origins of Accountability Training are found in the works of Beck (1970; Beck et al., 1993) Glasser (1963), Ellis (1973), Lazarus (1976), Carkhuff (1969), and in the 12-Step principles and traditions found in AA's Big Book (1939). From these theoretical foundations, Dr. Valle began formulating a new model for treating substance abuse offenders in mandated treatment settings in the late 1980s.

Beginning at MCI-Longwood (MA) in 1985, and continuing at the MCI Old Colony and Gardner (MA) program units in the late 1980s, the Accountability Training model crystallized in 1992, at the first Massachusetts Boot Camp program in Bridgewater. Thus, the origins of a new public safety treatment model, Accountability Training (Valle, 1991), was formulated in the Massachusetts Department of Correction's first substance abuse program units, the Longwood Treatment Center and in the original Massachusetts Boot Camp (1992-95). From these origins, Accountability Training has been implemented in several State Department of Corrections' programs including those in Florida, Maryland, North Carolina, and Texas. The Accountability Training model is currently being applied at the Barnstable County (MA) Shock Incarceration Program, several Sheriffs' Departments and at several Community Corrections Centers throughout the Commonwealth of Massachusetts.

In contrast to a mental health model which emphasizes treating the underlying causes of maladjustment, or a public health model which emphasizes the individual's growth and developmental needs, a public safety treatment model stresses the individual's accountability to others as the primary attitudinal and behavioral tenets for improving self-respect and enabling positive change to occur.

Accountability Training teaches the offender that addiction is a disease *and* a lifestyle disorder that results in such self-absorption that the individual's self-perception and view of reality becomes distorted through denial, delusion, and continual negative attitudes and behaviors. After first obtaining a solid baseline of sobriety, the principles of Accountability Training enables the individual to break this pattern of negativity and self-centeredness by teaching offenders the skills to be accountable for the consequences of their behavior. Learning to be accountable for the consequences of one's behavior is a pre-step to becoming responsible for one's behavior, a frequently stated goal of behavior change programs. For most substance abuse offenders whose developmental years were dominated with drug use and drug-seeking behavior, learning what it means to be accountable is a pre-step for becoming responsible. Offenders have developed such skills in manipulation, blaming, minimizing the impact of their actions on others, and living by their own social code, that the concept of accountability is foreign to their cognitive thinking processes. It is difficult to act responsibly if one does not first integrate the concept of accountability into their thinking styles. In Accountability Training programs, we have realized that the concept of accountability needs to be learned and relearned. Thus, Accountability Training is a teaching as "treatment model" where the emphasis is on learning new cognitive-behavioral skills and practicing these new skills and behaviors within the safety of the treatment group.

Accountability Training also gives offenders the skills to learn how to build self-respect by responding to the needs of others (learning to put "we before I"), and the skills of how to let go of a victim mentality and adopt an accountability mentality in both attitudes and behaviors. In formulating Accountability Training, the works of Glasser, 12-Step AA philosophy, and cognitive behavioral approaches to change that emphasize relearning positive skills and attitudes, were most influential in constructing this new approach to treating offenders.

## *CONCLUSION*

The past two decades have seen an explosion in the prison/jail population, most of which has been driven by the high prevalence of inmates with substance abuse problems. Over the past twenty years, particularly the last decade, there has been an increasing emphasis on providing alcohol/drug treatment for incarcerated offenders–with encouraging results. Correctional treatment programs of six months or more in duration significantly reduce recidivism and are cost beneficial. Still, the number of inmates receiving treatment remains far below the demand.

As alcohol/drug treatment in corrections has grown over the past twenty years, so has the awareness of the complexity of the problem. The needs of women offenders, youthful offenders, and inmates with co-occurring disorders all have special treatment needs that must be addressed more thoroughly as treatment in corrections evolves. Also, the need for cross training for corrections and treatment staff, better linkage with community-based providers of services that would assist in an inmate's reintegration, and stronger collaboration among public safety, mental health, and public health professionals, are all necessary to build upon the foundation that has been laid.

While the focus of this article has been on substance abuse and corrections, the developments in other areas of the criminal justice field have been significant and warrant attention in future publications. Alternative sanction programs as drug courts, community corrections, intensive supervision, and developments in reintegration services are but a few of the many encouraging developments that have occurred over the past two decades. These areas should be addressed in future reviews.

Great progress has been made over the past twenty years, but even greater progress needs to be attained to fully address the needs of offenders who present with alcohol and/or drug problems. The next generation of corrections and treatment professionals will need to improve upon the breadth, depth, and quality of services. From our observations of the commitment and professionalism of this cadre, it is a goal that will be attained.

## NOTE

1. All of the following institutional references are based on the NCJRS Abstract Database Document Details.

## REFERENCES

Alcoholics Anonymous (1939). *Alcoholics Anonymous, Publishing Inc.*, NY, New York.

American Bar Association (1992). *Responding to the Problem of Drug Abuse: Strategies for the Criminal Justice System.* Washington, DC.

Andrews, D. A. (1979). *The Dimensions of Correctional Counseling and Supervision Process in Probation and Parole.* Toronto: Ontario Ministry of Correctional Services.

Andrews, D. A. (1980). Some Experimental Investigations of the Principles of Differential Association Through Deliberate Manipulations of the Structure of Service Systems. *American Sociological Review*, 45, 448-462.

Andrews, D. A. (1983). The Assessment of Outcome in Correctional Samples. In M. L. Lambert, E. R. Christensen, & S. S. DeJulio (Eds.), *The Measurement of Psychotherapy Outcome in Research and Evaluation.* New York. Wiley.

Andrews, D. A. (1989). Recidivism is Predictable and Can Be Influenced: Using Risk Assessments to Reduce Recidivism. *Forum on Corrections Research*, 1 (2), 11-18.

Andrews, D. A., Hoge, R. D., Bonta, J., Gendreau, P., & Cullen, F. T. (1990). Does Correctional Treatment Work? A Clinically-Relevant and Psychologically-Informed Meta-Analysis. *Criminology*, 28, 369-404.

Andrews, D. A., & Kiessling, J. J. (1980). Program Structure and Effective Correctional Practice: A Summary of the CaVIC research. In R. R. Ross & P. Gendreau (Eds.), *Effective Correctional Treatment*, Toronto: Butterworth.

Austin, J. (Fall, 1998). Limits of Prison Drug Treatment. *Corrections Management Quarterly*, 2 (4), 66-74.

Ball, J. C., Rosen, L., Flueck, S. A., & Nurco, D. N. (1982). Lifetime Criminality of Heroin Addicts in the United States. *Journal of Drug Issues*, 3, 225-239.

Ball, J. C., Rosen, L., Flueck, S. A., & Nurco, D. N. (1981). The Criminality of Heroin Addicts When Addicted and When Off Opiates. In Inciardi, J.S. (Ed.), *The Drugs-Crime Connection* (pp. 39-65). Beverly Hills, CA: Sage.

Ball, J. C., Shaffer, J., & Nurco, D. (1983). Day to Day Criminality of Heroin Addicts in Baltimore–A Study in the Continuity of Offense Rates. *Drug Alcohol Dependence*, 12, 119-142.

Basta, J. M., & Davidson, N. S. (1988). Treatment of Juvenile Offenders: Study Outcomes Since 1980. *Behavioral Sciences and the Law*, 6, 355-384.

Beck, A. (1970). *Cognitive Therapy and Emotional Disorders*. Meridian.

Beck, A. T., Wright, F. D., Newman, C. F., & Liese, B. S. (1993). *Cognitive Therapy of Substance Abuse*. New York, Guilford Press.

Begleiter, H., Porjesji, B., & Kissen, B. (1984). Event-Related Brain Potential Boys at Risk of Alcoholism. *Science*, 225, 1493-1496.

Bronstein, A. (1990). *National Prison Project*, Brookings Institute.

Bureau of Justice Statistics. *Prisoners in 1999*, Washington, DC: U.S. Department of Justice, August 2000.

Bureau of Justice Statistics. *Correctional Populations in the United States*, 1992, Washington, DC: U.S. Department of Justice, January 1995.

Bureau of Justice Statistics. *Drug Use, Testing, and Treatment in Jails*, Washington, DC: U.S. Department of Justice, May 2000.

Bureau of Justice Statistics. *Substance Abuse and Treatment, State and Federal Prisoners*, 1997, Washington, DC: U.S. Department of Justice, January 1999.

Bureau of Justice Statistics. *Drug Use, Testing, and Treatment in Jails*, Washington, DC: U.S. Department of Justice, May 2000.

Bureau of Justice Statistics. *Probation and Parole in the United States*, 1999, Washington, DC: U.S. Department of Justice, July 2000.

Camp, C. G., & Camp, G. M. (1999). *The 1998 Corrections Yearbook*, South Salem, NY: Criminal Justice Institute, Inc.

Carhhuff, R. R. (1969). *Helping and Human Relations*. New York: Holt, Rinehart, & Winston.

Center on Addiction and Substance Abuse (CASA). (1998). *Behind Bars: Substance Abuse and America's Prison Population*. Columbia University. New York.

Chaiken, M. R., & Johnson, B. D. (1989) *Prison Programs for Drug-Involved Offenders*, Washington, DC. National Institute of Justice.

Chaiken, J. M., & Chaiken, M. R. (1982). *Varieties of Criminal Behavior*. Santa Monica, CA: The Rand Corporation.

Chaiken, J. M., & Chaiken, M. R. (1983). Crime Rates and the Active Offender. In J.Q. Wilson (Ed.), *Crime and Public Policy* (p. 1129). New Brunswick, NJ: Transaction Books.

Chaiken, M. R. (1986). Crime Rates and Substance Abuse Treatment Among Types of Offenders. In Johnson, B.D., & Wish, E. (Eds.), *Crime Rates Among Drug-Abusing Offenders*. Final Report to the National Institute of Justice. New York: Narcotic and Drug Research, Inc.

Chavaria, F. (1992). Successful Drug Treatment in a Criminal Justice Setting. *Federal Probation*, March, 48-52.

Cullen, F., & Gendreau, P. (1989). The Effectiveness of Correctional Rehabilitation. Reconsidering the "Nothing Works" Debate.

Cullen, F., & Gendreau, P. (1989). The Effectiveness of Correctional Rehabilitation. In L. Yoodstein, & D. L. Mackenzie (Eds.), *The American Prison. Issues in Research Policy*. New York, Plenum.

De Leon, G. (1998). *Therapeutic Community: Theory and Research*. Video Produced By Mid America Addiction Technology Transfer Center. Kansas City, Missouri.

DesJarlais, D., & Wexler, H. K. (1979). *Internal Report for the New York Division of Substance Abuse Services*, Albany, New York.

Deykins, E., Levy, J., & Wells, V. (1987). Adolescent Depression, Alcohol and Drug Abuser. *American Journal of Public Health*, 77 (2), 178-182.

Ellis, A., McInery, J., DiGruseppe, R., & Yaeger, R. (1973). *Rational Emotive Therapy with Alcoholics and Substance Abusers*. New York: Pergamon Press.

Fair, M. (1986). Operating Under the Influence: Programs and Treatment for Convicted Offenders in Massachusetts. In *Drunk Driving in America: Strategies and Approaches to Treatment*. The Haworth Press, Inc.

Federal Bureau of Investigation. *Crime in the United States in 1980 Through 1999, Uniform Crime Reporting Program*, Washington, DC: U.S. Department of Justice, October 2000.

Federal Bureau of Prisons. *Federal Bureau of Prisons Quick Facts*, Washington, DC: U.S. Department of Justice, February 2000.

Federal Bureau of Prisons. *TRIAD Drug Treatment Evaluation Six-Month Report: Executive Summary*, Washington, DC: U.S. Department of Justice, February 1998.

Gendreau, P. (1981). Treatment in Corrections: Martinson Was Wrong. *Canadian Psychology*, 22, 332-338.

Gendreau, P., & Andrews, D. A. (1990). Tertiary Prevention: What the Meta Analysis of the Offender Treatment Literature Tells Us About "What Works," *Canadian Journal of Criminology*, 32, 173-184.

Gendreau, P., Coggin, C., & Annis, H. (1990). Survey of Existing Substance Abuse Programs. *Forum on Corrections Research*, 2, 608.

Gendreau, P., & Ross, R. R. (1987). Revivification of Rehabilitation: Evidence from the 1980's. *Justice Quarterly*, 4 (3), 349-407.

Gendreau, P., & Ross, R. R. (1981). Correctional Potency: Treatment and Deterrence on Trial. In R. Roesch & R. R. Corrado (Eds.), Evaluation and Criminal Justice Policy. Beverly Hills, CA: Sage.

Gendreau, P., & Ross, R. R. (1979). Effective Correctional Treatment: Bibliography for Cynics. *Crime and Delinquency*, 25 (4), 463-489.

Gendreau, P., & Ross, R. R. (1984). Correctional Treatment. Some Recommendations for Successful Intervention. *Juvenile and Family Court Journal*, 34, 31-39.

Glasser, W. (1963). *Reality Therapy*. Harper & Row, New York, NY.

Gorenstein, E. (1987). Cognitive-Perceptual Deficits in Alcoholism Spectrum Disorder. *Journal of Studies on Alcohol*, 48 (4), 310-318.

Inciardi, J. A., Lockwood, D., & Pottleger, A. E. (1993). *Women and Crack-Cocaine*. New York. Macmillian Publishing Company.

Inciardi, J. A. et al. (Spring, 1997). Effective Model of Prison-Based Treatment for Drug-Involved Offenders. *Journal of Drug Issues*, 27 (2).

Johnson, B., Hamid, A., & Sanbria, H. (1992). Emerging Models of Crack Distribution. In T. Mieczkowski (Ed.), *Drugs, Crime, and Social Policy: Research, Issues and Concerns* (pp. 58-78). Boston: Allyn and Bacon, Inc.

Johnson, B., Taylor, A., Golub, A., & Eterno, J. (2001). *Monitoring Impacts of Policing Initiatives on Arrestees in New York City*. Final report submitted to the National Institute on Justice, U.S. Department of Justice, Washington, DC.

Lazarus, A. (1976). *Multi-Modal Behavior Therapy*, Springer Publishing Co., NY, New York.

LeClair, D. P. (1987). *Evaluation Study: Longwood Treatment Facility*, Mass. Department of Corrections.

LeClair, D. P., & Guarino-Ghezzi, S. (1997). Prison Reintegration Programs: An Evaluation. *Corrections Management Quarterly*, 1 (4).

Lipton, D. S. (1995). *The Effectiveness of Treatment for Drug Abusers Under Criminal Justice Supervision*. Washington, DC: National Institute of Justice.

Lipton, D. S. (1995). Successful Correctional Treatment Programming for Drug Abusers. Presented at the NIC meeting on effective treatment, Ellicott City, Maryland.

Lipton, D. S. (1998). Therapeutic Community Treatment Programming in Corrections. *Psychology, Crime & Law*, 4, 213-263.

Lipton, D., Fallkin, G., & Wexlar, H. (1992). "Correctional Drug Abuse Treatment in the United States: An Overview". *National Institute on Drug Abuse Research Monographs Series*, 118, 8-30.

Lipton, D. S., Martinson, R., & Wilks, J. (1975). *The Effectiveness of Correctional Treatment: A Survey of Treatment Evaluation Studies*. New York: Praeger.

Lu, N., Taylor, B. G., & Riley, K. J. (2001). The Validity of Adult Arrestee Self-Reports of Crack Cocaine Use. *American Journal of Drug and Alcohol Abuse*, 27 (3), 399-420.

MacKenzie, D. L., & Hickman, L. J. (1998). What Works in Corrections? *An Examination of the Effectiveness of the Type of Rehabilitative Programs Offered by Washington State Department of Corrections: Report to the State of Washington Legislature Joint Audit and Review Committee*, College Park, MD: University of Maryland.

Martin, S. S., Inciardi, J. A. et al. (September, 1999). Three-Year Outcomes of Therapeutic Community Treatment for Drug-Involved Offenders in Delaware: From Prison to Work Release to Aftercare. *Prison Journal*, 79 (3).

Martinson, R. (1974). What Works?–Questions and Answers About Prison Reform. *Public Interest*, 35, 22-25.

Martinson, R. (1979). New Findings, New Views: A Note of Caution Regarding Sentencing Reform. *Hofstra Law Review*, 243-258.

National Center on Addiction and Substance Abuse. *Behind Bars: Substance Abuse and America's Prison Population*, New York, NY: Columbia University, January 1998.

National Institute of Drug Abuse (NIDA). (1992). Drug Abuse Treatment in Prisons and Jails, U.S. Department of Health and Human Services. *Research Monograph*, 118.

National Institute of Justice. Drug Use Forecasting Program Annual Report, 1989.

Office of National Drug Control Policy (ONDCP). *Drug Policy Information Clearing-house Fact Sheet*, Rockville, MD: Executive Office of the President, March 2001.

Ross, R., & Gendreau, P. (Eds.). (1980). Effective Correctional Treatment, Toronto, Canada, Butterworths.

Ross, R., & Fabiano E. (1985). Time to Think: A Cognitive Model of Delinquency Prevention and Offender Rehabilitation. *Institute of Social Sciences and Arts*. Johnson City, TN.

Rothman, D. J. (1971). *The Discovery of the Asylum: Social Order and Disorder in the New Republic*. Boston: Little, Brown.

Substance Abuse and Mental Health Services Administration (SAMHSA), Center for Substance Abuse Treatment, National Evaluation Data Services. *The Cost and Benefits of Substance Abuse Treatment: Findings From the National Treatment Improvement Evaluation Study*, August 1999.

Tims, F. M. (1981). *Drug Abuse Treatment in Prisons. Treatment Research Reports*. Washington, DC. Superintendent of Documents U.S. Government Printing Office.

Tims, F. M., & Ludford, J. P. (1984). *Drug Abuse Treatment Evaluation: Strategies, Progress, and Prospects*. NIDA Research Monograph 51. DI HIS Pub. No. (ADM) 84-1349. Rockville, MD: National Institute on Drug Abuse.

U.S. Department of Justice, Office of Justice Programs. *An Analysis of National Data on the Prevalence of Alcohol Involvement in Crime*, NCJ-168632, April, 1998.

U.S. Department of Justice, Office of Justice Programs, Bureau of Justice Statistics. (1992). *Drugs, Crime and the Justice System: A National Report from the Bureau of Justice Statistics*. Washington, DC.

Valle, S. K. (1996). *Right Turn: Getting Tougher and Smarter with Repeat Drunk Driving Offenders*. Pioneer Institute for Public Policy Research. Boston, MA.

Valle, S. K. (1991). *Accountability Training for Addicted Inmates*. The Counselor, March/April, National Association of Alcoholism and Drug Abuse Counselors, Arlington, VA.

Valle, S. K. (Ed.). (1986). *Drunk Driving in America: Strategies and Approaches to Treatment*. The Haworth Press, Inc., New York.

Valle, S., Kerns, T., & Gaskell, A. (1986). *The Longwood Treatment Center: A Residential Program for Multiple D.U.I. Offenders*. In Drunk Driving in America: Strategies and Approaches to Treatment. The Haworth Press, Inc., New York.

Walters, G., Whitaker, D., Dial, S., Dairosow, S., & Chianciulli, J. (1992). Characteristics & Adjustments of Federal Inmates Enrolled in a Comprehensive Residential Drug Treatment Program. *Federal Probation*, June.

Wexlar, H. K., Blackmore, J., & Lipton D.S. (1991). Project Reform. Developing a Strategy for Correction. *The Journal of Drug Issues*, 21 (2), 469-490.

Wexler, H. K., Falkin, G., & Lipton, D. (1988). Outcome Evaluation of a Prison Therapeutic Community for Substance Abuse Treatment. *Criminal Justice and Behavior*, 17 (1), 71-92.

Williams, L. T. (1984). *County Commitments for Driving Under the Influence of Alcohol 1976-1983*, Massachusetts Department of Correction, Boston.

Wormer, K. (1988). All-or-Nothing Thinking and Alcoholism: A Cognitive Approach. *Federal Probation*, June.

Wormith, J. S. (1984). Attitudes and Behavior Change of Correctional Clientele. A Three Year Follow-Up. *Criminology*, 22, 595-612.

# Alcoholism/Addiction as a Chronic Disease: From Rhetoric to Clinical Reality

William L. White, MA
Michael Boyle, MA
David Loveland, PhD

**SUMMARY.** Although characterized as a chronic disease for more than 200 years, severe and persistent alcohol and other drug (AOD) problems have been treated primarily in self-contained, acute episodes of care. Recent calls for a shift from this acute treatment model to a sustained recovery management model will require rethinking the natural history of AOD disorders; pioneering new treatment and recovery support technologies; restructuring the funding of treatment services; redefining the service relationship; and altering methods of service evaluation. Recovery-oriented systems of care could offer many advantages over the current model of serial episodes of acute care, but such systems will bring

William L. White is Senior Research Consultant, Chestnut Health Systems, and Associate Director of the Behavioral Health Recovery Management (BHRM) project. Michael Boyle is Executive Vice President, Fayette Companies, a behavioral health management organization, and Director of the BHRM project. David Loveland is Senior Research Professional at the University of Chicago Center for Psychiatric Rehabilitation, and Associate Director of the BHRM project.

The preparation of this paper was supported by the Behavioral Health Recovery Management (BHRM) project, a collaborative effort of Fayette Companies of Peoria, IL, and Chestnut Health Systems of Bloomington, IL, a project funded by the Illinois Department of Human Services Office on Alcoholism and Substance Abuse.

The views expressed here are those of the authors and do not necessarily reflect the policies of IDHS/OASA.

[Haworth co-indexing entry note]: "Alcoholism/Addiction as a Chronic Disease: From Rhetoric to Clinical Reality." White, William L., Michael Boyle, and David Loveland. Co-published simultaneously in *Alcoholism Treatment Quarterly* (The Haworth Press, Inc.) Vol. 20, No. 3/4, 2002, pp. 107-130; and: *Alcohol Problems in the United States: Twenty Years of Treatment Perspective* (ed: Thomas F. McGovern, and William L. White) The Haworth Press, Inc., 2002, pp. 107-130. Single or multiple copies of this article are available for a fee from The Haworth Document Delivery Service [1-800-HAWORTH, 9:00 a.m. - 5:00 p.m. (EST). E-mail address: getinfo@haworthpressinc.com].

with them new pitfalls in the personal and cultural management of alcohol and other drug problems. *[Article copies available for a fee from The Haworth Document Delivery Service: 1-800-HAWORTH. E-mail address: <getinfo@haworthpressinc.com> Website: <http://www.HaworthPress.com> © 2002 by The Haworth Press, Inc. All rights reserved.]*

**KEYWORDS.** Chronic disease, disease management, recovery management

Alcoholism and other addictions have long been characterized as chronic diseases, but their treatment continues to be marked by serial episodes of acute care (O'Brien and McLellan, 1996; Kaplan, 1997; McLellan et al., 2001). There is growing disillusionment with this acute care model of intervention, and rising interest in the stages and processes of long-term addiction recovery. This confluence may mark an emerging shift from a treatment paradigm to a recovery paradigm in the clinical management of severe and enduring AOD problems. This essay will:

1. outline the history of the conceptualization of addiction as a chronic illness,
2. identify current clinical practices that continue to reflect an acute model of intervention,
3. summarize key concepts that undergird the shift toward a recovery management intervention model,
4. explore areas of contemporary clinical practice that will change within this new recovery focus, and
5. discuss potential pitfalls in the movement toward a recovery management.

## ADDICTION AS "CHRONIC" DISEASE: A BRIEF HISTORY

The conceptualization of repeated and destructive episodes of drunkenness as a disease rather than a vice (or as a vice that could become a disease) rose in the late eighteenth century at a time when American alcohol consumption virtually exploded (Rorabaugh, 1979; Levine, 1978). The late eighteen and nineteenth century writings of Anthony Benezet, Benjamin Rush, Samuel Woodward and William Sweetser conceptualized the nature of this newly perceived disease and catalogued the consequences that resulted from prolonged and repeated intoxication. Collectively, these writings portrayed intemperance as a disease that is chronic and progressive (Benezet, 1774; Rush, 1814; Sweetser, 1828; Woodward, 1838).

In the mid-to-late nineteenth century, this disease received new medical labels: *dipsomania, chronic alcoholism,* some of which–*inebrism, inebriety*–reflected the extension of the disease concept to embrace addiction to narcotics, cocaine, chloral and ether (Crothers, 1893; White, in press). During this same period, the disease concept of inebriety spawned a network of inebriate homes, inebriate asylums and private addiction cure institutes. Nineteenth-century addiction medicine journals and texts characterized alcohol and other drug addiction as a chronic, relapsing disease (Marcet, 1868; Brown, 1872; Crothers, 1893; Parrish, 1883). In 1879, Dr. T. D. Crothers, editor of the *Journal of Inebriety*, typified comparison of addiction to other chronic disorders during this era:

> *The permanent cure of inebriates under treatment in asylums will compare favorably in numbers with that of any other disease of the nervous system which is more or less chronic before the treatment is commenced.*

The disease concept fell out of favor in the early decades of the twentieth century. A wave of therapeutic pessimism and new alcohol and other drug prohibition laws led to a collapse of most treatment institutions. A reformulated disease concept emerged following the repeal of Prohibition that, by defining alcohol problems in terms of a vulnerable minority rather than the alcohol itself, provided a way to address alcohol problems while escaping a century of acrimonious Wet-Dry debates (Roizen, 1991). This reborn disease concept became the centerpiece of the "modern alcoholism movement" (Anderson, 1942; Mann, 1944). The documents of this movement consistently depict alcoholism as a disease and, more specifically, a chronic disease. As early as 1938, a report of the Scientific Committee of the Research Council on Problems of Alcohol noted:

> *An alcoholic should be regarded as a sick person, just as one who is suffering from tuberculosis, cancer, heart disease, or other serious chronic disorders.* (quoted in Johnson, 1973)

In the late 1940s and 1950s, Pioneer House, Hazelden, and Willmar State Hospital developed what came to be known as the "Minnesota Model" of chemical dependency treatment. This model, which philosophically dominated the treatment of alcoholism in the second half of the twentieth century, was a reaffirmation of the belief that alcoholism was a "chronic, primary, progressive disease" (Cook, 1988; Spicer, 1993). The conceptualization of addiction as a chronic disease subsequently became the rhetorical centerpiece of late twentieth-century policy positions taken by such organizations as the National Council on Alcoholism and Drug Dependence and the American Society of Addiction Medicine (1976, 1990). The proposition that addiction was a disease and the characterization of its chronicity (Vaillant, 1983; Lewis, 1993; Leshner, 1997) subsequently came under serious attack (Fingarette, 1989; Peele, 1989; Peele and Brodsky, 1992; Schaler, 2000) and sparked acrimonious debates regarding the nature of severe and persistent alcohol and other drug problems and how such problems could be best resolved (White, 2001a).

## RHETORIC VERSUS CLINICAL PRACTICE

In spite of the recent challenges, the long tradition of depicting addiction as a chronic, relapsing disease continues. Treatment practices, however, continue to be designed and delivered in self-contained, acute episodes of care (Ethridge et al., 1995). Historically, professionals *assess* and *admit* a *patient* to a course of inpatient or outpatient *treatment*, *discharge* that patient to *aftercare*, and then evaluate whether treatment "worked" by measuring the effect of this single episode of care upon the patient's post-treatment alcohol/drug consumption and psychosocial adjustment over a brief follow-up period. Such a model of intervention assumes an intervention process whose beginning, middle and end can be plotted over a brief period of time, not unlike interventions used to treat acute trauma, appendicitis, or a bacterial infection.

Refusing to admit clients to treatment because of "poor prognosis" (prior treatment "failures") and administratively discharging clients for using alcohol or other drugs (exhibiting inability to abstain/loss of control) also reflect the failure to perceive these conditions as chronic in character. Where durability and exacerbation of symptoms in other chronic disease states is viewed as validating evidence of the disorder and grounds for an altered type and intensity of service intervention, the display of, or exacerbation of, symptoms in the addiction treatment arena has historically constituted grounds for service refusal or termination.

Arguments over whether addiction treatment should be inpatient or outpatient, whether it should consist of 5 days or 28 days or 5 sessions or 10 sessions, or whether cognitive behavioral therapy is more effective than family therapy or "step work" are all arguments inside the acute care treatment paradigm. Even extended treatment, where it still exists, is often simply a longer version of the same cycle of admit, stabilize, and discharge in which clients briefly participate in "aftercare" and mutual aid groups. In spite of the treatment field's rhetoric that addiction is a chronic disease, its primary interventions do not reflect a model of chronic disease management.

For fear of overstating this point, it should be noted that there are episodes in the history of addiction treatment and recovery that do exemplify a vision of long-term recovery management. Nearly all of the alcoholic mutual aid societies in American history have taken this longer view of chronic disease (recovery) management (White, 1998; White, 2001d). When Synanon, the first ex-addict directed therapeutic community, encountered a high relapse rate among its first graduates, it shifted its goal of returning rehabilitated addicts to the larger community and replaced that goal with the creation of an alternative drug-free community where one could live forever (Mitchell, Mitchell, and Ofshe, 1980). Methadone maintenance, as pioneered by Dole and Nyswander, reflected a medically-directed model of long-term addiction recovery management (Dole, 1988, 1997).

What these quite different approaches share in common is that they were all severely criticized for their longer vision of recovery management. Mutual aid groups have been (and continue to be) criticized for shifting the addict's dependency on a drug to prolonged dependency on the support group, Synanon was criticized for its failure to return addicts to the larger community, and methadone was criticized for the very aspects that exemplified the chronic disease management model: prolonged maintenance of narcotic addicts on a stabilizing, opiate agonist and sustained psychosocial supports. This history would suggest that new efforts to shift from an acute to chronic disease management model of addiction treatment might well face similar resistance.

## TOWARD A CHRONIC DISEASE/ RECOVERY MANAGEMENT MODEL

If one were searching for a pivotal breakthrough of consciousness about the distinction between acute and chronic models of addiction disease intervention, it might very well be found in George Vaillant's 1983 work, *The Natural History of Alcoholism*. Vaillant's longitudinal study of alcoholism and recovery challenged three historical assumptions about the disorder and its treatment: (1) alcoholism can be effectively treated with a single episode of acute care, (2) a treatment episode that is followed by relapse is a failure, and (3) repeated relapses following multiple episodes of acute treatment mean that either the condition or the particular patient is untreatable (Vaillant, 1983). Vaillant's overall work was so pregnant with new ideas that his challenge of these basic premises was lost.

The acute care model of intervening in alcohol- and other drug-related (AOD) problems dominated the explosive growth of treatment in the 1970s and 1980s. In failing to consistently initiate enduring sobriety following a single episode of treatment, the model, by consequence rather than intent, blamed clients for poor clinical outcomes. The model also contributed to the rise of therapeutic pessimism within the larger culture, and helped fuel an ideological and financial backlash against the addiction treatment industry in the 1990s (White, 1998). As an aggressive system of managed care dramatically short-ened both inpatient and outpatient treatment, there was growing unease within the treatment community regarding the practice of placing clients with high problem severity and duration through multiple episodes of unlinked, brief treatment that for many did little to alter the long-term course of their disor-ders. This practice proved as demoralizing to treatment staff as it was to the cli-ents and families to which it was applied.

In the October 4, 2000, issue of the *Journal of the American Medical Asso-ciation (JAMA)*, a potentially historic article appeared entitled "Drug Depend-ence, a Chronic Medical Illness: Implications for Treatment, Insurance, and Outcomes Evaluation" that was authored by Drs. McLellan, Lewis, O'Brien, and Kleber. The report marks the most complete elaboration to date of the con-cept of chronic addiction disease. The *JAMA* article reflects several factors now pushing the addiction treatment field away from an acute care model and toward a chronic disease (recovery management) model of problem interven-tion.

First, there is a growing recognition that managing severe and persistent AOD problems through single or serial episodes of acute treatment is clini-cally ineffective and constitutes poor stewardship of individual, family and community resources. The "treatment careers" research conducted at the Uni-versity of California's Drug Abuse Research Center underscores several key points in this emerging view:

- A single, acute intervention rarely has sufficient effect to initiate stable and enduring recovery in those with severe and persistent alcohol and other drug problems.
- Multiple episodes of treatment may be viewed not as failures but as in-cremental steps in the developmental process of recovery.
- Treatment episodes may have effects that are cumulative (Hser et al., 1997).

Second, there is a growing recognition that addiction disorders are often chronic and relapsing in nature (Simpson et al., 1986), have much in common with other chronic diseases (O'Brien and McLellan, 1996), and that new tech-nologies of managing chronic disease could and should be adapted for the treatment of addiction (Lewis, 1993; McLellan, Lewis, O'Brien, and Kleber, 2000).

Third, the same managed care system that has lowered treatment dose and intensity and shifted the focus of intervention from one of recovery to that of cost-containment has spawned a treatment renewal movement and a new grassroots recovery advocacy (consumer) movement. These movements are developing a deeper understanding of the long-term addiction recovery process and how indigenous community resources may support this time-enduring process (White, 2000c).

Federal and state agencies that fund addiction treatment services have also begun to reevaluate the traditional acute models of professional intervention. In Illinois, the Department of Human Service's Office of Alcoholism and Substance Abuse has funded the Behavioral Health Recovery Management (BHRM) project to conduct such a reevaluation. The BHRM project is a multidisciplinary effort to develop service principles and clinical care practice guidelines for the long-term management of severe and persistent behavioral health disorders (Boyle, White, and Loveland, 2000). Such efforts are part of a more global interest in models of "disease management" that hold promise in improving the quality of health care while reducing health care costs (Lazarus, 2001).

## THE NATURE OF CHRONIC DISEASE

*Chronic diseases are disorders whose symptoms and their severity ebb and flow over an extended period of time.* Such disorders are often characterized by periods of remission and relapse of varying duration over an extended period of one's life. There are hundreds of thousands of people who have achieved stable and sustained recovery from severe and persistent AOD problems. Many individuals who never achieve full remission can and do achieve long periods of symptom remission and an enhanced quality of life.

*Acute versus Chronic Disorders: Problematic alcohol and other drug use may be just that–problematic–without constituting a chronic disorder. Alcoholism/addiction exists within a larger arena of persons who experience alcohol- and drug-related problems.* Models of sustained recovery management should not be applied to transient, though problematic, episodes of excessive AOD use. Many persons have utilized natural supports, mutual aid involvement or a single episode of treatment to initiate permanent resolution of their AOD-related problems.

Acute disease is culturally viewed as something that happens to you; chronic disease is viewed as a defect in who you are. The challenge of chronic disease management is to manage the disease without turning a person into a thing and contributing to the social stigma associated with the condition.

*The Etiology of Chronic Disease: Chronic addiction disease emerges and intensifies through the interaction of multiple factors*: the potency of the infectious agent (the drug), the biological and developmental vulnerability of the host; and the physical, political, economic, and social/cultural environment in which the person-drug relationship occurs.

A large number of chronic diseases have been called "diseases of lifestyle" because they are characterized by risk/resiliency factors related to such areas as daily diet, work habits, frequency and type of exercise, sleep patterns, medication compliance, style of stress management, drug use, exposure to environmental toxins, specifically contra-indicated (high risk) behaviors, and family and social relationships (Nicassio and Smith, 1995).

*The Onset of Chronic Disease: Chronic diseases can have either a sudden onset or a gradual onset* (Rolland, 1987).

The process through which an acute disorder migrates to the status of a chronic disorder is not fully understood. There is in all probability a priming dose of symptom activation necessary to move an acute disorder to the status of a chronic disease. Each acute episode of a chronic disease lowers the kindling point of symptom activation for the next episode. The priming process varies by many factors, including age of exposure. The lower the age of onset of regular use, the greater the potential for addictive disease and the greater the severity and chronicity of addictive disease (Chou and Pickering, 1992; Grant and Dawson, 1997). The kindling point can be raised by postponing age of onset of regular drug use and by enhancing biological resistance (medication, exercise, diet), cognitive abilities (coping and problem solving skills) and social supports (pro-recovery family and peer relationships).

*Disease Course and Variability: Chronic diseases exhibit a high degree of variability in pattern of onset, course (life trajectory), intensity, and outcome.* Chronic diseases may present as steadily self-accelerating (progressive), constant, or with alternating cycles of symptom remission and symptom reactivation (relapse) (Rolland, 1987). Most chronic diseases are also subject to unexplained, sustained remission—what in the addiction literature has been referred to as spontaneous remission, auto-remission, natural recovery, maturing out or self-cure (Granfield and Cloud, 1999). Chronic addiction disease also varies widely in its degree of incapacitation and in the speed and timing of such incapacitation. Addiction disease varies in physiological severity (morphological changes that threaten biological homeostasis and viability), functional severity (impact on quality of life and performance of life roles), and burden of illness (costs to the individual, family and society) (Rolland, 1987; Stein et al., 1987; Starfield, 1974). Such variability demands a high level of commitment to individualized assessment and treatment—both across clients and at different points of time in the life of the same client.

*Disease/Problem Co-Existence and Interaction: Chronic diseases heighten vulnerability for other acute and chronic diseases.* Alcoholism and other addictions invite other diseases that debilitate and threaten premature death. Acute and chronic diseases interact in ways that amplify their combined intensity and duration and the costs incurred in their management (Stein et al.,

1987). The longer an addiction disease is active, the higher the risk for acute physical toxicity (overdose), chronic physical toxicity (addiction-related tissue damage, e.g., cancer, emphysema, liver disease), behavioral toxicity (trauma or death via accident/violence), infectious diseases (e.g., HIV/AIDS, hepatitis B and C, tuberculosis), and co-morbid psychiatric illness. All programs serving individuals with severe and persistent AOD disorders must become dual and multiple disorder programs that serve the whole person/family through integrated models of care (Lebowitz and Harris, 2000; Drake et al., 1998; Minkoff, 1989; Norquist, Lebowitz, and Hyman, 1999; Osher, 1996).

*Family and Intimate Social Networks and Chronic Diseases: The individual and collective resources of families and social networks are strained (and drained) by adaptation to chronic disease.* A family's *capacity for adaptation* changes across the family life cycle (Goodheart and Lansing, 1997). The family's *style of adaptation* to a chronic illness is often shaped by the transgenerational history of responding to crisis, illness, loss and death (Rolland, 1987). Chronic disease of a family member can, by disrupting family rituals, realigning family roles, and by altering the allocation of family resources, impact the health and development of all family members as well as the health of adult intimate relationships and parent-child relationships.

### CONCEPTS AND PRINCIPLES OF RECOVERY MANAGEMENT

The shift from acute intervention models to recovery management models of intervening in severe and persistent AOD problems requires new ways of conceptualizing these problems and their resolution or amelioration.

*Disease Management: Persons suffering from chronic, incurable disorders need models of intervention that focus on the* management *of these disorders rather than the* cure *or* treatment *of these disorders. Disease management or, as we prefer, recovery management, provides an alternative to the traditional mode of reacting to life-impairing and life-threatening episodes of chronic disorders with unrelated, serial episodes of acute, emergency-oriented care.*

Recovery management implies a longer term vision of influencing the course of a disorder to enhance length and quality of life. It is about learning, in the absence of a cure, to contain a disorder and to optimize personal and family health over time.

*Chronic Disease and Recovery:* The shift from perceiving and treating addiction as an acute disorder to treating it as a chronic condition requires a shift in focus from the pathology of addiction to the nature of, and processes involved in, long-term addiction recovery. It extends the concepts of "addiction career" and "treatment career" (Hser et al., 1997) to encompass a third concept, "recovery career." There are a number of concepts that constitute important building blocks in the construction of recovery-oriented systems of care for severe and persistent AOD problems.

- There are many pathways and styles of recovery (White, 1990, 1996) and many legitimate sobriety-based support structures. Recovery styles and viable support structures vary by developmental age, gender, ethnicity, social class, and profession and they vary by one's "recovery capital" (the intrapersonal, interpersonal and community resources that can be brought to bear on the initiation and maintenance of recovery) (Granfield and Cloud, 1999).
- The mechanisms and processes that sustain recovery are different than the factors that initiate recovery (Humphreys et al., 1995).
- Addiction recovery can be self-directed and incremental in nature (Prochaska, DiClimente, and Norcross, 1992), a process of unconscious "drift" (Granfield and Cloud, 1999), or a process of sudden, climactic transformation (Miller and de Baca, 2001).
- Addiction recovery most often involves a process of developmental change, the stages of which can be identified and to which stage-appropriate interventions can be designed and delivered (Brown, 1985; DiClimente et al., 1992).
- Recovery can be professionally-guided (treatment), peer-guided (mutual support groups) or "solo"/"natural" (use of resources within the self and family/social network). Factors that distinguish those in the former from the latter include problem severity, co-morbidity, levels of family/social/occupational support, and social class (Sobell et al., 1993; Sobell et al., 1996a; Larimer and Kilmer, 2000).
- Styles of recovery vary considerably based on whether one does or does not incorporate addiction/recovery as a core element of personal identity, and whether one does or does not maintain active contact with other recovering people as a recovery maintenance activity. These dimensions of style may evolve through the stages of recovery.
- Recovery outcomes vary considerably in terms of primary and secondary drug consumption: abstinence, subclinical (nonproblematic) use, and problem reduction (partial recovery). Recovery outcomes also vary in the broader dimensions of global (cognitive, emotional, family, social, occupational) functioning.
- Post-treatment outcomes are characterized by subgroups who: (1) sustain problematic use, (2) sustain uninterrupted abstinence, and (3) who in the weeks/months/years following treatment vacillate between problematic use, non-problematic use, and experiments in abstinence. Fluid states

of addiction/recovery typified by this sizeable third group offer significant opportunities to enhance outcomes via recovery management models of intervention.

- A vision of long-term, staged recovery posits treatment and support services (e.g., harm reduction, motivational interviewing, pharmacological adjuncts, cognitive-behavioral therapies, mutual aid groups) not as competing and mutually exclusive technologies but as interventions that can be matched, not just to different individuals, but to the same individual at different stages of his or her addiction/recovery careers.

Because recovery-oriented systems of care are shifting from a treatment lexicon to a recovery lexicon, it will be tempting to view the recovery model as simply a new "buzz" word for treatment as usual. To do so would be a failure to recognize the quite fundamental conceptual and technical shifts implicit within the recovery model.

### TOWARD A RECOVERY-ORIENTED MODEL OF CARE

The shift from an acute treatment model to a recovery management model requires a fundamental redefinition of the service target; the nature, timing and duration of services; the locations in which services are delivered; the composition of the service delivery team, and the methods and criteria through which services are evaluated. We have been involved at many levels with recovery management models and believe the following are among the most significant of the changes in clinical practice that follow their implementation. We will focus this discussion on how the actual processes of service delivery change rather than on how the move to recovery-oriented systems of care will reshape health care policy and the organization and financing of such services.

*1. Service Integration: Recovery management models seek to strategically combine and refine the resources of human service agencies, primary health care providers, and indigenous supports into an integrated system of care that can address stage-specific needs across the span of long-term recovery.* Strategies of integration include the creation of multi-agency service delivery teams, cross-training of service professionals, and integrated (and often centralized) outreach, case management, and recovery support services. The primary mechanisms of service integration include a global assessment process/instrument, regular interdisciplinary conferences with the client/family, and the use of a single treatment/recovery plan that directs the allocation of resources drawn from multiple service institutions and indigenous support structures. There is growing evidence that integrated models of care are superior in terms of clinical outcomes and stewardship of community resources than are models that rely on either parallel or serial models of treating chronic and co-occurring problems (Miller, 1994; RachBeisel, Scott, and Dixon, 1999; Drake et al., 1989; Drake et al., 2001).

*2. Identification and Engagement: Recovery management models utilize population-based identification strategies, assertive community outreach, low thresholds of service entry, multiple points of entry, patient registries, and seamless movement between levels of care to locate, engage, retain and reengage people with AOD problems.* These interventions recognize and seek to work through the many sources of personal ambivalence and environmental obstacles that impede recovery. Engagement is viewed not as an event, but as a process that continues throughout the recovery management partnership.

The very things that are the hallmark of effective brief interventions–feedback of risk, emphasis on personal responsibility, prescriptive advice, a menu of change options, expression of empathy and encouragement, and enhancement of self-efficacy via expression of confidence in client's ability to change (Bien, Miller, and Tonigan, 1993)–are all integrated within this process of engagement. Such outreach and engagement techniques have been found effective in initiating change in multiple populations: women, ethnic minorities, youth, and drug injectors (Brown and Needle, 1994).

*3. Assessment: Assessment activities within recovery management models are a continuous rather than an intake activity, are global rather than categorical, and integrate traditional "treatment plans" into a larger "recovery plan."* The high degree of individual variability in AOD problems, the changing status of these problems over time, unique patterns of problem co-occurrence, and concerns regarding the misapplication of recovery management approaches all require rigorous, ongoing and global assessment activities. Global assessment assumes that the germination and development of severe AOD problems spring from multiple elements of the personal, family and cultural ecosystem and that the resources needed to resolve these problems are located within these same arenas.

Recovery management models integrate the traditional medical model "treatment plan" with the "recovery plan" utilized within social model alcoholism treatment programs (Borkman, 1998b). In contrast to a treatment plan, the recovery plan: (1) is prepared and regularly updated by the client, (2) documents the goals and planned activities of the client, and (3) covers such life domains of the client as finances, social life, legal difficulties, education, employment, and spirituality (Borkman, 1998a). Recovery management models provide a structured and individualized transition between professionally-directed treatment planning and self-directed recovery planning.

*4. Definition of "Client": In recovery management models, the definition of "client" shifts from the symptomatic individual to the family and cultural milieu and the individual nested within it.* In recovery management, family members and social network members are all co-providers of recovery support services and legitimate recipients of services in their own right. Recovery priming can occur by moving the family and social network toward greater health and understanding of addiction disease even without the symptomatic individual's direct participation. The focal point of action in the recovery management model is not on what the treatment professional does but on the client and family's capacity to self-direct their own recovery.

*5. Service Goals: The mission of recovery management is to help each person suffering from addiction disease to achieve their optimal long-term outcome (as measured by the quality and duration of life, achievement of personal goals, and his or her impact on family and society).* Recovery management strategies are aimed at multiple stage-specific goals:

- slowing the speed of disease acceleration and the speed of decline in biopsychosocial functioning,
- initiating, strengthening and extending periods of symptom remission (reducing the number, intensity and duration of relapse events),
- preventing the onset of, or reducing the severity of, co-morbid conditions,
- producing full and sustained symptom remission where possible,
- achieving the maximum level of age (stage)–appropriate functioning and health for the individual/family, and
- reducing the personal, family and social costs associated with addiction and recovery management.

The focus of recovery management is on reducing addiction-related mortality, decreasing the duration and degree of addiction-related incapacitation, and promoting the development of long-term processes of disease stabilization and recovery. Recovery management services seek to enhance the capacity of each client/family to achieve their highest degree of functioning, regardless of whether that level is one of full or partial recovery.

*6. Service Scope and Technologies: For clients whose patterns of AOD use reflect chronicity and severity, the best strategy for long-term recovery is proactive engagement, disease stabilization (acute treatment), recovery management education, ongoing recovery support, monitoring with feedback, and, when necessary, early reintervention and restabilization.* Recovery management doesn't so much replace the acute model as much as wrap that model in a larger continuum of support services and shift the focus from one of treating the acute manifestations of addiction to building a life of recovery.

These "recovery support services" focus on eliminating barriers to recovery and on enhancing what Granfield and Cloud (1999) have christened "recovery capital"–the intrapersonal, interpersonal and environmental resources that can be drawn upon to aid recovery. Such services encompass traditional clinical services but extend further into such areas as sober housing, pro-recovery educational and employment opportunities, day care and transportation services, and pro-recovery leisure activity. The essence of recovery management involves sustained monitoring of the status of a chronic disease, sustained monitoring of the effectiveness of recovery management strategies, and continual, stage-appropriate refinements in recovery support services.

7. *Timing and Duration of Services: The temporal focus of recovery management services is on interrupting the acceleration of AOD problems before the crises that generally initiate acute treatment episodes and sustaining support long after such episodes are traditionally defined as completed.*

By metaphorically changing the role of the addiction treatment specialist from that of an emergency room physician to that of a primary physician managing the long-term course of diabetes or hypertension, the recovery management model renders the concepts of "discharge" and "aftercare" anachronistic. In the recovery management model, all care is an element of continuing care. Continued telephonic, electronic (e-mail) and postal delivery of recovery education; monitoring; support; and, where needed and desired by the client and not otherwise available in the community, ongoing face-to-face group and individual support, are routine elements of the recovery management model. Within this model, intensity of services decrease over time but the commitment to and access to sustained recovery support remains constant.

8. *Delivery Locus: The locus of service activity within the recovery management model combines the primary health care institution (the inpatient/residential institution and the centralized outpatient clinic) with home-based, neighborhood-based service delivery, with a particular emphasis on the latter.* Two principles–personal autonomy and pro-recovery social support–guide recovery management models. First, persons suffering from AOD problems and addictive diseases seeking help are served within the least restrictive, least isolating and least coercive environments and methods possible. Second, transfer of learning is directly related to the degree of physical, psychological, and cultural distance between service delivery site and the client's natural environment. In the recovery management model, services are delivered as close as possible to the natural living environment of the client. Any isolation of the client from that environment is accompanied by intensive transition services aimed at transferring learning from the institutional environment to the client's natural environment. In the recovery management model, as much effort is

spent focusing on developing ecosystem supports for recovery as is spent on focusing on pro-recovery, intrapersonal changes.

9. *Service Relationship: With recovery management, the service relationship shifts from a "dominator model" to a "partnership model."* The traditional relationship between addiction treatment providers is time-limited, hierarchical, and commercialized. Power, status and strength lie on one side of the relationship and stigma, powerlessness and problems lie on the other side. The patient seeks the help of the expert who diagnoses the patient, prescribes what the patient must do to get well, and then seeks to manipulate the patient's compliance.

Recovery management replaces this expert-centered service relationship with what Eisler (1987) has characterized as a "Partnership Model" and what Lazarus (2001) has characterized as "consumercentric care." The focus is on creating a collaborative alliance that shifts the focus of recovery from the treatment professional to the person seeking and experiencing recovery. The service professional shifts from the roles of diagnostician and treater to the roles of long-term ally and recovery consultant. One of the essential dimensions of recovery management is continuity of contact over time in a primary service relationship.

This partnership requires the deep involvement of clients in the design, implementation, and evaluation of services. In the recovery management model, treatment professionals and their institutions become students and allies of the growing consumer/survivor movement in the United States (Anthony, 1993; Kaufmann, 1999; Chamberlin, 1990; White, 2000c). The recovery management model could help the field of addiction treatment face in the twenty-first century what it has never faced in its history: a strong consumer movement led by recovering people/families who are knowledgeable, articulate, well-organized, and angry at their historical exclusion from policy and clinical decision-making.

10. *The Role of Community in Recovery: The goal of recovery management is not to forever enmesh all persons with severe and persistent AOD problems in professionally-directed treatment services; it is to open resources in the wider community that will enhance each client's own capacity for recovery self-management. The goal is to help nest the client within a physical, psychological and social space where long-term recovery can be nurtured. This involves enmeshing the client in recovery-supportive relationships that are natural (rather than professionalized), enduring (rather than transient) and reciprocal (rather than fiduciary and commercialized).*

The community, when organized and educated, can be a reservoir of hospitality and support for recovering people. Professionally directed treatment services should be the last, not the first, line of defense in the management of chronic addictive diseases. The first lines of resources for the management of alcohol and other drug problems consists of the individual's own natural resiliencies, family and intimate social networks, and other nonprofessional support systems within the individual's natural environment. Interventions that inadvertently undermine and replace the natural support functions of the self, the family, and the community with professionalized and commercialized supports fail both on technical and ethical grounds (McKnight, 1995).

*11. The Recovery Management Team: The recovery management model places greater emphasis on the use of the client, his or her family, natural helping systems within the community, and on indigenous recovering people within the recovery management team.* In the future, many recovery support services will be provided by recovered and recovering persons and by recovery-based service organizations which will utilize recovering individuals, family members and other "folk healers" from within the community as recovery support specialists. Such individuals will fill both volunteer and paid staff positions.

*12. Service Evaluation: The evaluation of recovery management strategies involves the client/family as the primary evaluator, measures client/family functioning over a much longer (5-15 years) period of time (Vaillant, 1983), and assesses the synergistic interaction and cumulative effects of multiple interventions. If the transition to a recovery management model is achieved, addiction treatment and recovery support services will be judged by the same standards that are used to evaluate the treatment and management of other chronic diseases (as advocated by O'Brien and McLellan, 1996).*

The essence of the acute care model is to deliver a single treatment episode, and then to evaluate that episode based on symptom remission or reactivation during the months following "discharge" from that service episode. In contrast, the recovery management model assumes that a return of symptoms following a single treatment episode does not mean that a particular intervention was a failure, nor that sustained remission following an intervention reflects success where earlier episodes had failed. Recovery management models assume that symptom remission or relapse can occur independent of service interventions and that interventions can have delayed, cumulative or synergistic effects. The focus thus shifts to evaluating extra-treatment factors as well as evaluating particular combinations and sequences of interventions as they interact with the evolving life of the client/family.

Recovery management models include consumer participation and use of consumer-influenced evaluation criteria (Sloves, 2000). Like the assessment process, evaluation shifts from an end-of-service-episode or follow-up event to a continuous process and shifts from a categorical evaluation (focus on presence or absence of alcohol/drug use) to a global evaluation (focus on the health, quality of life and social functioning of the individual/family as well as the impact of intervention on the community, e.g., social costs, reduced threats to public safety).

## PITFALLS

The chronic disease recovery management model described in this paper is not without its potential pitfalls.

*Funding:* Virtually all funding of addiction treatment is currently set up to reimburse episodes of acute care provided by categorically segregated service specialists. A shift to the recovery management model will require population-based funding for longitudinal care delivered by multiple providers organized into integrated systems of care (Pawlson, 1994). Fundable services will need to include outreach, early intervention, case management, monitoring, harm reduction services, and a broad spectrum of recovery support services. There is a danger that the recovery management model could be manipulated by funding organizations to eliminate high intensity/high cost components of service continuum. There is also a danger that a greater responsibility for recovery support could be shifted to the community while all the financial resources remain within professional agencies and managed care entities.

*Service Capacity:* The shift from an acute intervention to a recovery management model will require new strategies for defining and managing service. Recovery management will require larger caseloads as service professionals maintain contact with a mix of people in widely varying stages of recovery. The increased numbers of people will be mirrored by a smaller percentage of clients with high intensity service demands. This will require new systems of defining and managing service caseloads.

*Stigma and Therapeutic Pessimism:* If not handled with great care, the "chronicity" language may undermine belief in the potential for permanent resolution of addiction (Brown, 1998). We feel very strongly that the presentation of this model needs to be framed as "recovery management" and not "chronic disease management" to both consumers and the community. We must be able to convey two messages: (1) uninterrupted remission of addiction is possible and a reality in the lives of hundreds of thousands of people, and (2) active recovery management can reduce the frequency, intensity and duration of relapse episodes as it enhances the quality of life and global functioning of those persons who have yet to achieve uninterrupted sobriety.

*Iatrogenic Effects from Model Misapplication:* There is a danger that a chronic disease management model will be misapplied to individuals whose AOD problems represent not chronic disorders but transient problems that will quite likely spontaneously remit with time and maturation or respond to brief intervention. The potential indiscriminate application of a chronic disease management model to children and adolescents presenting with AOD use is of particular concern.

*Service Provider Accountability:* "Chronic Disease" could become a shroud that hides and decreases the accountability of service providers for clinical outcomes. Service providers cannot be allowed to blame clients and the nature of their disorder on poorly designed and executed service technologies. Recovery management models should be subjected to more, not less, accountability for long-term clinical outcomes (Brown, 1998).

*Financial Exploitation:* The chronic disease/recovery management model could be financially exploited by treatment institutions who "capture" a population of chronic alcoholics/addicts and provide a high frequency of long-term billable services rather than linking these clients to indigenous resources that would diminish their need for these agency-provided services.

*Ethical Dilemmas:* The recovery management model raises a whole spectrum of ethical issue that will need to be addressed. These include:

- What is the boundary between appropriately assertive outreach and inappropriately intrusive outreach ("stalking")?
- When are we doing too much or too little?
- What relationship boundaries should guide this prolonged "partnership" with clients/families?
- Does a client have the right to not be "monitored and managed"?
- Who is the client (when an agency is contracted to provide prolonged case management services to reduce a client's threat to public safety or to reduce the client's consumption of scarce community resources)?

*From Dynamic to Static Model:* There is a danger that clinical care guidelines used within the recovery management model could reduce the treatment of complex disorders to "cookbook medicine." This is not a rational for avoiding evidence-based practice guidelines, but a caution that an adequate "toolbox" must be complemented with clinical training and clinical supervision to assure proper clinical judgement in applying techniques in an individualized manner.

*Staff Support:* In an acute care model, staff working with the most difficult of clients take solace from the fact that this involvement is short term and will be replaced in a few weeks with a new, perhaps less difficult client. The recovery management model will place staff in contact with these most difficult clients for much more prolonged periods of time. Without special supports (clinical supervision, team models of service delivery, etc.), this model could face challenges related to staff morale and retention. Continuity of contact is crucial to the success of the recovery management model; staff turnover must be kept at a low level.

## CONCLUSION

Chronic diseases possess many characteristics that distinguish them from acute disorders. They tend to have complex etiologies in which behavioral choices play a role in symptom onset, severity and duration. Their courses are prolonged and often characterized by periods of remission and relapse. They lack definitive cures but can be effectively managed by combinations of interventions. Although severe AOD problems have long been characterized as chronic diseases, their treatment has more closely resembled acute care interventions. The shift to a (chronic disease) recovery management model will require changing our very understanding of the nature of severe and persistent AOD problems and changing the timing and duration of service intervention, the composition of the service delivery team and the methods and criteria used to evaluate our interventions into these problems.

Traditional models of care will continue to meet the needs of many individuals who have sufficient "recovery capital" to resolve their AOD-related problems through a single episode of care. Clients who do not respond to such acute care will require recovery management models that sustain contact longer and place greater emphasis on recovery education, long-term monitoring and support, and early reintervention. The potential pitfalls in this shift toward recovery management models include the demands that will be required to change how services are funded and organized, the potential misapplication of chronic disease models to persons whose AOD-related problems are transient in nature, and the need to manage new and complex ethical issues that will arise within the context of long-term service relationships. Models of recovery management offer great promise in the future treatment of severe and persistent alcohol and other drug problems. We must be careful, however, in reaching for this future to not lose what is most valuable within the current system of care.

## REFERENCES

American Society of Addiction Medicine & National Council on Alcoholism and Drug Dependence. (1976). Disease definition of alcoholism. *Annals of Internal Medicine* 85(6): 764.

American Society of Addiction Medicine & National Council on Alcoholism and Drug Dependence. (1990). Disease definition of alcoholism revised. Joint News Release, April 26.

Anderson, D. (1942). Alcohol and public opinion. *Quarterly Journal of Studies on Alcohol*, 3(3): 376-392.

Anthony, W.A. (1993). Recovery from mental illness: The guiding vision of the mental health service system in the 1990s. *Psychosocial Rehabilitation Journal*, 16: 11-23.

Benezet, A. (1774). *The Mighty Destroyer Displayed (in some account of the dreadful havoc made by the mistaken used as well as abuse of spiritous liquors)*. Philadelphia: Joseph Crukshank.

Bien, T., Miller, W., and Tonigan, S. (1993). Brief interventions for alcohol problems: A review. *Addiction*, 88: 315-336.

Borkman, T. (1998a). Is recovery planning different from treatment planning? *Journal of Substance Abuse Treatment*, 15(1): 37-42.

Borkman, T. (1998b). Borkman, T., Kaskutas, L., Room, J., Bryan, K., and Barrows, D. (1998). A historical and developmental analysis of social model programs. *Journal of Substance Abuse Treatment* 15: 7-17.

Boyle, M., White, W., Loveland, D., Godley, M., and Hagen, R. (2000). The Behavioral Health Recovery Management project: Project summary and concept. *www.bhrm.org*

Brown, B.S. (1998). Drug use: Chronic and relapsing or a treatable condition? *Substance Use and Misuse*, 33(12): 2515-2520.

Brown, H. (1872). *An Opium Cure: Based on Science, Skill and Matured Experience*. New York: Fred M. Brown & Co. (Advertising Book for Antidote and Restorative) In: Grob, G. (1981). *American Perceptions of Drug Addiction*. New York: Arno Press.

Brown, B. and Needle, R. (1994). Modifying the process of treatment to meet the threat of AIDS. *International Journal of the Addictions*, 29: 1739-1752.

Brown, S. (1985). *Treating the Alcoholic: A Developmental Model of Recovery*. New York: Wiley.

Chamberlin, J. (1990). The ex-patients' movement: Where we've been and where we're going. *The Journal of Mind and Behavior*, 11: 323-336.

Chou, S.P. and Pickering, R.P. (1992). Early onset of drinking as a risk factor for lifetime alcohol-related problems. *British Journal of Addiction*, 87: 1199-1204.

Cook, C. (1988). Minnesota Model in the management of drug and alcohol dependency: Miracle, method or myth? Part I. The philosophy and the programme. *British Journal of Addiction*, 83(6): 625-634.

Crothers, T.D. (1879). Editorial: Practical value of inebriate asylums. *Journal of Inebriety* 3(4): 249.

Crothers, T.D. (1893). The disease of inebriety from alcohol, opium and other narcotic drugs. New York: E.B. Treat, Publisher.

DiClemente, C.C., Carbonari, J.P., and Velasquez, M.M. (1992). Treatment mismatching from a process of change perspective. In: R.R. Watson, (Ed.), *Alcoholism Treatment Mismatching from a Process of Change Perspective. Drug and Alcohol Abuse Reviews, Vol. 3: Alcohol Abuse Treatment*. Totowa, NJ: The Humana Press, pp. 115-142.

Dole, V. (1988). Implications of methadone maintenance for theories of narcotic addiction. *Journal of the American Medical Association*, 260(20): 3025-3029.

Dole, V. (1997). What is "methadone maintenance treatment"? *Journal of Maintenance in the Addictions*, 1(1): 7-8.

Drake, R.E., Essock, S.M., Shaner, A., Carey, K.B., Minkoff, K., Kola, L., Lynde, D., Osher, F.C., Clark, R.E., and Rickards, L. (2001). Implementing dual diagnosis services for clients with severe mental illness. *Psychiatric Services*, 52(4): 469-476.

Drake, R.E., Mercer-McFadden, C., Muesser, K.T., McHugo, G.J., and Bond, G.R. (1998). A review of integrated mental health and substance abuse treatment for patients with dual disorders. *Schizophrenia Bulletin*, 24: 589-608.

Drake, R.E. and Wallach, M.A. (1989). Substance abuse among the chronically mentally ill. *Hospital and Community Psychiatry*, 40(10): 1041-1045.

Drake, R.E. and Wallach, M.A. (2000). Dual diagnosis: 15 years of progress. *Psychiatric Services*, 51: 1126-1129.

Eisler, R. (1987). *The Chalice and the Blade: Our History, Our Future*. Cambridge, MA: Harper and Row.

Ethridge, R.M., Craddock, S.G., Dunteman, G.H., and Hubbard, R.L. (1995). Treatment services in two national studies of community-based drug abuse treatment programs. *Journal of Substance Abuse*, 7: 9-26.

Fingarette, H. (1989). *Heavy Drinking: The Myth of Alcoholism as a Disease*. Berkeley: University of California Press.

Goodheart, C.D. and Lansing, M.H. (1997). *Treating People with Chronic Disease: A Psychosocial Guide*, American Psychiatric Association.

Granfield, R. and Cloud, W. (1999). *Coming Clean: Overcoming Addiction Without Treatment*. New York: New York University Press.

Grant, B.F. and Dawson, D.A. (1997). Age at onset of alcohol use and its association with DSM-IV alcohol abuse and dependence. *Journal of Substance Abuse*, 9: 103-110.

Hser, Y-I, Anglin, M.D., Grella, C., Longshore, D., and Pendergast, M. (1997). Drug treatment careers: A conceptual framework and existing research findings. *Journal of Substance Abuse Treatment*, 14(6): 543-558.

Humphreys, K., Moos, R. H., and Finney, J. W. (1995). Two pathways out of drinking problems without professional treatment. *Addictive Behaviors*, 20: 427-441.

Johnson, B. (1973). *The Alcoholism Movement in America: A Study in Cultural Innovation*. Urbana, IL: University of Illinois Ph.D. Dissertation.

Kaplan, L. (1997). A disease management model for addiction treatment. *Behavioral Health Management*, 17(4): 14-15.

Kaufmann, C. L. (1999). An introduction to the mental health consumer movement. In: A. Horwitz and T. Scheid (Eds.), *A Handbook for the Study of Mental Health: Social Contexts, Theories, and Systems*. Cambridge: Cambridge University Press, pp. 493-507.

Labouvie, E., Bates, M.E., and Pandina, R.J. (1997). Age of first use: its reliability and predictive utility. *Journal of Studies on Alcohol*, 58: 638-43.

Larimer, M. E. and Kilmer, J. R. (2000). Natural history. In: G. Zernig, A. Saria, M. Kurz, and S. S. O'Malley, *Handbook of Alcoholism*. Boca Raton, FL: CRC Press.

Lazarus, A. (2001). Economic grand rounds: The promise of disease management. *Psychiatric Services*, 52(2): 169-171.

Lebowitz, B.D. and Harris, H.W. (2000). Efficacy and effectiveness: From regulatory to public health models. In: I. Katz & D. Oslin (Eds.), *Annual Review of Gerontology and Geriatrics: Focus on Psychopharmacologic Interventions in Late Life* (vol. 19). New York: Springer, pp. 3-12.

Leshner, A.I. (1997). Addiction is a brain disease, and it matters. *Science*, 278: 45-47.

Levine, H. (1978). The discovery of addiction: Changing conceptions of habitual drunkenness in America. *Journal of Studies on Alcohol*, 39(2): 143-174.

Lewis, D.C. (1993). A disease model of addiction. In: N.S. Miller (Ed.), *Principles of Addiction Medicine*. Chevy Chase, MD: American Society on Addiction Medicine, pp. 1-7.

Mann, M. (1944). Formation of a National Committee for Education on Alcoholism. *Quarterly Journal of Studies on Alcohol*, 5(2): 354.

Marcet, W. (MD) (1868). *On Chronic Alcoholic Intoxication*. New York: Moorhead, Simpson, & Bond, Publishers.

McElrath, D. (1997). Minnesota model. *Journal of Psychoactive Drugs*, 29(2): 141-144.

McLellan, A.T., Lewis, D.C., O'Brien, C.P, and Kleber, H.D. (2000). Drug dependence, a chronic medical illness: Implications for treatment, insurance, and outcomes evaluation. *Journal of the American Medical Association*, 284(13): 1689-1695.

McNight, J. (1995). *The Careless Society: Community and Its Counterfeits*. New York: Basic Books.

Miller, N. (1994). Psychiatric comorbidity: Occurrence and treatment. *Alcohol Health and Research World*, 18(4): 261-264.

Miller, W. and C' de Baca, J. (2001). *Quantum Change: When Epiphanies and Sudden Insights Transform Ordinary Lives*. New York: Guilford Press.

Minkoff, K. (1989). An integrated treatment model of dual diagnosis of psychosis and addiction. *Hospital and Community Psychiatry*, 40: 1031-1036.

Mitchell, D., Mitchell, C., and Ofshe, R. (1980). *The Light on Synanon*. Wideview Books.

Nicassio, P.M. and Smith, T.W. (Eds.) (1995). *Managing Chronic Illness: A Biopsychosocial Perspective*. Washington, DC: American Psychological Association.

Norquist, G., Lebowitz, B., and Hyman, S. (1999). Expanding the frontier of treatment research. Prevention and Treatment, 2 [On line], Available: *http://journals. apa.org/prevention/volume2/pre0020001a.html*

O'Brien, C. and McLellan, T. (1996). Myths about the treatment of addiction. *Lancet*, 347: 237-240.

Osher, F. (1996). A vision for the future: Toward a service system responsive to those with co-occurring addictive and mental disorders. *American Journal of Orthopsychiatry*, 66: 71-76.

Parrish, J. (1883). *Alcoholic Inebriety: From a Medical Standpoint*. Philadelphia: P. Blakiston, Son & Company.

Pawlson, L. (1994). Chronic illness: Implications of a new paradigm for health care. *Journal of Quality Improvement*, 20(1): 33-39.

Peele, S. (1989). *The Diseasing of America*. Lexington, MA: Lexington Books.

Peele, S. and Brodsy, A. with Arnold, M. (1992). *The Truth About Addiction and Recovery*. NY: Simon and Schuster.

Prochaska, J., DiClimente, C., and Norcross, J. (1992). In search of how people change. *American Psychologist*, 47: 1102-1114.

RachBeisel, J., Scott, J., and Dixon, L. (1999). Co-occurring severe mental illness and substance use disorders: A review of recent research. *Psychiatric Services*, 50(11): 1427-1434.

Roizen, R. (1991). *The American Discovery of Alcoholism, 1933-1939.* Ph.D. Dissertation. Berkeley: University of California.

Rolland, J. (1987). Chronic illness and the life cycle: A conceptual framework. *Family Process,* 145: 203-221.

Rorabaugh, W. (1979). *The Alcoholic Republic: An American Tradition.* Oxford: Oxford University Press.

Rush, B. (1814). *An Inquiry into the Effect of Ardent Sirits upon the Human Body and Mind (with an account of the means of preventing and of the remedies for curing them),* 8th rev. ed. Brookfield: E. Merriam & Company.

Schaler, J. (2000). *Addiction is a Choice.* Chicago: Open Court.

Simpson, D.D., Joe, G.W., and Lehman, W.E. (1986). *Addiction careers: Summary of studies based on the DARP 12-year follow-up.* National Institute on Drug Abuse. Treatment Research Report (ADM 86-1420).

Sloves, H. (2000). Reintegration: New technologies and the new consumer social services market transforms consumers into consumers. *www.foun-tainhouse.org*

Sobell, L. C., Cunningham, J. A., and Sobell, M. B. (1996). Recovery from alcohol problems with and without treatment: Prevalence in two population surveys. *American Journal of Public Health,* 86: 966-972.

Sobell, L. C., Sobell, M. C., Toneatto, T., and Leo, G. I. (1993). What triggers the resolution of alcohol problems without treatment? *Alcoholism: Clinical and Experimental Research,* 17: 217-224.

Spicer, J. (1993). *Minnesota Model: The Evolution of the Multidisciplinary Approach to Addiction Recovery.* Center City, MN: Hazelden Educational Materials.

Starfield, B. (1974). Assessment of morbidity. In: D. Grave and I.H. Pless, (Eds.), *Chronic Childhood Illness: Assessment and Outcome.* Washington, DC: US Department of Health, Education and Welfare.

Stein, R., Bauman, L., Westbrook, L., Coupney, S., and Ireys, H. (1997). Framework for identifying children who have chronic conditions: The case for a new definition. *The Journal of Pediatrics,* 122(3): 342-347.

Sweetser, W. (1828). *A Dissertation on Intemperance, to Which Was Awarded the Premium Offered by the Massachusetts Medical Society.* Boston: Hilliard, Gray, and Company.

Vaillant, G. (1983). *The Natural History of Alcoholism: Causes, Patterns, and Paths to Recovery.* Cambridge, Massachusetts: Harvard University Press.

White, W. (1990, 1996). *Pathways from the Culture of Addiction to the Culture of Recovery.* Center City, MN: Hazelden.

White, W. (1998). *Slaying the Dragon: The History of Addiction Treatment and Recovery in America.* Bloomington, IL: Chestnut Health Systems.

White, W. (2000a). Addiction as a disease: The birth of a concept. *The Counselor,* 1(1): 46-51, 73.

White, W. (2000b). The rebirth of the disease concept of alcoholism in the 20th century. *The Counselor,* 1(2): 62-66.

White, W. (2000c). Toward a new recovery movement: Historical reflections on recovery, treatment and advocacy. Presented at the Center for Substance Abuse Treatment Recovery Community Support Program Conference, April 3-5, 2000, posted at *www.treatment.org* and *www.defeataddiction.org*

White, W. (2001a). Addiction disease concept: Advocates and critics *The Counselor*, 2(1): 42-46.

White, W. (2001b). An addiction disease concept for the 21st century. *The Counselor*, 2(2): 44-52.

White, W. (2001c). A lost vision: Addiction counseling as community organization. *Alcoholism Treatment Quarterly*, 19(4): 1-32.

White, W. (2001d). Pre-AA alcoholic mutual aid societies. *Alcoholism Treatment Quarterly*, 19(2): 1-21.

White, W. (in press). The lessons of language: Historical perspectives on the rhetoric of addiction. In: S. Tracy and C. Acker (Eds.), *Altering American Consciousness: Essays on the History of Alcohol and Drug Use in the United States, 1800-1997*. Amherst, MA: University of Massachusetts Press.

Woodward, S. (1838). *Essays on Asylums for Inebriates*. Worcester, MA.

# A VIEW FROM THE FIELD

# Twenty Volumes of *ATQ*:
# A Content Analysis

Jerome R. Koch, PhD
Jean A. Lewis, MSEd

**SUMMARY.** *Alcoholism Treatment Quarterly* is a "resource for practitioners." This paper represents an analysis of the types of research published in *ATQ* in an effort to meet that goal. Data reveal that the majority of articles are designed to inform clinicians of the latest strategies and techniques for improving their practice. However, an increasing number of articles are being published which report results from analysis of primary and secondary data. Also on the increase is the proportion of authors who are affiliated with academic institutions and who are trained at the doctoral level. *[Article copies available for a fee from The Haworth Document Delivery Service: 1-800-HAWORTH. E-mail address: <getinfo@haworthpressinc.com> Website: <http://www.HaworthPress.com> © 2002 by The Haworth Press, Inc. All rights reserved.]*

**KEYWORDS.** Content analysis, alcoholism treatment, clinical and professional resources

Jerome R. Koch is Associate Professor of Sociology at Texas Tech University. Jean A. Lewis is a lifelong parent, educator, and counselor.

[Haworth co-indexing entry note]: "Twenty Volumes of *ATQ*: A Content Analysis." Koch, Jerome R., and Jean A. Lewis. Co-published simultaneously in *Alcoholism Treatment Quarterly* (The Haworth Press, Inc.) Vol. 20, No. 3/4, 2002, pp. 131-142; and: *Alcohol Problems in the United States: Twenty Years of Treatment Perspective* (ed: Thomas F. McGovern, and William L. White) The Haworth Press, Inc., 2002, pp. 131-142. Single or multiple copies of this article are available for a fee from The Haworth Document Delivery Service [1-800-HAWORTH, 9:00 a.m. - 5:00 p.m. (EST). E-mail address: getinfo@haworthpressinc.com].

## INTRODUCTION

Like individuals, organizations experience and pass through predictable life-events and passages. Adolescence, midlife, and end-of-life provide individuals with opportunities for reflection and retrospection. Reflective individuals often ask themselves these types of questions: *Where have the decisions I've made in the past taken me? Is this where I intended to go? Where am I headed?* These sorts of questions are equally relevant to bring to bear on the state of this journal. *ATQ* presents itself as "A Resource for Practitioners." What sorts of issues initiated its creation? In what manner have early efforts in presenting the theory and practice of treating addictions persisted? What has changed? What is to follow next?

After twenty years of responding to the needs and reflecting the principles of the professionals it serves, *Alcoholism Treatment Quarterly* has become a well-established forum for reporting and exchanging ideas. Contributors provide up-to-date insight and information to inform and enhance the practice of intervention and therapy. They also engage intellectual and practical debates relevant to the discipline of treating addiction.

This paper represents a content analysis of the work that has been presented to colleagues in this forum over the past twenty years. Its methods are by no means exclusive to this work, or exhaustive of efforts others might make. This is simply an attempt to concisely describe, and in some sense quantify for comparative purposes, where *ATQ* has been and what its identity has become. In so doing, this analysis provides *ATQ*'s constituency some insight into mapping its future.

## METHOD

The twenty volumes of *ATQ* published to date were analyzed in an effort to quantify elements of their content, but also with an eye for developing an interpretive summary of the body of work the journal itself represents. Two distinct categories of content are reported:

1. The demographic characteristics of the authors;
2. A typology describing the nature of the articles they wrote.

Finally, several of the volumes contain special issues that deal more specifically with topics amplifying a central theme. These are discussed in a separate portion of *Results*, below.

### Demographic Variables

The following variables were used to describe the authors:

1. Is the author Male or Female?[1]

2. What is the author's highest level of educational attainment?

> Doctoral degree (PhD, ScD, EdD, etc.)
> Physician (MD or DO)
> Academic, clinical/professional master's degree (MA, MS, MSEd, MSW, MDiv, etc.)
> Other (BA, BSN, RN, etc.)

3. What is the author's primary institutional affiliation or work environment?

> Academic institution (college or university)
> Clinical setting (hospital, clinic, private practice)
> Government agency (NIH, NIDA, etc.)
> Other (unable to determine)

## *Types of Articles*

The five categories that comprise the typology appear below.[2]

*1. Clinical or Management Techniques.* The primary purpose of this article type is to provide the reader with strategies or techniques which may improve clinical or management skills. Archetypical examples of articles such as this include:

Washousky, R. C., P. Muchowsky-Conley, and D. E. Shrey. 1984. "Sobriety Planning Activities: A Model for Treating the Alcoholic Client." *ATQ* 1(4): 85-98.

Hanson, G., and G. Liber. 1989. "A Model for the Treatment of Adolescent Children of Alcoholics." *ATQ* 6(2): 53-70.

Weinstein, B. A., and E. Slaght. 1995. "Early Identification of Alcoholism: A New Diagnostic Tool for Clinicians." *ATQ* 12(4): 117-125.

Dundas, I. 2000. "Cognitive/Affective Distancing as a Coping Strategy of Children of Parents with a Drinking Problem." *ATQ* 18(4): 85-98.

*2. Data Report.* The primary purpose of this article type is to inform the reader of evidence from surveys or secondary analysis which relate to the field of addiction recovery and therapeutic intervention. Archetypical examples of articles such as this include:

Filstead, W. J. 1984. "Gender Differences in the Onset and Course of Alcoholism and Substance Abuse." *ATQ* 1(1): 125-132.

Craig, R. J., and D. Dres. 1989. "Predicting DUI Recidivism with the MMPI." *ATQ* 6(2): 97-104.

Hanson, M., W. Gross, V. Pressley, and J. Quintana. 1995. "AIDS Knowledge and Risk Behaviors Among Alcoholic Adults." *ATQ* 12(3): 19-32.

Hartmann, D. 2000. "Locus of Control and Program Completion for State Funded Alcohol Clients." *ATQ* 18(2): 27-35.

*3. Ideological Discussion or Debate.* The primary purpose of this article type is to inform and engage the reader of the ideological, social, or political issues that comprise and challenge the discipline of addiction recovery and therapeutic intervention. Archetypical examples of articles such as this include:

Kurtz, L. F. 1984. "Ideological Differences Between Professionals and AA Members." *ATQ* 1(2): 73-86.
Goodyear, B. 1989. "Unresolved Questions About Alcoholism: The Debate (War?) Goes On–Is a Resolution Possible?" *ATQ* 6(2): 1-28.
Wade, T. 1995. "What if Alcohol and Other Drug Dependencies Are Not Diagnoses? A Call for a Paradigm Shift." *ATQ* 12(1): 97-106.
Culbreth, J. R. 2000. "Substance Abuse Counselors With and Without a Personal History of Chemical Dependency: A Review of the Literature." *ATQ* 18(2): 67-82.

*4. Spirituality.* The primary purpose of this article type is to address specific issues related to the concept of spirituality and its use in recovery and/or therapy. Archetypical examples of articles such as this include:

Booth, L. 1984. "Aspects of Spirituality in San Pedro Peninsula Hospital." *ATQ* 1(2): 121-124.
Brown, H. P., Jr., and J. H. Peterson, Jr. 1989. "Refining the BASIC-ISs: A Psychospiritual Approach to Comprehensive Outpatient Treatment of Drug Dependency." *ATQ* 6(3/4): 27-62.
Mariolini, N., and J. Rehm. 1995. "Alcoholics Anonymous and Its Finances: The Interrelationship of the Material and the Spiritual." *ATQ* 12(4): 39-59.
Jarusiewicz, B. 2000. "Spirituality and Addiction: Relationship to Recovery and Relapse." *ATQ* 18(4): 99-110.

*5. Ethnic Issues.* The primary purpose of this article type is to address specific issues related to the manner in which race or ethnicity impacts and affects recovery and/or therapy. Archetypical examples of articles such as this include:

Wolf, A. S. 1984. "Alcohol and Violence in the Alaskan Native: A Follow-Up and Theoretical Considerations." *ATQ* 1(1): 133-138.
Willie, E. 1989. "The Story of Alkali Lake: Anomaly of Community Recovery or National Trend in Indian Country?" *ATQ* 6(3/4): 167-174.
Delgado, M. 1995. "Hispanic Natural Support Systems and Alcohol and Other Drug Services: Challenges and Rewards for Practice." *ATQ* 12(1): 17-32.
Hohman, M. 1999. "Treatment Experiences of Women in a Recovery Home for Latinas." *ATQ* 19(3): 67-78.

Data in each category of the above variables were gathered for each volume of *ATQ* and are reported below. Included are summaries of the entire twenty volumes as well as data aggregated into five-year segments.

## RESULTS

Twelve hundred nineteen authors in volumes 1-20 of *ATQ* wrote six hundred seventeen articles. Each of the four sets of variables that describe this body of work is detailed as follows.

### Gender Ratio

Overall, 705 (60 percent) of the 1,169 authors that we were able to identify by gender were male; 464 (40 percent) were female. Figure One represents this in graphical form. The overall trend for this distribution very closely approximates the gender ratio of authors in each of the five-year increments. Essentially, male authors outnumber female authors by about two to one.[3]

### Authors' Educational Attainment

Overall, 61 percent of all authors hold a doctoral degree of some type. These include the PhD, EdD, ScD and the like. Figure Two indicates that the percentage of authors who hold the doctorate rises somewhat incrementally over time. Fifty percent of the authors in volumes 1-5 have doctoral degrees. This rises to 59 percent in volumes 6-10; 64 percent in volumes 11-15; and 69 percent in the final five volumes. Similarly, there is a steady, but less pronounced decrease in the percentage of authors who hold master's degrees of one form or another (MA, MS, MSW, MDiv, etc.). Nearly one-third (32 percent) of the authors in volumes 1-5 hold master's degrees; this drops to 23 percent of the authors in the last five volumes. A small percentage of physicians and others (BA, RN, etc.) round out the field of authors.

### Authors' Institutional Affiliation

A parallel finding is reported below regarding the settings in which these researchers do their work. Overall, the percentage of authors who work in academic settings (44 percent of the total) is roughly equal to that of the clinicians (41.5 percent of the total). However, the graph in Figure Three shows a rather dramatic shift in these data. Clinicians outnumber academics in the first ten volumes; the converse is the case in the last ten volumes. These two types of researchers have essentially switched places in the extent to which their work is published in *ATQ*. This is not surprising given the incremental increase over time of those authors who hold doctoral degrees as compared to others.

### Article Type

There has been a subtle but pronounced shift in the type of research that has appeared in *ATQ* over time. This is consistent with the evidence showing an

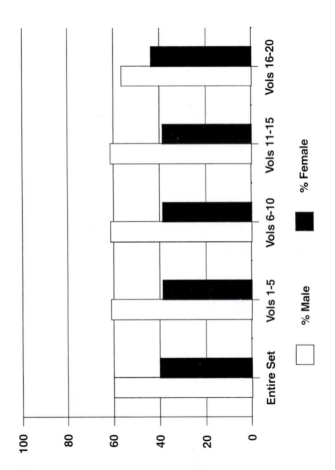

FIGURE 1. Gender Ratio of Authors

FIGURE 2. Authors' Educational Attainment

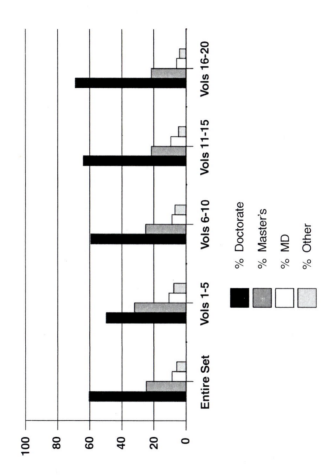

increasing trend toward doctorally trained authors who work in academic settings. Figure Four shows that a significant majority of the articles in *ATQ* are
designed to enhance the clinical or management skills of the readership. This
has remained the case throughout the entire twenty-volume set. However, the
"Data Report" has attained an increasingly prominent second place.

In the first five years of its existence, less than three percent of the articles
reported results from analysis of survey or secondary data. By the last five
years, this increased seven-fold to nearly 21 percent. This finding amplifies the
apparent increasing priority the editorial board places on data analysis to support the work that is published to enhance clinical and management skills.

Finally, there is a mildly increasing emphasis over time with regard to publishing articles dealing with ethnic issues and spirituality. This is discussed in
more detail below in the context of a brief report on the special issues that have
appeared in *ATQ* on a regular basis.

### The Special Issues

Thirteen of the twenty volumes of *ATQ* contain issues that are guest-edited
and all the articles discuss aspects of a specific topic. Several are double issues.
Volume eleven, for example, is entirely devoted to the same special topic. The
special issues are as follows:

1. 1984. Volume 1(3): "Alcohol and Sexual Dysfunction: Issues in Clinical Management."
2. 1985. Volume 2(2): "Psychosocial Issues in the Treatment of Alcoholism."
3. 1985-86. Volume 2(3-4): "Treatment of Black Alcoholics."
4. 1986. Volume 3(2): "Drunk Driving in America."
5. 1987. Volume 4(2): "The Treatment of Shame and Guilt in Alcoholism Counseling."
6. 1989. Volume 6(1): "Co-Dependency: Issues in Treatment and Recovery."
7. 1990. Volume 7(1): "Treating Alcoholism and Drug Abuse Among
   Homeless Men and Women: Nine Community Demonstration Grants."
8. 1993. Volume 10(3-4): "Treatment of the Chemically Dependent
   Homeless: Theory and Implementation of Fourteen American Projects."
9. 1994. Volume 11(1-4): "Self-Recovery: Treating Addictions Using
   Transcendental Meditation and Maharishi Ayur-Veda, Parts I and II."
10. 1995. Volume 12(2): "Treatment of the Addictions: Applications of
    Outcome Research for Clinical Management."

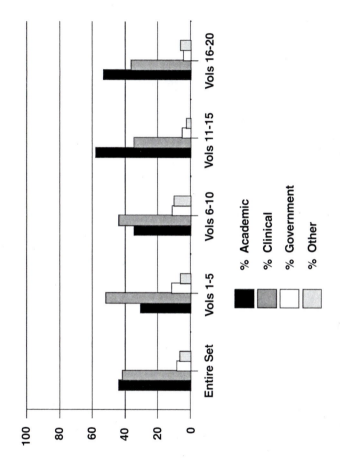

FIGURE 3. Authors' Institutional Affiliation

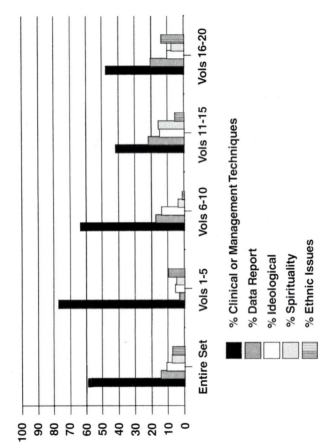

FIGURE 4. Article Type

% Clinical or Management Techniques
% Data Report
% Ideological
% Spirituality
% Ethnic Issues

11. 1998. Volume 16(1-2): "Alcohol Use/Abuse Among Latinos: Issues and Examples of Culturally Competent Services."
12. 1999. Volume 17(1-2): "Homelessness Prevention in Treatment of Substance Abuse and Mental Illness: Logic Models and Implementation of Eight American Projects."
13. 2000. Volume 18(3): "Women, Alcohol/Other Drugs and Trauma: The Interface Between Treatment and Research."

Disenfranchised groups are of significant interest to the editors of these special issues. For example, three of these thirteen publications are devoted to the needs of the homeless. African-American and Hispanic concerns are each covered by one special issue. Women and spirituality are also treated separately in these special reports.

Overall, a substantial proportion of the articles dealing with ethnic concerns and spirituality appear in special issues of *ATQ*. Over half (54.4 percent) of all articles addressing ethnic concerns appear in volume 2(3-4) and volume 16(1-2). Finally, over a third (38.3 percent) of all articles concerned mainly with spirituality appear in volume 11(1-4).

## *DISCUSSION*

"A Resource for Practitioners" continues its work. *Alcoholism Treatment Quarterly* has been remarkably consistent for twenty years in publishing timely and up-to-date insight and information to enhance the work of clinicians and managers working in the field of addiction recovery. The most consistent finding in this content analysis is the predominance of the "Clinical/Management Technique" article type.

Even so, there have been some gradual but pronounced changes over time in the other emphases reflected in the published work. We would note three trends:

1. An increasing tendency for authors to hold academic doctorates.
2. An increasing tendency for authors to be affiliated with academic institutions.
3. An increasing proportion of the articles published to be data reports.

The body of work *ATQ* represents is now comprised of work that emerged from the academic and practical sides of the discipline in relatively equal terms. However, this finding has taken twenty years to develop. The first ten years reflect a disproportionate emphasis on practical matters; the converse is true for the past ten years. The extent to which the shifting trend continues toward more academically trained authors who are affiliated with universities remains to be seen. The constituency served by the authors and editors of *Alcoholism Treatment Quarterly* will determine this.

## NOTES

1.   In cases where this was not obvious by the name, the two authors offered "best-guess" opinions and, if both agreed, a determination was made. In fifty cases (out of 1,219), this was left undetermined.

2.   While many of the articles categorized as "Spirituality" or "Ethnic Issues" could also have been categorized as "Clinical or Management Techniques," their primary purpose tended to highlight the special needs of ethnic populations or a specifically spiritual approach to treatment.

3.   While not reported in a graph or table, it is useful to note that this basic two to one ratio of male to female authors also describes lead authors. Sixty-three percent of all first authors were male; 37% were female.

# Youthful Drinking

## Gail Gleason Milgram, EdD

**SUMMARY.** The issue of adolescent drinking is reviewed to provide a perspective to the statistics on use and related problems. Since the percentage of adolescents who have consumed alcohol has remained fairly constant during the past fifty years, prevention and education programs should consider focusing on the reality of the youthful experience. Goals of such programs would target specific issues (e.g., drinking with peers, heavy drinking, drinking and driving, etc.). *[Article copies available for a fee from The Haworth Document Delivery Service: 1-800-HAWORTH. E-mail address: <getinfo@haworthpressinc.com> Website: <http://www.HaworthPress.com> © 2002 by The Haworth Press, Inc. All rights reserved.]*

**KEYWORDS.** Introduction to alcohol, adolescent alcohol use statistics, prevention and education

The majority of adults in the U.S.A. today indicate that they consume alcohol (National Institute of Alcohol Abuse and Alcoholism, 1997). Most young people also indicate that they have consumed alcohol. The introduction to alcohol usually takes place at home between the ages of 10 and 15 (Milgram, 1990). In *Alcohol and Youth: An Analysis of the Literature 1960-75*, Blane and

---

Gail Gleason Milgram is affiliated with the Center of Alcohol Studies, Rutgers–The State University of New Jersey.

Address correspondence to: Gail Gleason Milgram, EdD, Education and Training Division, Center of Alcohol Studies, Rutgers–The State University of New Jersey, 607 Allison Road, Piscataway, NJ 08854-8001.

[Haworth co-indexing entry note]: "Youthful Drinking." Milgram, Gail Gleason. Co-published simultaneously in *Alcoholism Treatment Quarterly* (The Haworth Press, Inc.) Vol. 20, No. 3/4, 2002, pp. 143-146; and: *Alcohol Problems in the United States: Twenty Years of Treatment Perspective* (ed: Thomas F. McGovern, and William L. White) The Haworth Press, Inc., 2002, pp. 143-146. Single or multiple copies of this article are available for a fee from The Haworth Document Delivery Service [1-800-HAWORTH, 9:00 a.m. - 5:00 p.m. (EST). E-mail address: getinfo@haworthpressinc.com].

Hewitt concluded that the age at which youngsters consumed their first drink had not changed significantly over the past twenty-five years; they indicated that the first exposure often occurs before the age of twelve (1977). Botvin and Wills indicated that initial experimentation and the development of patterns of alcohol use usually occur during pre-adolescence and adolescence (1985). Zucker and Harford obtained data as part of the Gallup Youth Survey of young people between the ages of 13-18 and determined that not only do the majority of adolescents drink but that adolescent drinking is related to age, sex, and grade in school (1986). Most adolescents perceive drinking as adult behavior and as a social act (Maddox and McCall, 1964). Drinking is viewed by the young as legitimate behavior, which is engaged in by the majority of adults; it is a pivotal part of the developmental process from adolescence to adulthood.

The question at hand is whether the statistics on adolescent drinking have changed in the past twenty years; the answer is an emphatic no. In fact, one can go back fifty years (i.e., 1952) and look at a study conducted in Nassau County, NY, of 1,000 high school students; 86% of the males and 85% of the females were identified as drinkers (Hofstra Research Bureau, 1953). A study of students in eighteen high schools in Oregon in 1967-68 found that 88% of the males and 84% of the females had consumed alcohol (Demone, 1966). A nationwide study of 4,918 students in 1978 found 87% of the students had tried alcohol and 77% of the males and 73% of the females were current users (Rachel et al., 1981). Johnston et al.'s national survey of school students found that 55% of eighth graders have consumed alcohol, 70% of tenth graders, 81% of twelfth graders, and 90% of college students (1996). These studies point out that the statistics on youthful drinking have remained fairly constant through time.

Ambivalence toward youthful drinking, which has also remained throughout the years, was discussed in "Youthful Drinking: Past and Present" and related to the various minimum ages of purchase throughout the U.S.A. (Milgram, 1982). Though the minimum age of purchase of alcohol in the U.S.A. in 2002 is 21, ambivalence still surrounds youthful drinking. One reason for this is the lack of clarification of the term drinking. When drinking is explained as consumption of a small amount of wine at dinner with parents, adults view this as part of family life. However, when drinking is described as occurring with friends outside of the home, adolescent drinking is considered negatively. The different meanings of the term drinking make it difficult to reach consensus on how much and what type of adolescent drinking is a problem.

A recent phenomena has been to look at the quantity of alcohol consumed by adolescents during a drinking occasion and attempt to determine potential problems. When occasions of heavy drinking (i.e., five or more drinks in a row at least once during the prior two weeks) were reported, 15% of the eighth graders indicated this occurrence, 24% of the tenth graders and 30% of the twelfth graders (Johnston et al., 1996). This finding demonstrates that the U.S.A. has an adolescent drinking population; it also indicates that a sizeable number of high school students engage in heavy drinking, putting themselves in risk situations. These young people arrive on college campuses with an established pattern of alcohol consumption, reasons for use, and attitudes toward drinking and intoxication. Johnston et al. indicate that 84% of college students have consumed alcohol within the previous year, and 70% within the previous month; consumption of five or more drinks during a drinking experience within the past two weeks is reported by approximately 40% of college students (Johnston et al., 2000). Another review of college drinking reported that 44% of college students drank heavily (i.e., five or more drinks by males, four or more drinks by females) on a drinking occasion within the previous two weeks (Wechsler et al., 1995). These recent studies make it clear that a majority of college students consume alcohol and many of them drink heavily (Anderson and Milgram, 2001). This finding is similar to those discussed by Warner (1970) and Rorabaugh (1979) many years ago.

It is now time for those of us in the alcohol field to design prevention and education programs that focus on the reality of the youthful experience. That is not to say that we are in favor of adolescent drinking; rather it is to understand that this phenomena has been with us for a long time. This realization will help us expand our focus on use to include minimization of alcohol related problems and alcohol abuse. Once we consider this issue more broadly, we will be able to determine what it is that we wish to deal with. Is it consuming alcohol at home with parents? Drinking with peers? Drinking heavily? Driving after drinking? Having problems related to drinking? Clearly stating the goal of our prevention and education program will assure that the other aspects (e.g., curriculum, teacher training, etc.) are in sync with the stated goal. Prevention and education programs need to be integrated into our institutions to facilitate change and achieve the desired outcome.

## REFERENCES

Anderson, D.S. and Milgram, G.G. (2001). *Promising Practices: Campus Alcohol Strategies*. Fairfax, VA: George Mason University.

Blane, H.T. and Hewitt, L.E. (1977). *Alcohol and Youth: An Analysis of the Literature, 1960-75*. National Institute on Alcohol Use and Alcoholism, Rockville, MD.

Botvin, G. J. and Wills, T. A. (1985). "Personal and Social Skills Training: Cognitive-Behavioral Approaches to Substance Abuse Prevention" in C.S. Bell and R. Battjes (Ed.), *Prevention Research: Deterring Drug Abuse Among Children and*

*Adolescents.* National Institute on Drug Abuse Monograph N. 63. Washington, DC: Government Printing Office.

Demone, H.W. (1966). *Drinking Attitudes and Practices of Male Adolescents,* Ph.D. Dissertation, Brandeis University, University Microfilms No. 66-13637.

Hofstra Research Bureau, Psychological Division, Hofstra College (1953). *Use of Alcoholic Beverage Among High School Students.* New York: Sheppard Foundation.

Johnston, L. D., O'Malley, P., and Bachman, J. G. (1996). *National Survey Results on Drug Use from Monitoring the Future Study, 1975-1995.* National Institute on Drug Abuse. Washington, DC: U.S. Government Printing Office.

Johnston, L. D., O'Malley, P. M., and Bachman, J. G. (2000). *National Survey Results on Drug Use: Vol. 11 College Students and Adults, 1979-1999.* Rockville, MD: National Institute on Drug Abuse.

Maddox G. L. and McCall, B. C. (1964). *Drinking Among Teen-Agers,* New Brunswick, NJ: Rutgers Center of Alcohol Studies.

Milgram, G. G. (1982). "Youthful Drinking: Past and Present." *Journal of Drug Education,* Vol. 12 (4).

Milgram, G. G. and the Editors of Consumer Reports Books (1990). *The Facts About Drinking: Coping with Alcohol Use, Abuse, and Alcoholism.* Mount Vernon, NY: Consumers Union.

National Institute on Alcohol Abuse and Alcoholism (1997). *Alcohol and Health: Ninth Special Report to the U.S. Congress.* National Institute of Health Publication No. 97-4017. Washington, DC: Department of Health and Human Services.

Rachel, J. V., Maisto, S. A., Guess, L. L., and Hubbard, R. L. (1981). "Alcohol Use Among Adolescents" in J. DeLuca (Ed.), *Fourth Special Report to the U.S. Congress on Alcohol and Health,* prepared for the National Institute on Alcohol Abuse and Alcoholism under Contract No. (ADM) 281-79-0022, U. S. Government Printing Office, Washington, DC.

Rorabaugh, W. (1979). *The Alcoholic Republic: An American Tradition.* New York: Oxford University Press.

Warner, H. (1970). "Alcohol Trends in College Life: Historical Perspective" in G. Maddox (Ed.), *The Domesticated Drug: Drinking Among Collegians.* New Haven, CT: College and University Press.

Wechsler, H., Moeykens, B., Davenport, A., Castillo, S., and Hansen, J. (1995). "The Adverse Impact of Heavy Episodic Drinkers on College Students." *Journal of Studies on Alcohol,* Vol. 56, No. 6.

Zucker, R. A. and Harford, T. C. (1986) "National Study of the Demography of Adolescent Drinking Practices in 1980" in C. M. Felsted (Ed.), *Youth and Alcohol Abuse: Readings and Resources.* Phoenix, AZ: Oryx Press.

# Reflections on the Past, Present and Possible Future of Women's Alcoholism Treatment

Jane M. Nakken, EdD

**SUMMARY.** The past twenty years have produced both good news and bad news in the treatment of alcoholic women. The impact of important strides in our clinical knowledge and skills is limited by the fact that women's access to effective alcoholism treatment peaked in the 1980s and is in decline. In 2002 we face the reality that providing excellent treatment for alcoholic women is as much a political and societal challenge as a clinical one; the treatment field must take on the challenge of opening our doors to all women in need of treatment. We must do this both by creating new, more accessible treatment models and through activism to push for increased access to current treatment resources. *[Article copies available for a fee from The Haworth Document Delivery Service: 1-800-HAWORTH. E-mail address: <getinfo@haworthpressinc.com> Website: <http://www.HaworthPress.com> © 2002 by The Haworth Press, Inc. All rights reserved.]*

**KEYWORDS.** Women, alcoholism, treatment

Jane M. Nakken is a consultant in private practice specializing in organization change and leadership. She retired in 2002 from her position as Executive Vice President of Hazelden, where she had worked since 1977 in a variety of clinical and leadership positions. She designed and implemented the Women & Children's Recovery Community and the Women Healing Conference Partnership, two cross-organizational partnerships that serve recovering women in innovative ways, and started Hazelden's Center for Public Policy.

[Haworth co-indexing entry note]: "Reflections on the Past, Present and Possible Future of Women's Alcoholism Treatment." Nakken, Jane M. Co-published simultaneously in *Alcoholism Treatment Quarterly* (The Haworth Press, Inc.) Vol. 20, No. 3/4, 2002, pp. 147-156; and: *Alcohol Problems in the United States: Twenty Years of Treatment Perspective* (ed: Thomas F. McGovern, and William L. White) The Haworth Press, Inc., 2002, pp. 147-156. Single or multiple copies of this article are available for a fee from The Haworth Document Delivery Service [1-800-HAWORTH. 9:00 a.m. - 5:00 p.m. (EST). E-mail address: getinfo@haworthpressinc.com].

## INTRODUCTION

Help for the woman alcoholic in America has improved dramatically over the last 50 years, and particularly in the most recent 20-year period. The trend toward women entering recovery established in the early part of the period, however, appears to have leveled off. One way to observe this is to examine women's membership in Alcoholics Anonymous (AA). Despite the fact that there have apparently always been women alcoholics, and many of them, the early members of AA were overwhelmingly male. Among the first 100 members, only one was a woman. AA's female membership climbed to 22 percent by 1968, and reached a peak of 35 percent in 1989 before leveling off, registering 33 percent in 1996 and 34 percent in 1998 (Alcoholics Anonymous, Inc., 1992).

Though women have made progress relative to their overall representation among AA members, there is also bad news in the fact that U.S. membership in AA has leveled off, perhaps as a result of declining availability of treatment programs based on AA's Twelve Steps. We know that this trend affects women, bad news at a time when nearly 4 million women meet the strictest criteria for alcohol dependence (NIAAA, 1997). The real severity of alcohol abuse and addiction among American women is much more staggering; for example, over 2.56 million women over the age of 60 are abusers of alcohol and other drugs, resulting in $30 billion annually in health care expenses for related illnesses (National Center on Addiction and Substance Abuse at Columbia University, 1998).

More than fifty years into the development of modem treatment methods, we find there are still major issues for alcoholic women in need of treatment:

- Although they represent forty percent of the nation's alcoholics, women make up only 28 percent of all people who receive treatment (NIAAA, 1997).
- Although women have better outcomes when treated in gender-specific programs, only about 10 percent of treatment programs are designed specifically for women (Alcohol and Drug Problems Association of North America [ADPA], 1996).
- Shame related to the stigma against alcoholic women remains one of the most important reasons women fail to seek treatment (Caron Foundation, 2001).

In 2002, the alcoholism treatment field is experiencing the passing of its heyday, and special treatment services for women are threatened even more specifically. This situation is deplorable and catastrophic, but it might have been predictable had we, as a field, paid closer attention to our history. It's not so much a case of "How could this happen?" as of "How could we let this happen again?"

## WHAT IT WAS LIKE: HISTORY AND LESSONS FROM THE PAST

History tells us that women have suffered with the disease of alcoholism through the ages. Mentioned in the Bible, punishable by death in ancient Rome, a reason for sterilization in the United States as recently as the 1950s: for women, alcoholism has always been attacked as a more serious "sin" than for men, and the harsh judgments of societies through the ages have led to shame that continues to this day (Straussner & Attia, 2002).

Women have played an important role in the emergence of concern about alcoholism in the United States. Whether suffering from the alcoholism of their men, medicating themselves with addictive elixirs, outlawing drinking, or winning the right for themselves to drink alcohol in public, alcohol issues have historically been related to the status of women in our society. "The history of women's use and abuse of alcohol in the United States," according to Straussner and Attia (2002), "is intertwined with the political movements of temperance, prohibition, and suffrage with the ever-changing role of women in political and family life."

For as long as drinking has been an issue in the Unites States, so has treatment of alcoholism. The current alcoholism treatment field is not our country's first. In *Slaying the Dragon*, William White (1998) chronicles the fortunes of our nation's earlier treatment approaches. From insane asylums to specialized asylums for the care of inebriates that emerged in the 1800s and early 1900s, to the Keeley Institutes of the 1800s, they served women, and they are gone.

### Emergence of the Classic Treatment Model

The birth of Alcoholics Anonymous (AA) provided the philosophical foundation of the modern treatment system. The culture and language of AA therefore addressed men; the characterization of the illness was dominated by masculine references. Women, when they were addressed or mentioned, were for the most part assumed to be in the role of the spouse of the alcoholic, not the alcoholic herself.

The alcoholic woman, in order to benefit from AA, had to search for the core essence of the AA message and try to translate it to her situation; it was her challenge to recognize that depression, anxiety, and withdrawing from others, for example, were her manifestations of the same core problems men acted out as anger, violence and abusive behavior. What a difficult intellectual task for a newly sober woman still struggling with denial of her disease! One can only guess that she felt out of place in the social setting of meetings, with the male alcoholic's views, humor, and conversational styles setting the tone.

Early treatment programs based on the Twelve Steps, adopting the premise that an alcoholic is an alcoholic, offered treatment to women only in coed settings, if at all. One of the early models of gender-specific treatment for women alcoholics was developed at Hazelden's Dia Linn Farm in 1956.

At Dia Linn, staff learned that alcoholism in women called for a more holistic approach than that offered to the men at Hazelden; it seemed more central to women's recovery process that the emotional, relationship, family, social, economic, and other issues in women's lives receive thoughtful attention as critical elements in recovery. The multidisciplinary approach that evolved was carried with Dia Linn as the program moved to Hazelden's main campus in 1961, changing the treatment offered to male patients. This model, combining the practical spirituality Twelve Step program of recovery with a holistic, multidisciplinary approach subsequently became known as the Minnesota Model or Hazelden Model of treatment which has been recognized, valued and replicated worldwide.

## WHAT HAPPENED: THE LAST TWENTY YEARS

The alcoholism treatment field has come a long way in accommodating women's needs by providing gender-specific treatment. There are specialized women's programs operating across the nation, and today even coed programs most often provide special treatment groups for women. Among programs and professionals identifying themselves as specializing in alcoholism treatment, the predominant clinical approach is still the classic Twelve Step-based, multidisciplinary model. Changes within the twenty-year time frame have been subtle but extremely important: women's programs supplement core AA literature with newer recovery materials written by women for women, substitute gender-neutral terminology when referring to a Higher Power, and address concurrent issues that are all-too-common for alcoholic women.

### New Literature Changed the Twelve Step Experience for Women

As the number of women seeking recovery in AA grew, so did women's dissatisfaction with that organization's predominantly masculine culture. While the structure of the Twelve Step Program, based on openness, fellowship, sponsorship and community is in itself a "feminine-friendly" model, the language, tone and personality of many AA groups were uncomfortable for women.

AA's emphasis on ego deflation and acceptance of powerlessness over alcohol piqued the anger and resistance of women who came of age in the feminist seventies. Like the suffragettes of an earlier era, recovering alcoholic women in the eighties were motivated to recognizing and honoring their value, potential, and personal power–not to admitting powerlessness over anything.

Alternative programs of recovery for women were started, though none took root as deeply and as ubiquitously as AA. These initiatives caught the attention of the treatment field, however, and new literature was written and published that helped women apply the AA program of recovery to their own lives.

The publication of *Each Day a New Beginning* in 1982 was a celebratory moment for women in recovery. This was the first widely available tool that brought women into the mainstream of Twelve Step recovery as addicts. For the first time, its author Karen Casey addressed the woman reader as the primary addict, not as the codependent. No longer did women have to translate the messages of the daily meditation books available up to that time, considering how the message might be appropriate to us if they just translated a more masculine character defect or behavior into one more typical of women. Stephanie Covington continued the feminization of recovery literature with her book *A Woman's Way Through the Twelve Steps* (1994). Today women's AA groups are common across the nation, supplementing the recovery experience available in for women in coed groups.

### New Theory and Research Emerge: Women Are Indeed Different from Men

Alcoholism treatment professionals working with women have increasingly attuned during the eighties and nineties to the fact that women experience their addictions and their recoveries differently from men. Counselors have noticed that women seem more affected by the circumstances of their lives, for instance. They seem less able to accept the traditional counselor's advice to "work a selfish program," advice readily adopted by many recovering male alcoholics. They also find it difficult to "stick with the winners," often returning instead to unhealthy relationships and families that demand compliance to lifestyles that threaten sobriety. Women also seem more vulnerable to relapse preceded by emotional stress, relationship problems, or poor self-care resulting from attending to the needs of others rather than themselves. In fact, sometimes it seems like women want or need *all* their problems solved, and their sobriety depends on it. Helping them stay sober, therefore, involves providing everything from relationship counseling to childcare to subsidized housing and transportation.

Within the last twenty years, a new theory of women's psychology has begun to emerge as an influence in the clinical treatment of women alcoholics. This theory, the Relational Model of Women's Psychology, proposed by Jean Baker Miller and her colleagues at Wellesley College's Stone Center, offers a theoretical framework that makes sense of the differences noticed by clinicians. A key premise is that women's healthy development does not aim toward the Freudian/Eriksonian goal of individuation and individualism, but rather aims toward functional positioning within a network of relationships as its goal and the expression of maturity.

While there are many interesting and unresolved issues that emerge in considering the application of the Relational Model, a top-side common-sense look at women's responses to treatment and recovery support their further exploration. For example, a recent *Time* magazine article cites research that finds that women are more sensitive than men to peer pressure. Women tend to integrate relationships and life experiences, rather than compartmentalize them. Women try to make things in their lives work together, or at least fit together. Therefore, culture and ethnicity, stage of life issues, and societal expectations matter deeply to women.

New biochemical research supports this idea that women are different from men in their approach to life, and, therefore, to establishing a sober lifestyle. Brand-new research regarding women's ways of handling stress suggests that women and men respond differently to stress. The human stress response has been characterized, both physiologically and behaviorally, as "fight-or-flight." This new research demonstrates that females' biochemical and behavioral responses are more marked by a pattern of "tend-and-befriend."

Incorporating emerging knowledge about women's physical, emotional and mental health into our holistic treatment models for alcoholism is well underway, thanks to the pioneering efforts of clinicians and trainers nationwide. Lala Straussner and Stephanie Brown have assembled a landmark collection of this work in *The Handbook of Addiction Treatment for Women* (2002). As a field, we are learning better to operationalize the belief that for women, the path to healthy sobriety leads through healthy self-concept, spirituality and relationships; integration of the many parts of our lives; and constructive use of support networks.

With the complexity of women's lives, it's easy to get distracted from the fact that spirituality and abstinence must be core to their recoveries from alcoholism. The real stresses of personal relationships, earning a living, childcare, and homemaking are necessary. They are real, critical, and the basis for a good life. But none of these will keep a woman sober. And without sobriety, she will not build success in these other areas.

## *Treatment Success and the Benefits of Gender-Specific Treatment*

When Hazelden began treating women in 1956, it had to be on a separate campus, since leadership decided that bringing women onto the hallowed Hazelden campus would spell nothing but trouble (McElrath, 1999).

Ironically, the decision made out of prejudice and stigma turned out to be a good thing; the treatment provided to the women at Dia Linn set a model for gender-specific treatment that has since proven to enhance the success of treatment for women. We know now that women treated in programs specifically for women have better success than women treated in coed programs, and that they have outcomes generally comparable to or better than men's, despite the fact that women have a higher prevalence of diagnosed coexisting disorders (Hazelden, 1999).

Researchers speculate that women may have such good outcomes because they have less severe addictions (Pettinati et al., 1997) or that they more readily engage in the treatment process (Gil-Rivas et al., 1996).

## *TREATMENT SYSTEMS IN 2002: WHAT'S HAPPENING*

More and more, holistic multidisciplinary alcoholism treatment, especially residential treatment, is unavailable to middle-class women alcoholics. Since health plans rarely cover this comprehensive approach to treatment, access is restricted to women who are: rich enough to pay for it from personal funds, poor enough to receive treatment through government funding, or incarcerated.

### *Treatment in the Health Care System in 2002*

Women who depend on their health care plans to provide treatment for their alcoholism are unlikely to receive comprehensive treatment in 2002. Most health coverage is provided under managed care plans that favor outpatient counseling of varying intensity, none of which have demonstrated outcomes as good as the classic intensive multidisciplinary model. Some plans deny treatment for anything beyond "medically necessary" care, a standard they often enact by providing no treatment beyond medical detoxification.

Yet another current response to the problems of alcoholic women is found in the physician's office. It seems always to have been the case that alcoholic women are often treated for depression or anxiety, but not for their alcoholism. The popularity of modern medications for mental illness raises the likelihood that these medications will be prescribed for alcoholic women by their physicians. But today's pharmacological treatments for depression or anxiety are no more likely (as far as we know) to cure alcoholism than medicine of the 1960s, when alcoholic women were given pills and sometimes shock treatments for relief of their alcohol-induced depressions.

Still more troubling is the possibility that the new medications being used for women seeking help will actually exacerbate addiction. "Throughout history, women's addictions are seen to arise as the unintended outcome of the latest well-meaning treatment approaches," write Straussner and Attia (2002). "For example, morphine was recommended as a cure for alcoholism, and coca syrup was touted as a cure for morphine addiction."

Current medical research on alcoholism is primarily aimed at biochemical causation and treatments. While new findings in brain research are interesting and affirming of the disease model of alcoholism, there is no realistic hope on the horizon that science will cure alcoholics with pharmacologic treatments, gene therapy or biofeedback any time in the near future. The health care system cannot expect to "cure" or even "manage" alcoholic women in the doctor's office.

### Women's Treatment in Public Systems

America's current initiatives on welfare reform and the "War on Drugs" have affected alcoholic women significantly. In some ways, the effect is deplorable: incarceration of women has increased 276% as compared to an increase of 165% for men (Rosenbaum, 1997). Yet is sad but true that without the treatment offered through the welfare and corrections systems, even fewer women would get treatment for their alcoholism and other addictions.

Alcoholic women who receive treatment through government-funded programs, whether freestanding, as part of their public housing programs, or in the correctional system, are more likely than other women to receive long-term treatment that is multidisciplinary in nature. They often do a credible job of addressing other critical issues such as childcare and parenting, domestic abuse, employment, and housing, though often these programs do not address spirituality as a component of recovery, or introduce women to the lifelong support found in AA.

### WHERE ARE WE GOING?

The future of treatment for alcoholic women will continue to be determined in the future, as in the past, as much by politics and public opinion as by clinical knowledge. At the same time we have been advancing our clinical models for understanding and more effectively addressing the needs of alcoholic women, access to alcoholism treatment for women has peaked and appears to be declining.

For the treatment field, there are burning challenges: How can we work together to better help chemically dependent women initiate and sustain recovery in an increasingly turbulent and unsupportive environment? We are all aware of ways the current social and political environment threatens effective treatment for chemically dependent women: cutbacks in healthcare dollars, the increasing prevalence of managed care, potential clients lacking financial resources to pay for treatment and continuing care, treatment models that are limited in scope and do not take into account the complex dynamics of a woman's life such as children and careers–and a social environment that produces isolation just when community is clearly needed. What's wrong with this picture and what are the alternatives to it?

Creating workable and effective treatment models in the current social, economic and political environment, like working a personal recovery program, is too big a job for any of us to do alone. But by working together, and in collaboration with other helping professions, the alcoholism treatment field may continue to facilitate the miracles that allow American women entry into recovery.

## REFERENCES

Alcohol and Drug Problems Association of North America. (1996). Conference proceedings.

Covington, S. (1994). A woman's way through the Twelve Steps. Center City, MN: Hazelden.

Gil-Rivas, V., Fiorentiine, R. and Anglin, M. (1996). Sexual abuse, physical abuse and post-traumatic stress disorder among women participating in outpatient drug abuse treatment. Journal of psychoactive drugs, 28, 95-102.

McElrath, D. (1999). A Place Called Hazelden. Hazelden Foundation, Center City, MN.

Morse, J. (April 1, 2002) Women on a binge. Time.

National Center on Addiction and Substance Abuse at Columbia University. (1998). Under the rug: Substance abuse and the mature woman.

Ninth Special Report to the US Congress on Alcohol and Health From the Secretary of Health and Human Services. (1997). National Institute on Alcohol and Alcoholism, USDHHS.

Owen, P. (1999). Women and substance abuse. Butler Center for Research and Learning Research Update. January 1999. Center City, MN: Hazelden.

Pettinati, H., Pierce, J., Wolf, A., Rukstalis, M. and O'Brien, C. (1997). Gender differences in comorbidly depressed alcohol-dependent outpatients. Alcoholism: Clinical and experimental research, 21, 1742-1746.

Rosenbaum, M. (1997).Women: Research and policy. In J. H. Lowinson, P. Ruiz, R.B. Millman & J. G. Langrod (Eds.), Substance abuse: A comprehensive textbook. Baltimore, MD: Williams & Wilkins.

Straussner, S. and Attia, P. (2002). Women addiction and treatment through a historical lens. In S. Straussner and S. Brown (Eds.), The handbook of addiction treatment for women. San Francisco: Jossey-Bass.

Straussner, S. and Brown, S. (2002). The handbook of addiction treatment for women. San Francisco: Jossey-Bass.

Taylor, S., Klein, L., Lewis, B., Gruenewald, T., Gurung, T. and Updegraff, J. (July 2000). Biobehavioral responses to stress in females: Tend-and-befriend, not fight-or-flight. Psychological review, 107(3), 411-429.

White, W. (1998). Slaying the dragon: The history of addiction treatment and recovery in America. Bloomington, IL: Chestnut Health Systems/Lighthouse Institute.

# Alcohol Problems in Native America: Changing Paradigms and Clinical Practices

Don Coyhis, BA
William L. White, MA

**SUMMARY.** Views about the sources and solutions to alcohol problems among Native Americans have undergone dramatic changes over the past quarter century. This brief article summarizes the nature of these changes, with particular emphasis on emerging principles and practices that underlie the resolution of alcohol problems among Native peoples. *[Article copies available for a fee from The Haworth Document Delivery Service: 1-800-HAWORTH. E-mail address: <getinfo@haworthpressinc.com> Website: <http://www.HaworthPress.com> © 2002 by The Haworth Press, Inc. All rights reserved.]*

**KEYWORDS.** Native American, cultural revitalization movements, "firewater" myths, culturally-informed treatment

Alcoholism and alcohol-related problems have long constituted a serious problem in Native American communities (Lender and Martin, 1982), but recent decades have witnessed substantial advances in understanding the sources and solutions of these problems. These advances include:

---

Don Coyhis is President and Co-founder of White Bison, Inc. and a member of the Mohican Nation from the Stockbridge-Munsee Reservation in Wisconsin. William L. White is Senior Research Consultant at Chestnut Health Systems, Bloomington, IL.

Address correspondence to: Don Coyhis, White Bison, Inc., 6145 Lehman Drive, Suite 200, Colorado Springs, CO 80918.

[Haworth co-indexing entry note]: "Alcohol Problems in Native America: Changing Paradigms and Clinical Practices." Coyhis, Don, and William L. White, Co-published simultaneously in *Alcoholism Treatment Quarterly* (The Haworth Press, Inc.) Vol. 20, No. 3/4, 2002, pp. 157-165; and: *Alcohol Problems in the United States: Twenty Years of Treatment Perspective* (ed: Thomas F. McGovern, and William L. White) The Haworth Press, Inc., 2002, pp. 157-165. Single or multiple copies of this article are available for a fee from The Haworth Document Delivery Service [1-800-HAWORTH, 9:00 a.m. - 5:00 p.m. (EST). E-mail address: getinfo@haworthpressinc.com].

1. new evidence of the historical roots of alcohol problems among Native tribes,
2. scientific challenges to the "firewater myths" that have permeated conceptions of the etiology of Native alcohol problems,
3. the beginning recognition of the role Native leaders played in organizing America's first sobriety-based, mutual aid societies,
4. Native adaptations of Alcoholics Anonymous,
5. a revival of Native cultural revitalization and therapeutic movements,
6. the development of culturally meaningful alcoholism treatment philosophies and techniques.

## THE RISE OF NATIVE ALCOHOL PROBLEMS

MacAndrew and Edgerton's (1969) landmark study, *Drunken Comportment*, and the historical investigations that followed (Mancall, 1995; Unrau, 1996), collectively challenge the long-held view that initial Native American contact with alcohol was one of instant personal and cultural devastation. Three conclusions stand out in this new historical research.

First, Native tribes had a commanding knowledge of botanical pharmacology, and many tribes had long ritualized the use of psychoactive drugs, including potent forms of tobacco, datura, and peyote, in ways that minimized their harmful effects and maximized their benefit to the individual and the tribe. Contrary to popular perception, there were also tribes such as the Pima, Papago, Apache, Coahulitec, Yuma, and Pueblo that had ritualized the use of fermented alcohol long before their first contacts with Europeans. While most Native tribes in what is today the United States and Canada were not exposed to alcohol prior to European contact, some tribes had culturally managed such use for centuries before the first Europeans arrived in the Americas (Westermeyer, 1996).

Second, the initial response of Native peoples to alcohol following European contact was not one of widespread alcoholism. Rather than infatuation, most Native peoples initially responded to alcohol with distaste and suspicion. They considered drunkenness "degrading to free men" and questioned the motives of those who would offer a substance that was so offensive to the senses and that made men foolish (Andersen, 1988). Most Native people who did drink alcohol were reported to show "remarkable restraint while in their cups." Most drank alcohol only during social or trading contact with Whites. As a result, early Native drinking, in its moderation and excess, tended to mirror the consumption patterns promoted by the English, Spanish, French, Dutch, and Russians from whom they learned the practice. Drinking and intoxication did not reflect their normal daily life and habits, but became increasingly disruptive as it was modeled on the "frontier drinking" patterns of soldiers, trappers, and traders (MacAndrew and Edgerton, 1969; Winkler, 1968).

Third, Native alcohol problems and alcoholism emerged as Native tribes came under physical and cultural assault, and as alcohol shifted from a benign token of social contact between Euro-Americans and Indians to a tool of economic, political and sexual exploitation. The new historical studies confirm an almost linear relationship between the rise of Native alcohol problems and the disruption or disintegration of tribal cultures.

## *"FIREWATER MYTHS"*

From their beginning, Native drinking behavior and alcohol problems were framed by Euro-Americans in ways that provided ideological support for the vision of "Manifest Destiny." White drunkenness was interpreted as the misbehavior of an individual; Native drunkenness was interpreted in terms of the inferiority of a race (Mosher, 1975). What emerged was a set of beliefs, known as "firewater myths," that misrepresented the history, nature, sources and potential solutions to Native alcohol problems. These myths proclaimed that Indian people:

1. had an insatiable appetite for alcohol,
2. were hypersensitive to alcohol (couldn't "hold their liquor"),
3. were dangerously violent when intoxicated,
4. were inordinately vulnerable to addiction to alcohol, and
5. could not resolve such problems on their own (Westermeyer, 1974; Leland, 1976).

The scientific literature of recent decades has challenged these myths by documenting the wide variability of alcohol problems across and within Native tribes, and by refuting claims of genetic or other biological anomalies that render Native peoples particularly vulnerable to alcoholism. Also criticized have been scientific and popular reports that, by framing all Native alcohol problems as "alcoholism" and by inflating and overdramatizing such problems, have stigmatized whole tribes (and a whole people) (Westermeyer and Baker, 1986; May, 1994; Mancall, 1995; Westermeyer, 1996). After reviewing the historical and scientific evidence, Dwight Heath (1983) concluded that the "stereotype of 'the drunken Indian' is not generally accurate today, and appears never to have been."

The "drunken Indian" stereotype, and the "firewater myths" that undergird it, have long served to sustain "systems of subordination and domination" (Morgan, 1983). Such perceptions and beliefs, by defining Indian peoples as biologically and culturally inferior, provided part of the conscience-salving justification for the decimation of Native tribes over the extended period of Indian-European contact and conflict. Several observers (see Mosher, 1975 and Holmes and Antell, 2001) have suggested that modern discussions of alcohol and Indians continue to reflect notions of inferiority and superiority, and may serve similar functions in maintaining relationships of unequal power and status. As these "firewater myths" and their political and economic functions have been exposed and challenged in recent decades, ethno-historical theories emphasizing social learning, cultural trauma and continued patterns of subjugation and domination are replacing biological theories on the root causes of Native alcohol problems. These emerging theories tend to shift the locus of intervention into alcohol problems from the individual alone to the community and the larger historical, political, economic and cultural contexts in which alcohol problems arise and are sustained.

## NATIVE RESISTANCE AND RECOVERY

The story of the rise of alcohol problems among Native tribes is not one of passive destruction, but of active resistance and recovery. Native leaders actively resisted the infusion of alcohol into tribal life by castigating alcohol as "fool's water," "the Devil'spittle," or "white man's poison" and calling attention to its destructive effects on Native peoples. They advocated the legal banishment of the exploitive whiskey trade–a practice in which traders would arrive in Native villages with 30 or 40 kegs of whiskey and, once the Natives were intoxicated, take a season's worth of skins in return for watered-down booze spiked with strychnine, red peppers, gunpowder and opium (Anderson, 1988; Kennedy, 1997).

Native leaders also birthed abstinence-based cultural revitalization and therapeutic movements that constitute the earliest organized frameworks for alcoholism recovery in America. It is only recently that the contributions of these movements to the history of alcoholism recovery in America have begun to be recognized (White, 2000, 2001). The beginning of alcoholic mutual aid societies is usually attributed to the Washingtonian revival of the 1840s, but abstinence-based support structures have much earlier and more enduring roots within Native America cultures.

Early Native recovery support structures included the Delaware prophet movements (Wyoming Woman, Papounhan, Wangomend, Neolin, and Scatttameck), the Christian Indian revivalists (William Apess and Samson Occom), the Handsome Lake movement–also know as the Longhouse Religion–the Shawnee Prophet (Tenskwatawa) and Kickapoo Prophet (Kennekuk) movements, the Indian temperance societies, the Indian Shaker Church and the Native American Church. These movements offered a culturally viable rationale for the rejection of alcohol, purification and healing rituals, a new code of living (the "Peyote Way," the "Red Road"), a new personal identity, sober role models, a means of repairing family and social relationships, and an esteem-affirming reconnection with ancestral and contemporary Native cultures. The rich and continuing history of these movements confirms that alcoholism recovery is a living reality in Native communities and has been for more than 250 years (White, 2001).

## THE "INDIANIZATION OF A.A."

Suggestions that Alcoholics Anonymous (A.A.) is not appropriate for Native Americans have been countered in recent decades by A.A. literature for Native Americans (*A.A. for the Native North American*, 1989), Native adaptations of A.A.'s Twelve Steps, Native refinement of A.A. meeting rituals, the growth of A.A. meetings conducted in Native languages, and an annual National/International Native American Indian A.A. (NAIAA) convention (Jilek-Aall, 1981; Coyhis, 1990, 2000). So-called "Indian A.A." meetings often start late and end late, provide long breaks for socializing, include family members and children, impose no time limits for speakers, integrate A.A. and Native cultural ideas and slogans, replace references to the Christian "God" with "the Creator" or "Great Spirit," and replace the affirmation of "powerlessness" with a focus on the acquisition of power over personal and tribal life (Jilek-Aall, 1981; Womak, 1996; Simonelli, 1993). A significant milestone in this "Indianization" of A.A. is the imminent release of a Native adaptation of the basic text of Alcoholics Anonymous by White Bison, Inc. that includes Native frameworks and stories of alcoholism recovery. The publication of this book culminates a trend of Indian people claiming and sharing their own stories of addiction and recovery (Manacle, 1993; Red Road).

## CULTURAL REVITALIZATION AND HEALING MOVEMENTS

Many of the earlier noted abstinence-based, religious and cultural revitalization movements such as the Native American Church and the Indian Shaker Church continue to flourish today in Native communities. What is equally noteworthy is the revival of earlier cultural practices such as the sweat lodge, the Gourd Dance, the Sun Dance and the Guardian Spirit Ceremony that some Native people are using therapeutically to initiate or anchor their recovery from alcoholism (Jilek, 1978; Jilek, 1994). New movements that are expanding cultural pathways to recovery include the Red Road approach to sobriety–created by Gene Thin Elk (Lakota-South Dakota), People in Prison Entering Sobriety (PIPES), and an emerging Wellbriety Movement that places sobriety within a larger framework of physical, emotional, spiritual and relational health. The Wellbriety Movement is serving as a focal point for organizing recovery support structures in Indian Country and incorporating culturally-based recovery tools into alcoholism treatment programs (Coyhis, 1999). The birth of organizations like White Bison, Inc. signals the involvement and leadership of Indian communities in a new grassroots recovery advocacy movement in the United States (www.whitebison.org; www.recoveryadvocacy.org).

## CULTURALLY-INFORMED TREATMENT

Native alcoholism treatment programs have evolved administratively through the Office of Economic Opportunity in the 1960s, the National Institute on Alcohol Abuse and Alcoholism in the early 1970s, the Indian Health Service's Office of Alcoholism Programs (beginning in 1976), and, recently, a trend toward tribal sponsorship. Through these transitions, treatment programs that serve Native populations have begun to incorporate more culturally-informed philosophies and techniques. These programs are linking treatment to Native communities via tribal sponsorship, involving tribal elders as advisors and teachers, integrating Native healers into the treatment team, recruiting and training Native addiction counselors, and using history and culture as tools of liberation. They are also incorporating culturally-grounded ideas such as medicine wheel teachings; traditional ceremonies like the Sacred Pipe and spirit dances; purification and healing rituals such as the sweat lodge and the peyote ritual; and engaging kinship and community networks for long-term support for recovery (Anderson, 1992; Abbott, 1998; McCormick, 2000). Culturally-informed treatment of Native alcohol problems is grounded in tribal values and folkways. Compared to traditional treatment, it utilizes less confrontation and questioning, is quieter (less pressure for self-disclosure and more respectful of silence), and places greater emphasis on spirituality (French, 2000).

Culturally-informed treatment seeks to understand the wounded individual in the context of the historical and continued wounding of the Native tribal culture of which he or she is a part. It recognizes that, as *The Red Road to Wellbriety* teaches, "healthy seeds cannot grow in diseased soil." It seeks not just the healing of the individual, but the healing of the community within which that individual is nested. As such, the goal of culture-congenial alcoholism treatment is viewed as a restoration of harmony between the individual, the family, the tribe, and the world. In contrast to interventions grounded in Western medicine, it is more holistic–more focused on creating a better person in the context of family and clan than on symptom suppression. Ernie Benedict, a Mohawk elder, explains:

> *The difference that exists is that the White doctor's medicines tend to be very mechanical. The person is repaired but he is not better than he was before. It is possible in the Indian way to be a better person after going through a sickness followed by the proper medicine.* (Quoted in Jilek, 1978)

### RECOVERY AND COMMUNITY

No recent tribal response to alcoholism has galvanized more public and professional notice than that of the community of Alkali Lake, British Columbia. The Shuswap tribal community in Alkali Lake was so plagued with alcoholism that surrounding communities referred to it as "Alcohol Lake." The change began in 1971, when Phyllis and Andy Chelsea made a commitment to stop drinking and to confront the pervasive problem of alcoholism in their community. When Andy Chelsea was subsequently elected Chief of the Shuswap Tribe, he began promoting A.A. meetings, arresting bootleggers (including his own mother), confronting the drunkenness of public officials, and staging interventions to get community members into treatment. Tribal traditions were revitalized for both the adults and children of the community. Educational and job development programs were initiated for those in recovery. Over a period of ten years, this sustained effort reduced alcoholism from nearly 100 percent of the tribe to less than 5 percent (Chelsea and Chelsea, 1985; Taylor, 1987).

The proclamation of Chief Andy Chelsea that "the community is the treatment center" (quoted in Abbott, 1998) illustrates a collectivist, as opposed to individualistic, approach to the resolution of alcohol problems. Native frameworks of recovery have always been, and continue to be, framed in terms of an inextricable link between hope for the individual and hope for a community and a people. Two and a half centuries of Native recovery movements, the current sobriety of Alkali Lake, the vitality of the contemporary Wellbriety Movement, and the infusion of tribal beliefs and ceremonies into alcoholism treatment collectively provide a compelling lesson: the most effective and enduring solutions to Native alcohol problems are ones that emerge from the very heart of tribal cultures.

## REFERENCES

Abbott, P.J. (1998).Traditional and western healing practices for alcoholism in American Indians and Alaskan Natives. *Substance Use and Misuse* 33(13): 2605-2646.

Anderson, E.N. (1992). A healing place: Ethnographic notes on a treatment centre. *Alcoholism Treatment Quarterly* 9(3-4): 1-21.

Anderson, T.I. (1988). *Alaska Hooch.* Fairbanks, AK: Hoo-Che-Noo.

Chelsea, P. and Chelsea, A. (1985). *Honour of All: The People of Alkali Lake.* (Video) British Columbia, Canada: The Alkali Lake Tribal Council.

Coyhis, D. (1990). *Recovery from the Heart: A Journey Through the Twelve Steps: A Workbook for Native Americans.* Center City, Minnesota: Hazelden.

Coyhis, D. (1999). *The Wellbriety Journey: Nine Talks by Don Coyhis.* Colorado Springs, CO: White Bison, Inc.

Coyhis, D. (2000). Culturally Specific Addiction Recovery for Native Americans. In J. Kristen (Ed.), *Bridges to Recovery,* pp. 77-114. New York: The Free Press.

French, L.A. (2000). *Addictions and Native Americans.* Westport, CT: Praeger.

Hall, R.L. (1986). Alcohol treatment in American Indian populations: An indigenous treatment modality compared with traditional approaches. *Annals of the New York Academy of Sciences* 472: 168-178.

Heath, D. (1983). Alcohol use among North American Indians: A cross-cultural survey of patterns and problems. In Reginald Smart et al. (Eds.), *Research Advances in Alcohol and Drug Problems,* Volume 7, pp. 343-396. NY: Plenum Press.

Holmes, M. and Antell, J. (2001). The social construction of American Indian drinking: Perceptions of American Indian and White officials. *The Sociological Quarterly* 42(2): 151-173.

Jilek, W. (1994). Traditional healing in the prevention and treatment of alcohol and drug abuse. *Transcultural Psychiatric Research* Review 31: 219-256.

Jilek, W.G. (1978). Native renaissance: The survival of indigenous therapeutic ceremonials among North American Indians. *Transcultural Psychiatric Research* 15: 117-147.

Jilek-Aall, L. (1981). Acculturation, alcoholism, and Indian-style Alcoholics Anonymous. *Journal of Studies of Alcohol* (Suppl. 9): 143-158.

Kennedy, M.A. (1997). *The Whiskey Trade of the Northwestern Plains: A Multidisciplinary Study.* New York: Peter Lang.

Leland, J. (1976). *Firewater Myths: North American Indian Drinking and Alcohol Addiction.* New Brunswick, NJ: Rutgers Center of Alcohol Studies Monograph No. 11.

Lender, M. and Martin, J. (1982). *Drinking in America.* NY: The Free Press.

MacAndrew, C. and Edgerton, R.B. (1969). *Drunken Comportment: A Social Explanation.* New York: Aldine.

Mancall, P. (1995). *Deadly Medicine: Indians and Alcohol in Early America.* Ithaca, NY: Cornell University Press.

Maracle, B. (1993). *Crazywater: Native Voices on Addiction and Recovery.* Toronto, Ontario: Viking.

May, P. (1994). The epidemiology of alcohol abuse among American Indians: The mythical and real properties. *American Indian Culture and Research Journal* 18: 121-143.

McCormick, R. (2000). Aboriginal traditions in the treatment of substance abuse. *Canadian Journal of Counseling* 34(1): 25-32.

Morgan, P. (1983). Alcohol, disinhibition, and domination: A conceptual analysis. In Room and Collins (Eds.), *Alcohol and Disinhibition: Nature and Meaning of the Link*, pp. 405-430. Washington, DC: U.S. Government Printing Office.

Mosher, J. (1975). Liquor legislation and Native Americans: History and perspective. Working Paper F 136. Berkeley: Social Research Group, University of California.

*The Red Road to Sobriety–Video Talking Circle.* San Francisco, CA: Kifaru Productions.

Simonelli, R. (1993). White Bison presents a Native view: Alcoholic recovery and the Twelve Steps. *Winds of Change* 8(3): 41-46.

Taylor, V. (1987). The triumph of the Alkali Lake Indian band. *Alcohol Health and Research World* Fall, 57.

Unrau, W. (1996). *White Man's Wicked Water: The Alcohol Trade and Prohibition in Indian Country, 1802-1892.* Lawrence: University Press of Kansas.

Westermeyer, J. (1974). "The drunken Indian:" Myths and realities. *Psychiatric Annals* 4(11): 29-36.

Westermeyer, J. (1996). Alcoholism among new world peoples: A critique of history, methods, and findings. *American Journal on Addictions* 5(2): 110-123.

Westermeyer, J. and Baker, J. (1986). Alcoholism and the American Indian. In N.S. Estes and M.E. Heineman (Eds.), *Alcoholism: Development, Consequences, and Interventions*, 3rd edition, pp. 273-282. St. Louis: Mosby.

White, W. (2000). The history of recovered people as wounded healers: From Native America to the rise of the modern alcoholism movement. *Alcoholism Treatment Quarterly* 18(1): 1-24.

White, W. (2001). Pre-AA alcoholic mutual aid societies. *Alcoholism Treatment Quarterly* 19(2): 1-21.

Winkler, A.M. (1968). Drinking on the American frontier. *Quarterly Journal of Studies on Alcohol* 29: 413-445.

Womak, M.L. (1996). The Indianization of Alcoholics Anonymous: An examination of Native American recovery movements. Master's thesis, Department of American Indian Studies, University of Arizona.

# The Response
# of African American Communities
# to Alcohol and Other Drug Problems:
# An Opportunity for Treatment Providers

Mark Sanders, LCSW, CADC

**SUMMARY.** The closing decades of the twentieth century were marked by a rise in culturally indigenous responses to alcohol and other drug problems in the African American community, and a consistent call for more culturally sensitive and competent addiction treatment services. This article provides a brief description of several indigenous recovery movements and discusses how addiction treatment agencies can collaborate with these movements to better respond to the needs of African American clients and families. *[Article copies available for a fee from The Haworth Document Delivery Service: 1-800-HAWORTH. E-mail address: <getinfo@haworthpressinc.com> Website: <http://www.HaworthPress.com> © 2002 by The Haworth Press, Inc. All rights reserved.]*

**KEYWORDS.** African American, addiction, religion, treatment

---

Mark Sanders is an international trainer and consultant in the addictions field. He is author of *Treating the African American Male Substance Abuser* and *Counseling Chemically Dependent African American Women*.

Address correspondence by e-mail at: <Sandersspeaks@aol.com>.

[Haworth co-indexing entry note]: "The Response of African American Communities to Alcohol and Other Drug Problems: An Opportunity for Treatment Providers." Sanders, Mark. Co-published simultaneously in *Alcoholism Treatment Quarterly* (The Haworth Press, Inc.) Vol. 20, No. 3/4, 2002, pp. 167-174; and: *Alcohol Problems in the United States: Twenty Years of Treatment Perspective* (ed: Thomas F. McGovern, and William L. White) The Haworth Press, Inc., 2002, pp. 167-174. Single or multiple copies of this article are available for a fee from The Haworth Document Delivery Service [1-800-HAWORTH, 9:00 a.m. - 5:00 p.m. (EST). E-mail address: getinfo@haworthpressinc.com].

## *INTRODUCTION*

In the late 1960s and early 1970s, a federal, state and local partnership was forged to create community-based alcoholism treatment programs across the United States. During this same period, there was a growing recognition of alcohol problems in the African American community (Larkin, 1965; Bourne, 1973) and documentation of the need for special responses to these problems (Davis, 1974). Harper's (1976) mid-1970 review of the alcoholism literature revealed only 11 of 1,600 indexed articles that dealt specifically with alcohol problems among African Americans. Growing agitation to respond to alcohol and other drug (AOD) problems by activist groups (Tabor, 1970) brought a heightened awareness of these problems within the African American community and set the stage for expanded treatment services. Treatment programs initiated by the anti-poverty and mental health programs of the 1960s were significantly expanded in the 1970s under the sponsorship of NIAAA and NIDA.

The 1980s brought a heightened interest in the history of alcohol and other drug problems in the African American community (Herd, 1983, 1985) and a growing body of literature calling for cultural frameworks for understanding and responding to the treatment of AOD problems (Bell and Evans, 1981), including calls for responses to the special needs of addicted African American women (Corrigan and Anderson, 1982). This period also witnessed the creation of organizations such as the National Black Alcoholism and Addictions Council and the Institute on Black Chemical Abuse.

These positive responses were overshadowed by contextual changes that exerted an enormous impact on the African American community. These changes included:

1. a perceived cocaine "epidemic," signaled most dramatically by the death of basketball star Len Bias in 1986 and the growth of cocaine-related urban violence,
2. a heightened "war on drugs" that called for "zero tolerance" of illicit drug users, and
3. virtual hysteria surrounding the phenomena of "crack babies."

Differential arrest and sentencing practices moved an ever-growing number of African Americans into the criminal justice system. While African Americans make up 15% of illicit drug consumers, they make up 37% of those arrested on drug offenses and 60% of felony drug offenders in state prisons (Human Rights Watch, 2001). These trends apply to African American women as well as men: incarceration rates for African American women increased 828% between 1986 and 1991 (Chavkin, 2001). The racialization of drug policy was further extended to responses to cocaine-exposed infants, the effect of which was to place a large number of African American infants and children in the custody of child protection authorities. This practice was based on a view of the prenatal effects of cocaine that is being increasingly challenged by research studies (Frank, 2001).

Growing concerns about alcohol and illicit drug problems and the consequences of drug policies on African American communities left these communities no recourse but to mount their own responses to AOD problems.

## INDIGENOUS RECOVERY MOVEMENTS

The 1980s and 1990s witnessed attempts to adapt traditional recovery support structures, such as Alcoholics Anonymous and Narcotics Anonymous, for increased cultural relevance, as well as attempts to develop culturally sensitive and competent treatment (Sanders, 1993). There were also a growing number of indigenous addiction recovery movements within African American communities. Five such recovery movements are briefly described below.

### Glide Memorial Methodist Church

Feeling a sense of hopelessness as crack cocaine invaded the poor San Francisco community where his church is located, Pastor Cecil Williams was excited when he received a phone call from William Bennett, the Drug Czar for President Bush's Administration. Bennett invited him to help with the "War on Drugs." Pastor Williams soon concluded that the War on Drugs was a war on Black males and the poor as thousands were imprisoned.

In 1989, Pastor Williams took matters into his own hands. He held a conference in San Francisco to which a network of Black leaders were invited, including medical and criminal justice professionals, addictions specialists, ministers, civil rights leaders, recovering addicts and community members. The purpose of the conference was to collectively come up with solutions to the addiction problem that plagues African Americans and poor people. Pastor Williams then created, as an offshoot of that conference, his own church-based recovery program. He described the program in his book, *No Hiding Place*.

At Glide, 80% of the congregation is working on recovery. The program is culturally based, as Pastor Williams believes that African Americans need a recovery effort that takes their culture into consideration, recognizes their history and socially spirited manner of relating to each other. Most of the members of Glide Church had tried traditional 12-step groups prior to joining Glide and felt isolated, as many were the only African Americans or the only crack addicts in the group.

Pastor Williams goes on to state that at Glide meetings, members are allowed to openly express their feelings of anger and rage. This is significant. In interviews I have conducted with African American male substance abusers regarding their treatment experiences, many stated that they feared being kicked out if they really expressed their anger and rage while in treatment. Expressing pent-up anger and rage is an important part of the recovery process.

The program differs from traditional 12-step groups in that anonymity is not an important part. The co-founders of Alcoholics Anonymous had to build an anonymous program. Most of the original core members of Alcoholics Anonymous had reputations to protect. Most were successful White males, as were co-founders Bill Wilson, a stockbroker, and Dr. Bob, a surgeon. Healing for members of Glide Church involves members empowering themselves by being able to stand up in front of the entire congregation or go out into the community and tell their stories. Members are historically poor and, for the most part, voiceless in the society. Acknowledging powerlessness is not a part of this program. So many members of Glide Church have felt powerless for most of their lives.

Finally, members of Glide Church are taught that their recovery is important to the African American community. This is significant for those who feel stigmatized because of their illness and that they don't matter.

### One Church–One Addict

Founded by the renowned Father George Clements in 1993, the purpose of the project is to recruit churches to help recovering addicts maintain their recovery. To date, over 900 churches in 31 states are involved with the project. At The Million Man March in October of 1995, Father Clements talked about his plans to launch, "One Church–One Inmate." The goal is to recruit faith communities (churches, temples and synagogues) to provide post-release aftercare for men and women leaving prison (Source: Father George Clements Biography).

### Free-N-One

Founded in 1987 by Ronald Simmons in Los Angeles, California, Free-N-One is a Christian-centered recovery program that provides support groups for addicts and their family members. The program has spread to African American churches throughout the country. There are over 50 churches in Illinois alone holding Free-N-One meetings weekly.

### Nation of Islam

The Nation of Islam is perhaps the most successful program in reaching African American male substance abusers in the criminal justice system. They began their efforts in the 1950s and continue their work today. In 1995, the author interviewed ten African American males who were chemically dependent, with criminal pasts and who credited their recoveries to the Nation of Islam. Some attended 12-step group meetings (Narcotics Anonymous) and were members of the Nation of Islam. All had been involved in two or more traditional treatment programs before establishing stable recovery within the Nation of Islam. They were asked what the Nation of Islam did for them that traditional treatment did not. Below are representative responses:

1. *A Sense of Hope.* "Malcolm X seemed to have a worse problem than mine. When I read his story I had hope that I could turn my life around."
2. *Physical Changes.* "I started wearing a suit and bow-tie everyday. This is important, because when I was a hustler, I never dressed up. I started noticing that, as I looked better externally, I started to feel better internally."
3. *Role Models.* "I met many other Black men in the Nation who had been in jail like me, drug addicted and now living productive lives. This gave me something to shoot for."
4. *Ethnic Pride and Dignity.* "Imams (ministers) would talk about the greatness of the Black man. Gradually I began to have more pride as a Black man."
5. *Encouraged to Read.* "The way you keep a slave a slave is to never allow him to read. Reading is freedom for the Black man. In the Nation, we're encouraged to read everything including the Qur'an, the Bible, and books on African American history. Reading changed my life."
6. *Proper Diet.* "For years we have eaten the diet that we were forced to eat in slavery, including the worst part of the hog–chitterlings. We don't eat pork and most of us don't eat a lot of fried foods. It is very liberating to not have to eat the food that our ancestors were forced to eat as slaves."
7. *Help with Employment and Classes on How to Live.* "I started out selling newspapers written by the Nation. They helped me find full-time employment. The classes taught me how to eat to live, how to treat women, and the responsibility of man."
8. *No Labels.* "I had been seeing counselors and psychiatrists since I was eleven years old, including counselors in jail. I always felt labeled by them. When members of the Nation of Islam came into the jails I felt loved" (Sanders, 1995).

The Nation of Islam also works with African American female inmates. Marilyn Muhammad was awarded the 2001 superintendent's volunteer service award for her efforts at Cook County Jail, Chicago. According to Marilyn Muhammad, the National of Islam is playing a very important role in the prison rehabilitation ministry of women. Muhammad teaches classes at Cook County Jail geared toward helping women develop self-esteem and turn their lives around (Muhammad, 2001).

### African American Survivors Organization

Founded by Benneth Lee of Chicago, Illinois, African American Survivors Organization provides recovering African American men a safe place to talk about issues they would be uncomfortable addressing in traditional, mixed-culture recovery support meetings. Lee explains:

> African Americans experience racism; yet this is rarely mentioned in 12-step group meetings. I chose the name African American Survivors Organization realizing that Blacks have been victimized in this society and that some have turned to drugs to deal with the victimization. A survivor is a person who overcomes the victimization.

The format of an African American Survivors meeting begins with a reading entitled, "Who Is a Survivor?" and "What Is an African American Survivors Group Meeting?" This is followed by reading the Seven Principles of Nguza Saba, which are followed during a Kwanzaa celebration, and teach group members some of the principles of African culture. They are unity, self-determination, collective works and responsibility, cooperative economics, purpose, creativity–You have a responsibility to do as much as you can to leave your community more beautiful than how you found it–and faith.

The eleven personal development principles, based on the work of Wade Nobel, are then read. This is followed by group members being allowed to share their life challenges and whatever else is on their minds in a supportive environment. Some talk about relationships, concerns about how to build relationships with their children, how to deal with racism, temptations to get high, and feelings of inferiority when they go for job interviews and see people from other ethnic groups sitting in the waiting room.

The group meetings both support and challenge group members. Principles of African culture are used to help members solve daily problems (Lee, personal communications).

The purpose of the above list was to introduce the reader to the ways in which the African American community has risen up to decrease the devastating impact of alcohol and drugs. This is by no means the complete story of the community's efforts. One could write volumes about the work of Pastor James

T. Meeks of Salem Baptist Church, Chicago, Illinois, who, in addition to having a drug ministry at the church, led a referendum prohibiting the sale of alcohol in parts of the Roseland Community, where his church is located. His community organizing efforts led to the closing of a liquor store in his community, which was later transformed into the largest religious bookstore in Chicago. He regularly organizes the men of his church to help addicts on the street within the community.

Every major church denomination within the African American community is involved in helping addicts. There are current efforts to work inter-denominationally. This is significant in that many African Americans begin their recovery efforts in traditional 12-step programs and combine this with church-related assistance.

## IMPLICATIONS FOR ADDICTION TREATMENT PROVIDERS

The professional community has an unprecedented opportunity to forge partnerships with indigenous recovery movements within the African American community. Such partnerships begin with becoming students of these movements. Treatment providers must move into the life of African American communities and build relationships with the indigenous healers and indigenous institutions. Treatment providers can learn from the therapeutic functions these movements meet in the lives of their members, whether it is the empowerment provided by Glide Church (an important function for a historically disenfranchised people), the self-esteem infused in members of the Nation of Islam, the ways in which One Church–One Addict provides long-term recovery supports, or the way in which African American Survivors Organization teaches how to address racism in the context of recovery. All of these indigenous movements contain lessons that can enhance the power of our service work with African American clients and families.

In the future, treatment programs serving African American clients will pioneer joint service delivery models with these indigenous movements and will use these movements as part of the menu of recovery support services. The African American community is not an homogenous community and no single recovery support structure can meet the needs of all its members who need such a structure. The task of the treatment provider is thus to enter into relationships with the African American community to expand this menu of recovery support services. The time for such partnerships is long overdue.

## REFERENCES

Bell, P. & Evans, J. (1981). *Counseling the Black Client: Alcohol Use and Abuse in Black America*. Minnesota: Hazelden Foundation.

Bourne, P. (1973). Alcoholism in the urban Negro populations. In: Bourne, P. & Fox, R. (Eds), *Alcoholism: Progress in Research and Treatment*. NY: Academic Press.

Chavkin MD, MPH, W. (2001). Cocaine and pregnancy. *JAMA, 285* (28): 12.

Corrigan, E. & Anderson, S. (1982). Black alcoholic women in treatment. *Journal of Addictions and Health, 3:* 49-58.

Frank, D.A., Augustyn, M., Knight, W.G. et al. (2001). Growth, development and behavior in early childhood following prenatal cocaine exposure: A systematic review. *JAMA, 285:* 1613-1625.

Harper, F. (1976). *Alcohol and Blacks: An Overview.* Alexandria, VA: Douglas Publishers.

Harper, F. (1979). *Alcoholism Treatment and Black Americans.* Rockville, MD: National Institute on Alcohol Abuse & Alcoholism.

Herd, D. (1983). Prohibition, racism and class politics in the post-reconstruction south. *Journal of Drug Issues, 13:* 77-94.

Herd, D. (1985). We cannot stagger to freedom: A history of blacks and alcohol in American politics. In Brill, L. & Winick, C. *The Yearbook of Substance Use and Abuse: V. III.* NY: Human Sciences Press, Inc.

James, W. & Johnson, S. (1996). *Doin' Drugs.* Texas: University of Texas Press.

Levinthal, C. (1999). *Drugs, Behavior, and Modern Society.* Needham Heights, MA: Allyn and Bacon.

Muhammad, D. *Prison Report: Paving the Way Out For Sisters in Prison, The Final Call.* Online: www.finalcall.com/index08.28.2001.htm

Robinson, R. (2002). *The Reckoning.* New York: Dutton.

Sanders, M. (1993). *Treating the African American Male Substance Abuser.* Chicago, IL: Winds of Change.

Tabor, M. (1970). *Capitalism Plus Dope Equals Genocide.* Black Panther Party, U.S.A.

Williams, C. (1992). *No Hiding Place.* San Francisco: Harper.

# Participation in Alcoholics Anonymous Among African-Americans

J. B. Kingree, PhD
Bryce F. Sullivan, PhD

**SUMMARY.** This paper examines the appropriateness of Alcoholics Anonymous as a resource for African-Americans with alcohol problems. The paper discusses features of the organization that may hold special appeal for African-Americans and reviews studies that have compared rates of AA involvement between African-Americans and Caucasians. Some conclusions are drawn from this research and suggestions for future research are made. *[Article copies available for a fee from The Haworth Document Delivery Service: 1-800-HAWORTH. E-mail address: <getinfo@haworthpressinc.com> Website: <http://www.HaworthPress.com> © 2002 by The Haworth Press, Inc. All rights reserved.]*

**KEYWORDS.** Alcoholics Anonymous, African-American, participation

J. B. (Kip) Kingree is Associate Professor, Department of Public Health Sciences, Clemson University. He holds a PhD in community psychology from Georgia State University. In addition to participation in Alcoholics Anonymous, his recent research has focused on marijuana use and risky sexual behavior among adolescent detainees.

Bryce F. Sullivan is Associate Professor and Chairperson, Department of Psychology, University of Southern Illinois, Edwardsville. He holds a PhD in clinical psychology from Ohio State University. In addition to issues related to the treatment of alcoholism, his research has focused on human aggression and couple relations.

Address correspondence to: J. B. Kingree, PhD, Department of Public Health Sciences, 517 Edwards Hall, Clemson University, Clemson, SC 29634.

[Haworth co-indexing entry note]: "Participation in Alcoholics Anonymous Among African-Americans." Kingree, J. B., and Bryce F. Sullivan. Co-published simultaneously in *Alcoholism Treatment Quarterly* (The Haworth Press, Inc.) Vol. 20, No. 3/4, 2002. pp. 175-186; and: *Alcohol Problems in the United States: Twenty Years of Treatment Perspective* (ed: Thomas F. McGovern, and William L. White) The Haworth Press, Inc., 2002, pp. 175-186. Single or multiple copies of this article are available for a fee from The Haworth Document Delivery Service [1-800-HAWORTH. 9:00 a.m. - 5:00 p.m. (EST). E-mail address: getinfo@haworthpressinc.com].

Alcoholics Anonymous (AA) is an international organization that assists problem drinkers to abstain from alcohol through a spiritually-oriented, 12-step approach. This approach is largely promulgated through mutual help group meetings that are sponsored by local chapters. The meetings are conducted according to a common set of guidelines published by the organization. The guidelines and one or more prayers are recited by participants at the outset and/or close of the meetings.

AA is a democratic and decentralized organization (Room, 1993). Each chapter is essentially autonomous and does not have any designated leaders. The mutual help group meetings are led by participants on a rotating basis and are typically conducted in one of two formats. In the "speaker format," participants give lengthy talks describing their experiences with alcohol, events surrounding their decisions to change, and what their lives have been like since they quit drinking. In the "discussion format," participants share their experiences and beliefs about a particular issue that is relevant to problem drinkers (Alcoholics Anonymous, 1976).

Since its inception in 1935, AA has exerted a tremendous influence on the treatment practices for alcohol and other drug problems in the United States. AA meetings are the most widely used form of alcohol treatment in the country (Hasin, 1994). The 12-step approach, including the emphasis on maintaining abstinence through participation in mutual help group meetings, serves as a model for organizations like Narcotics Anonymous (NA) and Cocaine Anonymous (CA) that assist persons with illicit drug problems. The emphasis on abstinence is widely accepted by the general public and substance abuse treatment personnel as the appropriate prescription for alcohol and other drug addictions (Humphreys, Greenbaum, Noke, & Finney, 1996; Leavy, 1991).

A rapidly growing research literature is emerging on AA. Much of this literature has addressed two questions: (a) Is AA effective? (b) Does participation in AA vary in relation to specific individual difference variables. In regard to the first question, there is substantial evidence that participation in AA is associated with a reduction in alcohol problems (Emrick, Tonigan, Montgomery, & Little, 1993; Tonigan, Toscova, & Miller, 1996). Unfortunately, this evidence is almost exclusively correlational and thus firm conclusions about the effectiveness of AA cannot be made. The absence of rigorous, experimental evaluations addressing this question can be attributed to various features of AA meetings that pose significant impediments for conducting experimental investigations of their effectiveness (Kingree & Ruback, 1994; Ogbourne, 1993).

In relation to the second question, many studies have examined individual difference variables as predictors of AA attendance. One influential book chapter (Emrick et al., 1993) examined 62 of these variables. Half of these variables had been examined in multiple studies and the other half had been examined only in single studies. Among the variables examined across multiple studies, only alcohol severity was consistently associated with AA attendance.

The authors reported that their conclusions were limited by variation in how AA meeting attendance had been operationalized across the studies they reviewed. Early studies on this topic usually specified attendance at AA meetings as the criterion. Some researchers assessed lifetime attendance whereas others assessed attendance over a defined period of time. Variation also existed in whether attendance measures were coded dichotomously or continuously. Given this situation it has been difficult if not impossible to discern if variation in the measurement of AA attendance was responsible for disparate findings across multiple studies.

Surprisingly, race was one of the individual difference variables examined in only one study. This study found that African-Americans and Caucasians did not differ significantly in recent attendance at AA meetings (Thurstein, Alfano, & Scherer, 1986). The inclusion of only one study that had examined race is surprising given the salience of race as a social issue as well as prior publications that have commented on the appropriateness of AA for African-Americans and other minority groups (Caldwell, 1983; Denzin, 1987; Harper, 1976; Hudson, 1985). However, it is less surprising when considering that African-Americans have been generally underrepresented in alcohol research (Caetano, Clark, & Tam, 1998).

The remainder of this article focuses on AA participation among African-Americans. We first discuss why AA is appropriate for this population by considering the nature of alcohol problems among African-Americans as well as features of AA meetings that they should find appealing. We then review recent studies that have compared African-Americans and Caucasians on different measures of AA involvement. Our review allows for some preliminary conclusions about the research findings as well as suggestions for future research on this topic.

## THE NEED FOR AA INVOLVEMENT AMONG AFRICAN-AMERICANS

Surveys that ask respondents about their recent alcohol use may suggest that African-Americans have less need to participate in AA than do Caucasians. For example, the most recent National Household Survey on Drug Abuse (Substance Abuse and Mental Health Services, 2001a) indicated that alcohol use during the preceding month was substantially lower for African-Americans (33.7%) than for Caucasians (50.7%). However, among persons who drink alcohol, African-Americans have higher levels of consumption and consumption-related problems than do Caucasians (Caetano & Kaskutas, 1995; Herd, 1994), including more alcohol-related medical problems and alcohol-related causes of death (Stinson, Dufour, Steffens, & DeBakey, 1993). Moreover, among persons who develop alcohol dependence, African-Americans show lower rates of remission than do Caucasians (National Longitudinal Alcohol Epidemiologic Survey, 1992). All of these factors contribute to relatively high levels of substance abuse treatment in public facilities for this population. In 1999, African-Americans comprised approximately 12 percent of the population in the United States but 23 percent of its admissions to publicly funded, substance abuse treatment centers. Among the African-Americans admitted to these treatment centers, alcohol abuse was the most common drug problem for males (35%) and the second leading problem for females (27%) (Substance Abuse and Mental Health Services, 2001b).

The drinking patterns and problems of African-Americans probably result from some interrelationship of individual attributes, environmental characteristics, historical experiences, and cultural factors (Caetano et al., 1998). Poverty, unemployment, and racial discrimination may also play a role (Mosely, Atkins, & Klein, 1988). Furthermore, alcohol problems in this population are perpetuated or exacerbated by inadequate access to health insurance and health care. Twenty-three percent of African-Americans in the United States are uninsured, which is one and a half times the rate for Caucasians. African-Americans are more likely than Caucasians to report an unmet need for alcohol treatment (Wells, Klap, Koike, & Sherbourne, 2001).

Significant structural changes in the governmental, economic and health care systems are necessary to establish equal access to the formal alcohol treatment system. Until such structural changes occur, the informal alcohol treatment system may bear the burden for serving African-Americans and other disadvantaged minority populations (Humphreys & Moos, 2001). AA meetings are the centerpiece of the informal treatment system. These meetings are widely available across the country, are open to anyone with a desire to stop drinking (Alcoholics Anonymous, 1976), and can be attended without cost to the participant. Whereas these features should appeal to all persons, the inherently social and spiritual nature of AA meetings may hold special appeal to African-Americans. African-Americans reportedly value social relations (Martin & Martin, 1995) and spirituality (Pargament, Poloma, & Tarakeshwar, 2001) more than do Caucasians. The social nature of the meetings is reflected in the considerable verbal and social exchange that occurs between participants. The spiritual nature is evident in the recitation of prayers and/or other AA literature with references to God (e.g., the 12 steps) at the beginning and end of individual meetings.

## AFRICAN-AMERICANS AND RESEARCH ON ATTENDANCE IN AA OR OTHER 12-STEP GROUP MEETINGS

Although not included in the Emrick et al. (1993) review cited above, some of the strongest data on AA involvement among African-Americans were generated through three community-based, national surveys conducted in 1979, 1984, and 1990 by the Alcohol Research Group in Berkeley, California (Caetano, 1993). Over 2,000 African-Americans and 4,500 Caucasians participated in one of the three surveys. Among respondents who had experienced an alcohol problem, the rate of prior participation in at least one AA meeting was identical (5%) for African-Americans and Caucasians. Additionally, African-Americans and Caucasians experienced similar increases in rates of AA participation between the first survey in 1979 and the third conducted in 1990.

In the national survey conducted in 1984, Caetano (1993) also examined the related issue of whether other individual difference variables predicted AA utilization for African-Americans and Caucasians. Analyses focused on four individual difference variables:

a. level of alcohol consumption;
b. education;
c. gender; and
d. marital status.

Heavier drinking was associated with more utilization for African-Americans but not Caucasians. Education was positively associated with utilization among Caucasians but not African-Americans. Gender and marital status were not associated with AA utilization for either ethnic group.

A more recently published study from the Alcohol Research Group reported on prior AA attendance among 253 African-Americans and 538 Caucasians who were admitted to treatment programs in Northern California (Kaskutas, Weisner, Lee, & Humphreys, 1999). Lifetime exposure to AA was very high but did not vary significantly between African-Americans (86%) and Caucasians (80%).

Other recent data on AA utilization among African-Americans is available from Project MATCH, a large multisite study funded by the National Institute on Alcohol Abuse and Alcoholism. Project MATCH evaluated three different types of psychosocial therapies:

1. cognitive behavioral therapy;
2. motivational enhancement therapy; and
3. 12-step facilitation therapy.

These therapies were evaluated in both aftercare and outpatient samples. Although attendance at in AA meetings was explicitly recommended by the 12-step facilitation therapy only, follow-up assessments indicated that over 70% of the Project MATCH participants attended at least one AA meeting over a 12-month posttreatment period (Tonigan, Conners, & Miller, 1998). The proportions of African-Americans and Caucasians who participated in AA during the follow-up did not differ in the outpatient samples. In the aftercare sample, AA participation during the follow-up was slightly less for African-Americans than for Caucasians.

Keith Humphreys (Humphreys, Mavis, & Stofflemayer, 1991; Humphreys & Woods, 1994) has published two studies that compared African-American and Caucasian substance abusers on posttreatment measures that reflected attendance in both AA and NA meetings. Use of criterion measures that tapped participation in AA and/or NA was reasonable for this line of work for the following reasons:

a. the majority of participants in many substance abuse treatment programs use both alcohol and illicit drugs;
b. many participants in substance abuse treatment programs attend both AA and NA meetings (Humphreys et al., 1991; Kaskutas et al., 1999; Kingree, 2001); and
c. AA and NA meetings are conducted similarly and based on the same 12-step model.

Respondents in both studies were recruited from outpatient and residential treatment programs in Michigan. One of the studies used a six-month follow-up assessment to compare 201 African-Americans and 89 Caucasians on whether they had attended at least one 12-step group meeting during the posttreatment period. Results from this study revealed a higher rate of attendance for African-Americans (65.3%) than Caucasians (54.7%). The second study used a 12-month follow-up assessment to compare 233 African-Americans and 267 Caucasians on whether or not they had attended a 12-step group meeting in the month preceding the assessment. Results from the second study revealed no significant differences in recent attendance between African-Americans (33.9%) and Caucasians (31.8%).

Humphreys and Woods (1994) also examined whether specific individual difference variables predicted 12-step group attendance at the 12 month assessment for each one of the two racial groups. Analyses focused on nine predictor variables. Three of these predictor variables (i.e., substance abuse severity, family/social problems, psychological problems) were related to the respondents' clinical issues or needs. Three other predictor variables (i.e., enrollment in an inpatient or outpatient program, length of the program, extent to which program staff endorsed AA principles) were related to the treatment that respondents received. The final three predictor variables (i.e., legal problems, whether respondents were pressured to enter treatment by a judge or lawyer, whether the program was located in Detroit vs. central or western Michigan) were ecological in nature.

For Caucasians, all of the predictor variables except two (i.e., psychological problems, family/social problems) were prospectively associated with 12-step group attendance. Caucasians who reported recent 12-step group attendance at follow-up had less substance abuse severity and fewer legal problems at treatment intake. They were more likely to have been treated in a program that was residential, long in duration, located in central or western Michigan, and staffed by persons who weakly endorsed AA principles. In contrast, only three of the nine variables were prospectively associated with 12-step group attendance among African-Americans. Those who reported recent attendance at the 12-month follow-up assessment had more psychological problems at intake and were more likely to have been treated in programs that were long in duration and located in Detroit.

### AFRICAN-AMERICANS AND RESEARCH ON MULTIPLE INDICATORS OF AA OR OTHER 12-STEP GROUP INVOLVEMENT

Several researchers have recently argued that attendance measures may not provide the best indication of the extent of an individual's involvement in AA (Humphreys, Kaskutas, & Weisner, 1998; Kingree, 1997; Morgenstern, Kahler, Frey, & Labouvie, 1996; Tonigan, Connors, & Miller, 1996). These researchers assert that composite measures of involvement should be used to tap not only attendance at meetings but also perceptions and other behaviors that come with affiliating with AA. Such perceptions include self-identification as an alcoholic or AA member as well as acceptance of the disease concept of alcoholism. Behaviors other than mere attendance that occur though affiliating with AA include chairing meetings, sharing in meetings, working the 12 steps, reading AA literature, using a sponsor, sponsoring other AA members, performing service work for AA, and having a primary AA (home) group. By tapping multiple domains of involvement, composite measures are believed to provide more reliability and validity than single-item attendance measures.

At least three published studies have compared African-Americans and Caucasians on composite measures of AA involvement. In addition to examining racial differences on single-item measures of meeting attendance, the recently published study of the Alcohol Research Group that was cited above compared African-Americans and Caucasians on a composite measure of 9 indicators (Kaskutas et al., 1999). Consistent with the analysis of prior meeting attendance, this study found no overall difference between the two racial groups on the composite measure.

The 9-item composite measure used by Kaskutas et al. (1999) was employed in a second study that compared responses of six racial or ethnic groups (Humphreys et al., 1998). This study was notable for its inclusion of large, treatment ($n = 927$) and community-based ($n = 674$) samples. Inferential statistical values from omnibus tests indicated that there was variation in overall levels of AA involvement in the treatment sample but not in the community sample. Although the authors did not present results of posthoc tests comparing specific racial/ethnic groups, an examination of mean scores on the composite indicated that African-Americans had higher levels of AA affiliation than did Caucasians.

A smaller study compared 80 African-American and 23 Caucasians enrolled in a residential treatment program on a composite measure of six indicators (Kingree, 1997). Most of the participants in this study were polysubstance abusers who had attended AA as well as NA and CA meetings. Therefore, the composite used in this study asked respondents about involvement in 12-step groups generally (AA, NA, CA) rather than AA exclusively. The composite included six indicators. Three indicators asked about perceptions associated with involvement:

a. subjective commitment to 12-step groups;
b. perceived comfort in sharing in 12-step group meetings; and
c. acceptance of the 12-step ideology.

The other three indicators tapped behaviors associated with involvement:

a. meeting attendance;
b. use of a sponsor; and
c. work on the 12-steps.

Single-item measures were used for all of the indicators except acceptance of the 12-step ideology, which used a 17-item measure. Comparisons between African-American and Caucasians were made when these persons were at the midpoint of their stay in the RTP. Consistent with the treatment sample in the Humphreys et al. study (1998), African-Americans reported a higher level of AA affiliation on the composite measure than did Caucasians.

## CONCLUSIONS

This article has considered whether AA is an appropriate resource for African-Americans. We have addressed this question by focusing upon the nature of alcohol problems among African-Americans, the format and characteristics of AA meetings, and prior research that has compared rates of AA participation between African-Americans and Caucasians.

AA appears to be appropriate for African-Americans when one considers the nature of AA meetings and alcohol problems in this population. Participation in AA meetings is open and free to all persons who desire to stop drinking regardless of their race or any personal characteristic. Because a relatively large proportion of African-Americans with alcohol problems lack health insurance, these persons should be inclined to make use of a therapeutic resource like AA that appears to be effective but does not require payments from recipients. Moreover, African-Americans should be comfortable with the way that AA meetings are conducted, particularly in relation to the emphases placed on spirituality and sharing with others.

We reviewed six studies that compared African-Americans and Caucasians on measures of AA or other 12-step group attendance. These studies included seven analyses, with six involving treatment samples and one involving a community sample. One of the studies made comparisons across both inpatient and outpatient treatment samples (Tonigan et al., 1996). Two of the analyses showed a higher level of attendance among African-Americans, one showed higher attendance among Caucasians, and four showed no differences in attendance between the two racial groups. Although the discrepant findings may be attributable to methodological variations between the studies, it appears that African-Americans and Caucasians do not show dramatic differences in AA meeting attendance.

In addition, we reviewed three studies that compared African-Americans and Caucasians on composite measures of AA involvement. These three studies included four analyses, with one of the studies making the comparison for both treatment and community samples (Humphreys et al., 1998). Two of the four analyses revealed a higher level of AA or 12-step group involvement for African-Americans than for Caucasians; the other two analyses found no overall difference between the racial groups.

More research is clearly needed before strong conclusions can be drawn about whether African-Americans and Caucasians differ in AA involvement. Since most of the studies involved treatment samples, additional studies with community-based samples are needed. These samples should be sufficiently large to allow for comparisons between specific subgroups (e.g., teenagers, incarcerated populations) of African-Americans and Caucasians with alcohol problems.

The absence of uniform findings on this topic may be due to differences in the respondents who were sampled as well as differences in the measures used for assessing attendance or involvement. Differences in findings may also stem from inadequate attention to within-group variations among African-Americans and Caucasians with alcohol problems. Future research should rely on multivariate frameworks to examine factors that may moderate the association between race and AA involvement. Potential moderators of this association include age, gender, personality characteristics, and the nature of an individual's alcohol or other drug problem(s).

Research is also needed to determine whether involvement in AA is a qualitatively different experience than involvement in other 12-step groups like NA and CA. Initially, this research could assess whether individuals perceive these groups differently. As pointed out above, many persons who seek treatment for alcohol problems also have problems with illicit drugs. These persons may participate in and benefit from more than one type of 12-step group. If substance abusers perceive these groups as similar, then it may be logical to use composite measures that reflect involvement in different types of 12-step organizations. Otherwise, relying on measures that tap AA involvement exclusively may not adequately reflect the extent to which an individual is involved in, and benefiting from, 12-step groups generally.

## REFERENCES

Alcoholics Anonymous. (1976). *Alcoholics Anonymous: The story of how many thousands of men and women have recovered from alcoholism (3rd edition)*. New York: Alcoholics Anonymous Services.

Caetano, R. (1993). Ethnic minority groups and Alcoholics Anonymous: A review. In B. McCrady & W. Miller (eds.), *Research on Alcoholics Anonymous: Opportunities and alternatives* (pp. 209-232). New Brunswick, NJ: Rutgers University Publications.

Caetano, R., Clark, C., & Tam, T. (1998). Alcohol consumption among racial/ethnic minorities. *Alcohol Health & Research World, 22,* 233-238.

Caetano, R., & Kaskutas, L. (1995). Changes in drinking patterns among whites, blacks, and Hispanics, 1984-1992. *Journal of Studies on Alcohol, 56,* 558-565.

Caldwell, F. (1983). Alcoholics Anonymous as a viable treatment source for black alcoholics. In T. Watts & R. Wright, Jr. (eds.), *Black alcoholism: Toward a comprehensive understanding* (pp. 85-99). Springfield, IL: Charles Thomas.

Denzin, N. (1987). *The recovering alcoholic*. Newbury Park, CA: Sage Publications.

Emrick, C., Tonigan, J., Montgomery, H., & Little, L. (1993). Alcoholics Anonymous: What is currently known? In B. McCrady & W. Miller (eds.), *Research on Alcoholics Anonymous: Opportunities and alternatives* (pp. 41-78). New Brunswick, NJ: Rutgers University Publications.

Harper, F. (1976). *Alcohol abuse and Black America*. Alexandria, VA: Douglass Publishers.

Hasin, D. (1994). Treatment/self-help for alcohol-related problems: Relationship to social pressure and alcohol dependence. *Journal of Studies on Alcohol, 55,* 660-666.

Herd, D. (1994). Predicting drinking problems among black and white men: Results from a national survey. *Journal of Studies on Alcohol, 55*, 61-71.

Hudson, H. (1985). How and why Alcoholics Anonymous works for blacks. *Alcoholism Treatment Quarterly, 2*, 11-30.

Humphreys, K., Greenbaum, M., Noke, J., & Finney, J. (1996). Reliability, validity, and normative data for a short version of the Understanding of Alcoholism Scale. *Psychology of Addictive Behaviors, 10*, 38-44.

Humphreys, K., Kaskutas, L., & Weisner, C. (1998). The Alcoholics Anonymous Affiliation Scale: Development, reliability, and norms for diverse treated and untreated populations. *Alcoholism: Clinical and Experimental Research, 22*, 974-978.

Humphreys, K., Mavis, B., & Stofflemayer, B. (1991). Factors predicting attendance at self-help groups after substance abuse treatment. *Journal of Consulting and Clinical Psychology, 59*, 591-593.

Humphreys, K. & Moos, R. (2001). Can encouraging substance abuse patients to participate in self-help groups reduce demand for health care? A quasi-experimental study. *Alcoholism: Clinical and Experimental Research, 25*, 711-716.

Humphreys, K. & Woods, M. (1994). Researching mutual help group participation in a segregated society. In T. Powell (ed.), *Understanding the self-help organization: Frameworks and findings* (pp. 62-87). Thousand Oaks, CA: Sage Publications.

Kaskutas, L., Weisner, C., Lee, M., & Humphreys, K. (1999). Alcoholics Anonymous affiliation at treatment intake among White and Black Americans. *Journal of Studies on Alcohol, 60*, 810-816.

Kingree, J. (1997). Measuring affiliation with 12-step groups. *Substance Use and Misuse, 31*, 181-194.

Kingree, J. (2001). Predictors of 12-step group preference among low-income persons with alcohol problems. *Alcoholism Treatment Quarterly, 19*, 57-66.

Kingree, J. & Ruback, R. (1994). Understanding self-help groups. In T. Powell (ed.), *Understanding the self-help organization: Frameworks and findings* (pp. 272-292). Thousand Oaks, CA: Sage Publications.

Leavy, R. (1991). Alcoholism counselors' perceptions of problem drinking. *Alcoholism Treatment Quarterly, 8*, 47-55.

Martin, E. & Martin, J. (1995). *The helping tradition in the black family and community*. Washington, DC: National Association of Social Worker Press.

Morgenstern, J., Kahler, C., Frey, R., & Labouvie, E. (1997). Modeling therapeutic response to 12-step treatment: Optimal responders, nonresponders, and partial responders. *Journal of Substance Abuse, 8*, 45-59.

Mosley, B., Atkins, B. J., & Klein, M. (1988). Alcoholism and blacks. *Journal of Alcohol & Drug Education, 33*(2), 51-58.

Ogbourne, A. (1993). Assessing the effectiveness of Alcoholics Anonymous in the community: Meeting the challenges. In B. McCrady & W. Miller (eds.), *Research on Alcoholics Anonymous: Opportunities and alternatives (pp. 339-356)*. New Brunswick, NJ: Rutgers University Publications.

Pargament, K., Poloma, M., & Tarakeshwar, N. (2001). Methods of coping from the religions of the world. The bar mitzvah, karma, and spiritual healing. In C. Snyder (ed.), *Coping with stress: Effective people and processes* (pp. 259-284). New York: Oxford University Press.

Room, R. (1993). Alcoholics Anonymous as a social movement. In B. McCrady & W. Miller (eds.), *Research on Alcoholics Anonymous: Opportunities and alternatives* (pp. 167-188). New Brunswick, NJ: Rutgers University Publications.

Stinson, F. S., Dufour, M. C., Steffens, R. A., & DeBakey, S. F. (1993). Alcohol-related mortality in the United States, 1979-1989. *Alcohol Health & Research World, 17*, 251-260.

Substance Abuse and Mental Health Services. (2001a). *Summary of Findings from the 2000 National Household Survey on Drug Abuse.* Office of Applied Studies, NHSDA Series H-13, DHHS Publication No. (SMA) 01-3549. Rockville, MD.

Substance Abuse and Mental Health Services. (2001b). *Treatment Episode Data (TEDS): 1994-1999. National Admissions to Substance Abuse Treatment Services.* Office of Applied Studies, DASIS Series: S-14, DHHS Publication No. (SMA) 01-3550, Rockville, MD.

Thurstein, A., Alfano, A., & Sherer, M. (1986). Pretreatment MMPI profiles of AA members and nonmembers. *Journal of Studies on Alcohol, 47*, 468-471.

Tonigan, J., Connors, G., & Miller, W. (1996). Alcoholics Anonymous Involvement Scale: Reliability and norms. *Alcohol, Health, and Research World, 22*, 281-285.

Tonigan, J., Connors, G., & Miller, W. (1998). Special populations in Alcoholics Anonymous. *Alcohol, Health, & Research World, 22*, 281-285.

Tonigan, J., Toscova, R., & Miller, W. (1996). Meta-analysis of the literature on Alcoholics Anonymous: Sample and study characteristics moderate findings. *Journal of Studies on Alcohol, 57*, 65-72.

Wells, K., Klap, R., Koike, A., & Sherbourne, C. (2001). Ethnic disparities in unmet need for alcoholism, drug abuse, and mental health care. *American Journal of Psychiatry, 158*, 2027-2032.

# Latinos and Alcohol:
# Treatment Considerations

Melvin Delgado, PhD

**SUMMARY.** The history of Latino-specific alcohol services is one that can best be measured in one or one-and-one-half decades. Although the Latino community has been severely affected by alcohol use and abuse, services have been slow to recognize the unique cultural needs of Latinos. The past decade, however, has witnessed a dramatic shift in this thinking and the future holds much promise for the field. *[Article copies available for a fee from The Haworth Document Delivery Service: 1-800-HAWORTH. E-mail address: <getinfo@haworthpressinc.com> Website: <http://www.HaworthPress.com> © 2002 by The Haworth Press, Inc. All rights reserved.]*

**KEYWORDS.** Latinos, programs, culture, diversity

## INTRODUCTION

The field of alcohol as it relates to communities of color has historically not received the attention that other drugs, particularly cocaine (crack) and heroin, have received. As a result, research and programming of services have suffered. Advocates of the attention given to other drugs would argue that the con-

Melvin Delgado is Professor of Social Work and Chair of Macro-Practice, Boston University School of Social Work, 266 Bay State Road, Boston, MA 02215 (E-mail: delgado@bu.edu).

[Haworth co-indexing entry note]: "Latinos and Alcohol: Treatment Considerations." Delgado, Melvin. Co-published simultaneously in *Alcoholism Treatment Quarterly* (The Haworth Press, Inc.) Vol. 20, No. 3/4, 2002, pp. 187-192; and: *Alcohol Problems in the United States: Twenty Years of Treatment Perspective* (ed: Thomas F. McGovern, and William L. White) The Haworth Press, Inc., 2002, pp. 187-192. Single or multiple copies of this article are available for a fee from The Haworth Document Delivery Service [1-800-HAWORTH, 9:00 a.m. - 5:00 p.m. (EST). E-mail address: getinfo@haworthpressinc.com].

sequences of their use and abuse have devastated families and communities, and are therefore worthy of increased attention. The crack epidemic of the 1980s has largely been credited for the increased use of the criminal justice system as the primary means of addressing substance abuse in communities of color. The crime associated with this epidemic received nationwide attention and this translated into "get tough" on crime policies.

However, alcohol as a drug is more widely available, used, and abused than any other drug within the Latino community, currently and historically. The role of sugar cane in Latino countries, for example, has played an influential role in making alcohol both available and profitable. This easy access has made the problem use and abuse much more endemic within Latino communities and much more arduous to identify and address. The "secondary status" of alcohol as a drug within this society has translated into less funding and less attention from the media, policy makers, researchers, and scholars. However, the past two decades have witnessed the emergence of a greater understanding of the deleterious impact of alcohol in the lives of people of color, and the Latino community has benefited from increased attention.

The past two decades, in addition, have also witnessed a tremendous upsurge in research and programming specifically focused at the Latino community across the United States, and has served as a foundation for dramatic advances in the early part of the twenty-first century. The days when there were no alcohol programs targeting Latinos seem like a distant memory for many who have worked in this field since the 1960s and 1970s. This is not to say that these programs are culture-specific to the extent that be, however.

Demographic trends and profiles have played a critical role in bringing national attention to the needs of Latino communities, urban as well as rural. Sizable Latino communities can be found in all fifty states and in numerous cities within these states. The continued dramatic demographic trends regarding the Latino community have translated into socio-economic-political changes, and have fueled the need for research and program models that take into account Latino culture (Delgado, 1998).

## *DEMOGRAPHIC TRENDS/PROFILE*

The Latino community first received increased national recognition in the 1980s when the entire decade was labeled "The Decade of Hispanics." Although this label was primarily fueled by the advertising industry, it nevertheless marked the awareness of how this ethnic group would help shape this country in the coming decades. The Latino community has continued to increase numerically since that proclamation with projections that it will be the largest ethnic group in this country by the year 2050. Between 1995 and 2025 the U.S. population is projected to increase by 34 percent. However, the Latino community will increase by 161 percent and are expected to number 36 million.

The Latino community historically consisted primarily of three groups–Mexicans, Puerto Ricans and Cubans. However, the past two decades have shown how the composition of the Latino community in the United States has become more diverse. It is not unusual to see communities that were historically Mexican now have a combination of groups from Central and South America having replaced Mexicans. In New York City, for example, Puerto Ricans were the largest Latino group. However, if current trends continue, Dominicans will be the largest Latino group. In Boston, Mexicans are the Latino group experiencing the greatest increase in numerical representation.

## IMPACT OF ALCOHOL ON THE LATINO COMMUNITY

The consequences of alcohol use and abuse on Latinos are quite evident (De La Rosa, 1998). In a 1997 study by the University of California, Berkeley's Prevention Center, found that Latino communities are very often targeted for alcohol ads and that these communities have higher rates of crime against women; alcohol is considered to be one of the strongest predictors of crime among Latinos; approximately 60 percent of all homicides and 75 percent of all rapes among Latinos involved alcohol; chronic liver diseases and cirrhosis are among the six leading causes of death in the Latino community (Hall, 1997).

## KEY SOCIOCULTURAL FACTORS

Organizations wishing to serve the Latino community can take any one of four possible approaches towards culture: (1) They can completely ignore it in all facets of service delivery. Unfortunately, this is the prevailing approach in many organizations across the United States. This can translate, for example, into intake procedures and forms that simply treat everyone who comes through the door the same. No effort is made to individualize the intake by expanding on the category of family composition (nuclear versus extended), religion (if asked, it is relegated to a box), or other important cultural factors. (2) Systematically undermining cultural values that have played critical roles in helping Latinos cope in their homeland. Efforts for Latinos to use Spanish in counseling may be discouraged, or in the case of Latinas, having their children with them in residential care where appropriate. (3) Modification of existing services to take into account the cultural heritage of Latinos. Intake forms will elicit information pertaining to religious beliefs and use the definition of family provided by the client. These two steps may appear innocuous. However, they reflect a high level of organizational sensitivity to culture. (4) Establishment of collaborative partnership with Latino indigenous (nontraditional settings) such as Pentecostal churches, beauty parlors, grocery stores, etc., as a means of developing bridges between programs and the community (Delgado, 1999).

Accessibility to alcohol-related services for Latinos in the United States requires that organizations address four key arenas:

1. geographical;
2. psychological;
3. cultural; and
4. operational.

Geographical accessibility usually refers to services being located within easy commutating distance for the person seeking services and their family and other social network. Locating services within public transportation system linkages is one way of facilitating geographical accessibility. Locating services within the Latino community, too, offers tremendous advantages, although fear of stigma is always present in those circumstances.

Psychological accessibility refers to the comfort level that Latinos experience in seeking services from an institution. This comfort level translates into a belief that they are welcomed and valued as people. Fear of discrimination, stigma, and retribution are very real in the lives of Latinos. Cultural accessibility, in turn, allows Latinos to be "themselves" through the use of the language of preference, cultural traditions, staffing with people of similar ethnic/cultural heritage as the consumer, and a profound understanding of cultural values and beliefs. Finally, operational accessibility refers to the days and hours of operation, and procedures employed throughout all facets of programming from intake through follow-up. It is not possible to have any three of these accessibilities, for example, and still be successful. All four types of accessibility are essential in effectively serving Latinos.

The days when alcohol-related programs, research, and scholarship could just get by labeling their activity "Latino" are long gone. These efforts, although well-intentioned, did a disservice to Latinos and the community. An in-depth understanding of the role of alcohol on the lives of Latinos necessitates placing this drug within a sociocultural context. The following five key sociocultural factors must be taken into account in any service delivery system:

1. *Documented/Undocumented Status:* The documented status of Latinos wield a tremendous amount of influence in dictating the help-seeking patterns they can safely exercise in this country. If they are citizens or

possess the requisite immigration status, then they can have free and safe access to care. However, being undocumented means that they must fear being deported back to their country and this will prevent them from getting services.

2. *Gender:* The last twenty years have taught us that gender cannot be ignored. The proliferation of gender-specific programs for Latinos stands as a testament to the importance of this factor. Historically, it was much easier for Latinos, when compared to their Latina counterparts, to receive services. The stigma that Latinas faced in seeking services was considerable, and effectively limited their access to treatment. However, the past two decades have witnessed an understanding of the needs of Latinas.

3. *Religious Beliefs/Affiliations:* Historically, when alcohol-related services were discussed regarding Latinos, rarely would religion and religious beliefs enter into the discussion. However, the presence of religious institutions, not necessarily Catholic, cannot be dismissed in any assessment of alcohol services for Latinos. Religious institutions such as Pentecostals and Seventh Day Adventists, for example, may well have a wide range of services from detoxification to inpatient treatment, along with support services for the family of the person in treatment.

4. *Urban/Rural:* Some service providers may well argue that alcohol-related problems are the same whether they transpire in urban or rural areas of the county. However, if context sets the stage for assessment and treatment, then nothing could be further from the truth. Setting influences how outreach is undertaken, the nature and extent of referrals, and the structure of services. Although a significant portion (over 90 percent) of the Latino community resides urban areas, there is still a large number of Latinos living in rural areas.

5. *Sexual Orientation:* The subject of sexual orientation and alcohol-related services has not received the attention that it deserves from academics, funders, and programs. We can no longer ignore the role of sexual orientation in any service provision. Clearly, the majority of Latinos are heterosexual, although a significant percentage is not. Consequently, the creation of services that are specific to gays and lesbians, for example, are not out of the ordinary, although they face incredible pressures from society and the Latino community.

## CONCLUSION

The early part of the twenty-first century will undoubtedly continue to witness the emergence of culture-specific alcohol-related services for Latinos taking into account sub-groups. These developments will prove fertile for advancing knowledge on how best to meet the needs of this emerging group within the country. This movement, however, cannot be expected to continue unabated without the requisite research, program evaluation, and scholarship that will help policy makers to in allocating funding. Alcohol-related services will continue to compete with other drug-related programs to receive the attention and resources they require to make a meaningful impact on this social problem in the Latino community and in the country. The continued dramatic numerical representation of the Latino community will require that service organizations be able to respond to a wide-range of alcohol and other forms of drug abuse without sacrificing any one form of abuse, particularly alcohol.

## REFERENCES

De La Rosa, M. (1998). Prevalence and consequences of alcohol, cigarette and drug use among Hispanics. In M. Delgado (Ed.), *Alcohol use/abuse among Latinos: Issues and examples of culturally competent services* (pp. 21-70). New York: The Haworth Press, Inc.

Delgado, M. (1999). *Social work practice in nontraditional urban settings*. New York: Oxford University Press.

Delgado, M. (Ed.). (1998a). *Alcohol use/abuse among Latinos: Issues and examples of culturally competent services*. New York: The Haworth Press, Inc.

Delgado, M. (1998b). Cultural competence and the field of ATOD: Latinos as a case example. In M. Delgado (Ed.), *Alcohol use/abuse among Latinos: Issues and examples of culturally competent services* (pp. 5-19). New York: The Haworth Press, Inc.

Hall, J. (1997, October 6). *New study on Latino communities links alcohol advertising with disease, crime, violence against women. (www.beveragenetwork.com/news/1997/10-06-1997-study.asp)*.

# PERSONAL PERSPECTIVES

# Trends in the Treatment of Alcohol Problems: 1980 to 2000

## Thomas F. McGovern, EdD

**SUMMARY.** The editorial board of *Alcoholism Treatment Quarterly* (ATQEB) was polled about their perceptions of significant trends in the treatment of alcohol problems, from 1980-2000. They identified the major influences, positive and negative, together with the effects on treatment initiatives in response to managed behavioral health care, the decline of inpatient services, increased emphasis on drugs other than alcohol, and the changing character of treatment providers. *[Article copies available for a fee from The Haworth Document Delivery Service: 1-800-HAWORTH. E-mail address: <getinfo@haworthpressinc.com> Website: <http://www.HaworthPress.com> © 2002 by The Haworth Press, Inc. All rights reserved.]*

Thomas F. McGovern is Professor, Department of Neuropsychiatry, Texas Tech University Health Sciences Center, Lubbock, TX. He also directs the program on Health Care Ethics and Humanities for the School of Medicine. He has been actively involved in the treatment of alcohol and other drug problems, as clinician, educator and researcher, for 25 years. He served on the committee which authored the Institute of Medicine Study, Broadening the Base of Treatment for Alcohol Problems (1990). He has served as Editor of *Alcoholism Treatment Quarterly* for 15 years.

[Haworth co-indexing entry note]: "Trends in the Treatment of Alcohol Problems: 1980 to 2000." McGovern, Thomas F. Co-published simultaneously in *Alcoholism Treatment Quarterly* (The Haworth Press, Inc.) Vol. 20, No. 3/4, 2002, pp. 193-197; and: *Alcohol Problems in the United States: Twenty Years of Treatment Perspective* (ed: Thomas F. McGovern, and William L. White) The Haworth Press, Inc., 2002, pp. 193-197. Single or multiple copies of this article are available for a fee from The Haworth Document Delivery Service [1-800-HAWORTH, 9:00 a.m. - 5:00 p.m. (EST). E-mail address: getinfo@haworthpressinc.com].

**KEYWORDS.** Treatment, alcohol problems, major influences, treatment providers, managed behavioral health care

The majority of the editorial board of *Alcoholism Treatment Quarterly* (ATQEB) have served on the board since the journal's inception. They represent many aspects of the treatment field, as treatment providers in a variety of settings, educators, policy makers and researchers. The average age of the board members is 55 years and the majority have worked in the field for more than 25 years. They have witnessed firsthand changes in the treatment field over the past 20 years. Compiling their responses to a survey requesting their perceptions of major trends and influences during the eighties and nineties was a difficult task. The narrative that follows represents an editorial effort to capture the voices of those whose collective wisdom and insight have contributed significantly to an understanding of the treatment of alcohol problems.

Bruce Carruth (2002), the founding editor, acknowledges the pioneers from the sixties and early seventies who led the treatment movement of alcohol problems into the closing decades of the twentieth century. He wonders if the early trailblazers like Vern Johnson, Marty Mann, Morrie Chefetz, Dan Anderson, Mark Keller, E. M. (Bunkie) Jellenek, LeClaire Bissell, among others are familiar names to those from the eighties onward who benefited from the legacy of expansion of services, knowledge, and changed attitudes towards all alcohol problems which they inherited. The ATQEB members readily identify the contributions of the early pioneers in their reflection on later developments in the field. The influences, positive and negative, which have been at work in addressing alcohol problems over the past twenty years are many. The respondents from the ATQEB, and in a special way, Bruce Carruth, identify the most obvious influence as resting on the lives of the millions of people successfully treated in their contributions to the well-being of our society. This is possible because of changed societal attitudes towards alcohol problems and especially from the acceptance of extreme alcohol problems as an illness. Carruth (2002) charts the change as follows: the missionary zeal of the late seventies and early eighties has been replaced by a more recent acceptance of what society is willing and not willing to do in response to alcohol and other drug problems in our culture. Changed societal attitudes, translated into federal funding, insurance coverage, increased inpatient and outpatient opportunities and professional awareness and research initiatives, have changed the face of treatment. The details of this transformation are covered by the articles in this volume and especially so by Wilborurne and Miller (2002) and Nace and Morse (2002). The comments of the ATQEB support the observation of these authors as the editorial board, in turn, identify the major influences as: managed care, the credentialing of counselors and other health professionals, Project Match studies, the acceptance of various treatment modalities, the recognition of alcohol problems along a degree of severity, and the growth of alternatives to intensive inpatient treatment.

The ATQEB also identify forces which have had a negative effect on efforts to address alcohol problems. Carruth (2002) is concerned about the inability of the research and treatment communities to integrate their findings into a more effective and comprehensive form of treatment. He writes (Carruth 2002): "Controlled studies of treatment effectiveness have demonstrated the efficacy of specific treatment approaches as well as the impact of treatment as a whole. And yet, in comparison to research and treatment of other disorders, addiction (alcohol and drug problems) research has failed to translate into the day to day practice of addiction treatment." His recommendation that the two communities work closer together, availing of initiatives like the federally funded supported "Technologies Center," is reechoed by the respondents from the ATQEB.

The absence of a widely accepted terminology, which describes alcohol and other drug problems along a spectrum of severity, is seen by the respondents as a limiting factor. A clearer way of differentiating between the terms use, misuse, abuse and dependence is necessary. Without such clarity, efforts to address issues across educational, prevention and treatment lines flounder and communication, designed to promote common goals, become a nightmare. Many of the respondents question the usefulness of the term "addiction" in its ability to cover the diversity of conditions resulting from the use of alcohol and other drugs. Of equal concern to the respondents is the merging of addiction treatment (including the treatment of alcohol problems) under the umbrella of behavioral health, including Managed Behavioral Health Care Organizations. Those, who see this trend as a positive influence rejoice that alcoholism is now viewed as a primary disorder like other psychiatric conditions. Others fear that an emphasis on the "behavioral" aspects of alcohol problems will reverse the gains which have resulted from the acceptance of severe alcohol/drug problems as an illness; this, in turn, may result in the restigmatization and the demedicalization of alcohol problems. There is no clear consensus among the respondents as to their determination of the effects of the new emphasis on behavioral health as positive, negative, or as a mixed blessing.

The status of training and expertise among health care professionals, as they deal with alcohol and other drug problems in a variety of treatment settings, is difficult to assess from the survey's responses. The contribution of alcohol and drug abuse counselors, described as such through much of their professional history towards the professionalization of their own specialty and of the treatment field as a whole is monumental. Carruth (2002), reflecting on the honored place counselors, often in recovery, occupy in the story of treatment over the past decades writes: "And these thousands of individuals not only provide direct services for clients and their families, but by their actions and involvement in communities across the country create awareness, credibility, compassion, and hope for people affected by the disorder." The influence of the individual counselors and of their professional organizations, like the National Association of Addiction Counselors (the newest title for the group), is profound. The education and training of physicians, nurses, social workers, and other professionals in the health care field has been uneven in character. One respondent notes that the impetus for improving professional appreciation of the dimensions of treatment issues has declined following a gratifying increase in the eighties. A further distinction between educational and training initiatives is identified by the respondents.

The ATQEB members comment on the alcoholism treatment field for its insistence from the beginning on the need to address the spiritual dimensions of alcohol and other drug problems. Kurtz (2002) and Morgan (2002), both members of the ATQEB, chronicle the contributions of AA and of like movements to our understanding of spirituality in the recovery process. They are joined in this sentiment by the voices of other members of the board in asserting that the current acceptance of spirituality as a legitimate component of holistic health can be traced to the influence of the alcoholism/drug dependency treatment field. The overarching power of spirituality is best reflected in the lives of recovering persons who are the face and voice of recovery and success.

The respondents experienced difficulty in identifying the significant institutional research and personages associated with the growth of treatment initiatives in the concluding decades of the twentieth century. At the risk of omitting equally important factors and persons involved in this period of change, they identified representative samples from each of the areas under consideration. The work and influence of the National Institute for Alcohol Abuse and Alcoholism (NIAAA) under the inspired leadership of Enoch Gordis is recognized for its special contribution. William Miller's research, which embraces many dimensions of the treatment of alcohol problems, enjoys a special place in defining our society's response to treatment issues. Of particular note are the outcome studies which he has sponsored/directed; the Project Match Studies are examples of his work. Broadening the Base of Treatment for Alcohol Problems, sponsored by the Academy of Medicine, has provided needed direction for expanding treatment, research and educational initiatives which embrace a community approach to alcohol problems. The respondents identify the leadership of David Lewis and note his role in organizing Physician Leadership on National Drug Policy as being an important element in fashioning federal programs. Some of the significant contributors to the field include such personalities as Ernie Kurtz, Vern Johnson, Mark Keller, Allan Marlatt, and Stephanie Brown.

Those polled in the survey recommend careful examination of programs which are dedicated to the needs of underserved populations including women, Latinos, African Americans and Native Americans. They stressed that funding such programs at all levels should be balanced and based on a consideration of all those who are in need. A lack of consistency in funding, which often responds to immediate political pressure, is viewed as a detriment in developing comprehensive approaches to alcohol problems.

Carruth (2002), in reflecting on the state of treatment issues in our day, writes: "The chorus of voices, advocating change, expansion and new directions has died or at least has become muted." One wonders if he is describing a period of change and evaluation rather than a period of stagnation. A need exists to carefully evaluate our experience in the treatment of alcohol problems over the past twenty years. The editorial board of ATQ, in their comments, identify the need for such a careful review. The story of the era from 1980 to 2000 needs to be told. This volume represents a modest effort towards the achievement of this goal.

## REFERENCES

Carruth, B. (2002). Issues in the treatment of alcohol/other drug problems, 1980-2000. Unpublished manuscript.

Kurtz, E. (2002). Alcoholics Anonymous and the disease concept of alcoholism. Alcoholism Treatment Quarterly, Vol. 20, No. 3-4, pp. 5-40.

Morgan, O. (2002). Spirituality, alcohol and other drug problems: Where have we been? Where are we going? Alcoholism Treatment Quarterly, Vol. 20, No. 3-4, pp. 61-82.

Nace, E. and Morse, R. (2002). A tale of two cities (and two programs): The rise and fall of alcoholism and drug dependence treatment at Mayo Clinic and Timberlawn Hospital, 1975-2000. Alcoholism Treatment Quarterly, Vol. 20, No. 3-4, pp. 211-226.

Wilbourne, P. and Miller, W. (2002). Treatment for alcoholism: Older and wiser? Alcoholism Treatment Quarterly, Vol. 20, No. 3-4, pp. 41-59.

# Treating Co-Occurring Alcohol-Drug Dependence and Mental Illness: A Personal Retrospective Reflection (1971-2001)

Jerome F. X. Carroll, PhD

**SUMMARY.** This personal retrospective reflection spans three decades of a conscious and purposeful effort to treat and study individuals with co-occurring alcohol-drug dependence and mental illness. Specific services and policies designed for this population are described, as well as efforts to integrate mental health services into a comprehensive, integrated holistic treatment program. The most recent efforts by New York State's Office of Mental Health and Office of Alcohol and Substance Abuse Services are described. Achievements realized and a significant barrier to further progress are included. *[Article copies available for a fee from The Haworth Document Delivery Service: 1-800-HAWORTH. E-mail address: <getinfo@haworthpressinc.com> Website: <http://www.HaworthPress.com> © 2002 by The Haworth Press, Inc. All rights reserved.]*

---

Jerome F. X. Carroll has been actively involved in the treatment of alcohol and other drug problems for 30 years. He has authored books, book chapters and articles on treatment issues. He has served as Executive Director of Eagleville Hospital, Pennsylvania, and of Protect Return Inc., New York.

[Haworth co-indexing entry note]: "Treating Co-Occurring Alcohol-Drug Dependence and Mental Illness: A Personal Retrospective Reflection (1971-2001)." Carroll, Jerome F. X. Co-published simultaneously in *Alcoholism Treatment Quarterly* (The Haworth Press, Inc.) Vol. 20, No. 3/4, 2002, pp. 199-210; and: *Alcohol Problems in the United States: Twenty Years of Treatment Perspective* (ed: Thomas F. McGovern, and William L. White) The Haworth Press, Inc., 2002, pp. 199-210. Single or multiple copies of this article are available for a fee from The Haworth Document Delivery Service [1-800-HAWORTH, 9:00 a.m. - 5:00 p.m. (EST). E-mail address: getinfo@haworthpressinc.com].

**KEYWORDS.** Co-occurring alcohol-drug dependence and mental illness, MICA, dual diagnosis, integrated mental health and substance abuse treatment, New York Model, Quad IV, barrier to further progress

This is a personal retrospective account of my professional experiences spanning three decades of treating and studying clients with co-occurring alcohol/other chemical dependence and mental health problems. They have been referred to as mentally ill chemical abusers (MICAs), dual diagnosis (DDs) clients, and clients with co-occurring psychiatric and addictive disorder (COPADs). My experiences stemmed mainly from clinical/administrative work and research done in two Therapeutic Communities (TCs). One was located in Pennsylvania and the other in New York.

In these TCs, we mainly treated adults (18 years and older, with an average age of 30 plus years), minorities (70 to 80% African Americans), and mostly males (60% male; 40% female). These clients typically were multiple substance abusers (i.e., clients abusing two or more illicit substances and alcohol) and presented with multiple, serious "problems-in-living," including legal, family, work, education, and housing problems.

In the 1970s, most of our Pennsylvania clients were primarily abusing alcohol or heroin, although most were abusing some combination of drugs and alcohol. In the mid-80s and throughout the 90s, heroin was replaced by crack-cocaine as the primary drug of abuse, especially among New York City area TC clients (called "residents" in the TCs) In the New York City area, alcohol typically was a secondary or tertiary substance of abuse.

When I arrived at Eagleville Hospital and Rehabilitation Center (EHRC) in 1971, I became the Director of the hospital's Psychology Department. EHRC was considerably ahead of the rest of the addictions field throughout most of the 1970s with respect to how it related to MICA clients. EHRC, for example, already had a Psychiatry and a Psychology Department, as well as a Social Services, a Recreational Therapy, and an Educational Department. Since it was a hospital-based program, it also had a Medical and a Nursing Department, and because its sole mission was to treat both alcohol dependent and other drug dependent persons, it also had a Substance Abuse Treatment Department. Most of EHRC's Substance Abuse Counselors (SACs) were men and women in recovery. Representatives from these departments would meet periodically to discuss the results of their respective assessments and treatments and to attempt to coordinate their respective services.

Any debate about the nature and extent of mental health problems to be found among alcohol/chemically dependent persons was very much in the background in the early 70s. At that time, the addictions field was debating whether or not "combined treatment" (i.e., treating alcohol dependent and drug dependent persons together in the same program) could/should be done with any degree of success. In 1968, Eagleville consciously and purposefully decided to change from being an alcohol-only treatment program to a combined treatment program. This decision was made in order to address the nation's need to provide treatment for the large number of returning Viet Nam veterans who had substance dependence problems.

To prepare itself to meet the treatment needs of the addicts, senior EHRC staff visited the Daytop treatment program in New York City. They were much impressed by what they witnessed and experienced there, and upon their return, they adopted the group interventions and some of the program structures employed by Daytop. However, some major modifications in the Daytop approach were made (e.g., about half of EHRC's staff were professionals and the clients did not cook and serve their meals, drive agency vehicles, or assist the building maintenance staff).

Since the hospital had pioneered combined treatment, Eagleville chose to host a series of national conferences to attempt to facilitate debate concerning the appropriateness and efficacy of this form of treatment. A small element of the first 10 conferences did address MICA issues, but it was not until 1978 that the 11th annual conference ("Treating Mixed Psychiatric-Drug Addicted and Alcohol Patients") was devoted exclusively to MICA issues.

While EHRC was openly pioneering combined treatment, it was simultaneously pioneering how to provide integrated alcohol/substance abuse and mental health treatment to its MICA clients (Carroll & Sobel, 1986), albeit with far less fanfare. All newly admitted clients were screened by both the Psychiatry and Psychology Departments, and when clients were identified as having significant psychopathology, they were placed on "alert/observation (A/O) status." These A/O clients received closer supervision and support until their condition improved. When and if a client experienced an emotional crisis, s/he received individual therapy from either a staff psychiatrist or psychologist. Such therapy was typically of short duration, and it supplemented rather than replaced the ongoing group counseling done by the SACs.

The psychiatrists were responsible for prescribing and monitoring all psychotropic medications. At that time, the majority of clients taking psychotropics presented with intensive borderline states of anxiety, depression, and dysphoria. The psychiatrists and psychologists also consulted with the SACs when the SACs needed help with differential diagnoses. For example, the SACs typically wanted to know how much "control" a particular client was capable of exercising, since any "acting out" had to be dealt with by the SACs. SACs also needed help in differentiating between a client's being "lazy" and attempting to avoid community responsibilities vs. his/her being lethargic due to severe depression.

Despite all of the above useful services and consultation, the level of integration of these mental health services still left room for improvement. For example, although mental status reports were routinely written and entered into the medical charts, for the most part, the SACs paid little heed to them. Except for those instances when a patient was undergoing a psychiatric crisis and/or needed a more intense level of psychiatric care than that provided by the hospital (e.g., restraints, 24-hour surveillance, or heavy psychotropic medications), the SACs made most of the important clinical decisions. These included decisions such as deciding whether or not to discharge a client, grant a visit, or to "shoot down" the client (i.e., demote the client from a higher to a lower status level), and the SACs typically did this without consulting either the Psychiatry or the Psychology Department.

One of the first things I did after assuming my position at EHRC was to seek out the SAC staff for some one-on-one talks about what they were getting out of the Psychology Department reports. The SACs did not perceive these reports as written to be very helpful–they were described as having "too much psychological jargon" and too "theoretical." I also asked the SACs what information they would like to receive in these reports. As a result of my "needs assessment," substantial changes were made in the battery of tests administered by the Psychology Department (e.g., they would no longer focus exclusively on "what was wrong with the clients"; strengths too would be assessed) and what was done with the results of the psychological testing.

A new, more comprehensive test battery was introduced which was administered over two half-days. The battery enabled the Psychology Department to assess each client's level of intellectual functioning, screen for any cognitive impairment, signs of organicity and/or brain damage, determine the client's basic educational skills and deficits in reading and math, examine underlying personality traits, assess the degree of integration and acceptance of the client's self-concept, and identify the level and type of any co-occurring psychopathology.

One of the early lessons learned from this testing was that the overwhelming majority of clients presented with some form(s) of psychopathology. The most commonly observed forms of which consisted of Personality Disorders (Antisocial, Dependent, and Borderline Personality Disorders were most common), Mood Disorders (especially Dysthymic Disorder), and various forms of Anxiety Disorders. Post Traumatic Stress Disorder (PTSD) was a very frequently encountered problem, especially among the women. Most of the PTSD was related to early childhood sexual and/or physical abuse.

More serious and persistent forms of psychiatric illnesses (SPMIs), such as schizophrenia, major depression, and paranoia, were seen far less frequently.

In part, this was because the EHRC Admissions Unit purposefully screened out persons with SPMI, since they would presumably require very intensive psychiatric care which the hospital did not provide. However, some SPMI clients always managed to get through this initial screening process. Mostly this occurred when no obvious SPMI symptoms had been observed during the admission process, and when the individual denied ever having had a SPMI, and/or s/he had not been referred to EHRC from a psychiatric treatment center.

In the late 70s and early 80s, I began recommending that clients whose co-occurring psychiatric disorders were less severe than their substance disorders be referred to as CAMIs (chemical abusers with mental illness, Carroll, 1990) in order to distinguish them from clients whose mental illness was more severe or as severe as their chemical dependence disorder. These clients would be referred to as MICAs. I now believe that this distinction between MICA and CAMI may create more problems than it solves. For example, a non-SPMI form of mental illness (e.g., Post Traumatic Stress Disorder) can, when undetected and/or untreated, significantly interfere with the recovery process and/or increase the likelihood of relapse. In such cases, it hardly makes much sense to consider the non-SPMI mental disorder as "minor" which is implied in CAMI.

All types of co-morbid psychiatric disorders need to be addressed in the client's treatment and aftercare plans. Ideally, they should be dealt with simultaneously according to a well coordinated and integrated treatment plan. The sequencing of the treatment, however, can vary according to the unique nature of the individual's co-occurring disorders which should dictate what problem is addressed first and in what manner.

At EHRC, the psychologists offered to provide each client tested with full and honest feedback on the results of the testing, either in an individual counseling session or in his/her primary alcohol/substance abuse treatment group. The overwhelming majority of clients opted to have their feedback done in their primary group, and this "psychological feedback" group did much to solidly integrate the work of the Psychology Department into the general rehabilitation process.

The psychological feedback sessions typically helped to strengthen group cohesion (everyone in the group could identify with some part of the client's feedback), and they also provided valuable insights to the client (and his/her SAC) about how certain personality traits and dynamics related to the client's abuse of alcohol or other substances. The SACs also benefitted in two other ways. They learned a lot about psychological testing and what psychologists could contribute to the rehabilitative process. They also were provided with some relief from the daily grind of running groups, since in the feedback sessions, they could assume the role of participant-observer rather than group leader.

While the feedback of psychological testing sessions proved to be highly popular with the clients and SACs, this specialized service was discontinued when the charismatic founder of the hospital's addiction treatment program, Dr. Donald J. Ottenberg, resigned his position. Under Dr. Ottenberg's leadership, EHRC had been administered as a hospital-based, modified TC which encouraged many innovative, alternative therapies (e.g., psychodrama, Gestalt techniques, minithons, and marathons) for its clients. He had also initiated many therapeutic processes that enabled the entire community to confront difficult and challenging social issues, such as racism and sexism. The new administrator, however, discouraged such activities in favor of operating a more traditional hospital program.

A number of the staff who valued what was eliminated at Eagleville sought employment elsewhere. I ended up in New York City, where, in 1986, I accepted the position of Vice President for Clinical Services at Project Return Foundation, Inc. In New York, I was surprised to learn that the drug treatment community was just beginning to discover that there were substantial numbers of substance abuse clients who had MICA problems. Dr. Marc Galanter and Dr. Bert Pepper were two of the principal early advocates in the area who spoke of the great need for providing mental health services to alcohol and other substance abusers. Coming from a combined treatment program, I was similarly taken aback by the drug treatment community's insouciance concerning the drinking of alcohol by recovering addicts.

In most of the TCs in the New York City area, there was little or no interest in admitting, screening, or treating MICA clients. From top management down to the direct line staff, mental illness and alcohol/substance abuse were perceived as separate and distinct disorders. Alcohol/substance abuse and mental health treatment agencies each remained on their "own turf," with their own philosophies of treatment, treatment/rehabilitation procedures, values, traditions, and means of conveying advancement and status to recognize patient progress and staff achievements. There was little or no attempt made by either field to promote integrated and coordinated care for their MICA clients, most of whom remained undiagnosed for the "other illness."

Therefore, the first two years of my work at Project Return Foundation were spent in building a comprehensive, holistic treatment program that addressed both co-existing psychiatric disorders and the dangers of relapse associated with drinking by recovering drug addicts. Addressing the MICA problems of our clients required the development of interdisciplinary treatment teams that included qualified mental health specialists. This was accomplished by very careful budgeting and winning a large Center for Substance Abuse Treatment (CSAT) grant.

Developing a program that addressed the needs of our MICA clients also entailed undertaking the difficult challenge of convincing both management and staff that most of the agency's clients had co-existing mental health problems, and that these problems could be successfully treated by our existing staff, with the infusion of some additional mental health specialists and interventions. This was not an easy sell, and it took more than two years of persistent persuading before PRF had achieved at least a workable level of integrated mental health-alcohol/substance abuse treatment services.

From that early platform of integrated MICA treatment services, more and more mental health services were added, including the prescribing of psychotropic medications. With each addition, the degree of integration of services was raised, albeit slowly and with many brief regressions before lasting advancements were achieved (Carroll, 1990).

One of the last innovations accomplished before I retired in July of 2000 was the introduction of a short, easy to use screening device (the Mental Health Screening Form III, MHSF III, Carroll & McGinley, 2001) designed to uncover mental health problems at the point of admission to treatment. The MHSF III can be administered by any staff member, with minimal training. It takes only about 15 minutes to complete. It can be done in a structured interview format with a staff member reading the items to the client and then following up any question answered with a "yes" with additional questions to determine how the mental illness relates to the client's alcohol/substance abuse problem. Or it can simply be given to the client to read and answer on his/her own. In this case the client must read at least at the fourth grade level. The former method is preferred to the latter.

After a client has answered the MHSF III's 17 items and the followup questions recommended for any "yes" answer (Carroll & McGinley, 2001), the results should then be reviewed by a qualified mental health professional who either works for the agency or who works in a cooperating mental health agency located in the area. The MHSF III provides diagnostic information on 13 different forms of mental illness, including: Schizophrenia; Depressive Disorders; Post Traumatic Stress Disorder; Phobias; Intermittent Explosive Disorder; Delusional Disorder, persecutory type; Sexual and Gender Identity Disorders; Eating Disorders; Manic Episodes; Panic Disorder; Obsessive Compulsive Disorders; Pathological Gambling; and Learning Disorders and Mental Retardation.

What was done at PRF, however, was not replicated generally throughout the TC network of service providers in the New York City area. Although certain TCs did go on to develop effective MICA services (e.g., Argus Community's Harbor House, Odyssey House, Aurora Concept, and Apple), most TCs resisted even acknowledging the need for such services. Those in leadership positions within the network of TC service providers who resisted making accommodations in their TCs for MICA clients mainly denied that such problems existed.

While attending one of the TC network meetings, I heard an agency representative remark that he could accept the fact that there probably were TC residents who had mental health problems in his TC. However, he went on to say that his agency would not screen for MICA problems, because if they found them, they would then have to do something about them. He did not believe that his agency had the resources to deal with MICA problems, nor did he have much confidence that the state funding agency would provide additional funds to acquire those resources.

Over the last ten years, considerable literature has appeared which documented a high level and variety of MICA problems to be found among substance abusing clients in diverse treatment settings (Brown, Stout, & Mueller, 1996; Calsyn & Saxon, 1990; Carroll & McGinley, 1998; Craig & Weinberg, 1992; Horner, Scheibe, & Stine, 1996; Karson & Gesumaria, 1995; Penick et al., 1990; Sacks, Sacks, De Leon, Bernhardt, & Staines, 1997). The literature is also quite clear and consistent in demonstrating that negative treatment outcomes are associated with the failure to identify and treat co-morbid disorders and that more favorable outcomes result when these disorders are identified and treated (Carroll et al., 1994; McLellan & Metzger, 1998; Mercer, Mueser, & Drake, 1998; Nuttbrock, Rahav, Rivera, Ng-Mak, & Struening, 1997; Woody, Luborsky, & O'Brien, 1995).

While some believe MICA is a new phenomenon, if not in kind than in scope and intensity, I believe that most alcohol/chemically dependent clients have always had co-occurring mental health problems that reflected their pathologically low levels of self-esteem. The only thing "new" is that the alcohol/chemical dependency treatment field is now more aware of and beginning to do a better job of identifying and treating MICA clients.

In addition to the research findings, a very significant and recent development occurred within two of New York State's major bureaucracies that fund treatment programs with MICA clients. The Commissioners of the New York State Office of Mental Health (SOMH), James L. Stone, and the New York State Office of Alcoholism and Substance Abuse Services (OASAS), Ms. Jean Somers Miller, agreed to hold ongoing interagency meetings to discuss how MICA clients were being treated in programs funded by their agencies. In 1998, Commissioners Stone and Miller issued a historic, joint Memorandum of Understanding (MOU) that officially recognized the high incidence of co-occurring psychiatric and addictive disorders that existed in their respective treatment agencies. The MOU also called attention to the need to improve the identification and treatment of these clients, and it stated that the two agencies would strive to better integrate their services.

To accomplish this goal, the two commissioners created an Interagency Workgroup charged with the responsibility of developing and recommending new policies and initiatives that would further improve and enhance coordination and cooperation between the two state agencies. The Interagency Workgroup was also charged with making recommendations on the screening, assessment, and treatment of individuals with co-morbid disorders, as well as how to provide the necessary training to upgrade the knowledge base and skills of the staff working in programs funded by the two state agencies.

A special New York four-celled model was created to illustrate the likely "locus of care" based on an individual's severity of mental illness and his/her alcohol and drug dependencies. The model especially focused on the "Quad IV" cell which contained MICA clients with both severe mental illness and severe alcohol/substance dependency. This "no man's land" was the location where MICA clients were believed to receive the least effective treatment, since neither the mental health nor the chemical dependency treatment systems had developed system-wide treatment protocols to effectively treat Quad IV MICA clients. Ironically, individual treatment programs within SOMH and OASAS had independently developed very effective MICA treatment programs using their own initiative and creativity.

To address the needs of Quad IV clients, the Interagency Workgroup formed a Quad IV Taskforce consisting of high ranking SOMH and OASAS staff and service provider representatives from agencies from all parts of the state. This taskforce met for more than two years to develop a plan (Quadrant IV Task Force, 2001) with specific recommendations to better serve MICA clients, especially those who fell in the Quadrant IV cell of the New York model.

First and foremost, there would no longer be any "wrong doors" for MICA clients seeking treatment. Ready access to a system of care which was "welcoming, integrated, and part of a seamless continuity of care" was a prime goal to be implemented. Some of the more important specific treatment recommendations from the Quad IV Taskforce included the following. Service providers in both the SOMH and OASAS systems would be mandated to screen and assess all clients for co-morbid psychiatric and alcohol/substance abuse disorders. More uniform charting and reporting standards would be developed that would promote coordinated and integrated delivery of simultaneous mental health and substance abuse services. Consensus psychopharmacological practices and guidelines would also be developed for various settings that serviced MICA clients. SOMH and OASAS would increase their collaborations with county Mental Hygiene Directors in developing dual recovery clinical practice and service provider guidelines.

Despite these very positive developments, there still exist very strong pockets of resistance within both the alcohol/chemical dependency and mental health fields to this "no wrong door" goal for MICA treatment. Some alcohol/chemical dependency treatment programs are still very wary of inviting mental health professionals into their programs who may challenge existing traditions, practices, and how treatment decisions are made. Mental health treatment programs, too, have serious reservations, especially about dealing with "forensic" substance abusing clients who have committed multiple felonies, violent acts, and who have antisocial personality disorders.

Although many challenges and obstacles still exist, it is my impression that real progress is being made. At least the MICA issue is very much more prominent in the minds of service providers in both systems. In New York State, a statewide Dual Disorders Advisory Council with consumer, provider, clinician, county, and other state agency representation is being created. In addition, special MICA curricula have been developed in the state to better educate treatment staff in both the alcohol/chemical dependency and mental health fields to identify and more effectively treat MICA clients. New standards for program staffing and services also have been promulgated to distinguish dual diagnosis "capable" and "enhanced" programs in both the alcohol/chemical dependency and the mental health fields.

The interagency group formed by the Commissioners of SOMH and OASAS continues to function to effect even greater integration of MICA services within and across both systems. In addition, the group has begun to explore ways of reaching out to other state agencies (e.g., the Office of Child and Family Services, The Criminal Justice System, the Office of Homeless Services) to encourage them to screen for alcohol/chemical dependency problems, mental health problems, and co-occurring disorders. A special Coordinator of Dual Recovery Services position has been created in order to promote and facilitate local networks of MICA service providers in selected counties and to provide advice and assistance to treatment agencies within these counties who are servicing MICA clients. Finally, some of the most resistant of TCs have recently begun to hire qualified mental health professionals to work in their programs.

There remains one significant barrier that prevents us from achieving even more progress in designing and implementing seamless loci and levels of care for individuals with co-occurring alcohol/chemical dependency and mental health disorders. This barrier is the continued avoidance of leaders in both the mental health and alcohol/chemical dependency fields to come to terms with the significant differences that underlie their respective philosophies/theories of treatment, and all of the associated values, clinical practices, and traditions that come with these very different perspectives of the MICA client and his/her treatment needs.

To date, the planners have chosen to let "sleeping dogs lie." It is my belief that these differences need to be discussed openly and frankly by reasonable people capable of appreciating and valuing different perspectives and experiences, and who can disagree with one another without rancor while searching for common ground and consensus. If this can be done, the future would indeed be very bright.

## REFERENCES

Brown, P.J., Stout, R.L., & Blow, F.C. (1992). Posttraumatic stress disorder and substance abuse relapse among women: A pilot study. *Psychology of Addictive Behaviors, 10*, 124-128.

Calsyn, D.A., & Saxon, A.J. (1990). Personality disorder subtypes among cocaine and opioid addicts using the *Milton Clinical Multiaxial Inventory. International Journal of the Addictions, 25*, 1037-1049.

Carroll, J.F.X. (1975). Are the addict and alcoholic mentally ill? In D.J. Ottenberg & E.L. Carpey (Eds.), *Proceedings of the 7th Annual Eagleville Conference: Critical issues in addiction-1974* (pp. 113-134). Washington, DC: U.S. Department of Health, Education and Welfare.

Carroll, J.F.X. (1990). Treating drug addicts with mental health problems in a therapeutic community. *Journal of Chemical Dependency, 3(2)*, 237-259.

Carroll, J.F.X. (1994). Clinical issues in therapeutic communities. In F.M. Tims, G. De Leon, & N. Jainchill (Eds.), *Therapeutic community: Advances in research and application* (U.S. DHHS, NIDA Research Monograph 144, NIH Publication No. 94-3633) (pp. 268-279). Rockville, MD: National Institute on Drug Abuse.

Carroll, J.F.X., & Klein, M.I. (1974). An exploratory study comparing the personality characteristics of alcoholic and drug dependent males as measured by the *Personality Research Form* (PRF) and *Tennessee Self Concept Scale* (TSCS). Paper presented at the meeting of the Alcohol and Drug Problems Association of North America, Research Section, San Francisco, December 1974.

Carroll, J.F.X., Malloy, T.E., Roscioli, D., Pindjak, G.M., & Clifford, J.S. (1982). Similarities and differences in self-concepts of alcohol and drug addicted women. *Journal of Studies on Alcohol, 43(7)*, 725-738.

Carroll, J.F.X., & McGinley, J.J. (1998). Managing MICA clients in a modified therapeutic community with enhanced staffing. *Journal of Substance Abuse Treatment, 15(6)*, 565-577.

Carroll, J.F.X., & Sobel, B.S. (1986). Integrating mental health personnel and practices into a therapeutic community. In G. De Leon, & J.T. Ziegenfuss, Jr. (Eds.), *Therapeutic communities for addiction* (pp. 209-226). Springfield, IL: Charles C. Thomas.

Carroll, K., Rousanville, B.J., Nich, C., Gordon, L.T., Wirtz, P.W., & Gawin, F. (1994). One-year follow-up of psychotherapy and pharmacotherapy for cocaine dependence: Delayed emergence of psychotherapy effects. *Archives of General Psychiatry, 51(12)*, 989-997.

Craig, R.J., & Weinberg, D. (1992). Assessing drug abusers with the *Millon Clinical Multiaxial Inventory*: A review. *Journal of Substance Abuse Treatment, 9*, 249-255.

Horner, B., Scheibe, K., & Stine, S. (1996). Cocaine abuse and attention-deficit hyperactive disorder: implications of adult symptomatology. *Psychology of Addictive Behaviors, 10*, 55-60.

Karson, S., & Gesumaria, R.V. (1995). A comparison of the benefits of two therapeutic community treatment regimens for inner-city substance abusers. In J.N. Butcher, & Speilberger (Eds.), *Advances in personality assessment* (Vol. 10, pp. 109-120). Hillsdale, NJ: Lawrence Erlbaum.

McLellan, A.T., & McKay, J.R. (1998). The treatment of addictions: What can research offer practice? In S.J. Lamb, M.R. Greenlick, & D. McCarty (Eds.), *Bridging the gap between practice and research: Forging partnerships with community-based drug and alcohol treatment* (pp. 125-154). Washington, DC: National Academy Press.

Mercer, C.C., Mueser, K.T., & Drake, R.E. (1998). Organizational guidelines for dual disorders programs. *Psychiatric Quarterly, 69(3)*, 146-168.

Nuttbrock, L., Rahav, M., Rivera, J., Ng-Mak, D., & Struening, E. (1996). Mentally ill chemical abusers in residential treatment programs: Effects of psychopathology on levels of functioning. *Journal of Substance Abuse Treatment, 14(3)*, 269-274.

Penick, E.C., Nickel, E.J., Cantrell, P.F., Powell, B.J., Read, M.R., & Thomas, M.M. (1990). The emerging concept of dual diagnosis: An overview and implications. (Special Issue: Managing the dually diagnosed patient: current issues and clinical approaches). *Journal of Chemical Dependency Treatment, 3*, 1-54.

Quadrant IV Task Force (2001). *Treating co-occurring mental health and addictive disorders in New York state: A comprehensive view.* Albany, NY: NYS Office of Mental Health and NYS Office of Alcohol and Substance Abuse Service.

Sacks, S., Sacks, J.Y., De Leon, G., Bernhardt, A.I., & Staines, G. L. (1997). Modified therapeutic community for mentally ill chemical abusers: Background; influences; program description; preliminary findings. *Substance Use & Misuse, 32(9)*, 1217-1259.

Woody, G.E., Luborsky, L., & O'Brien, C. P. (1995). Psychotherapy in community methadone programs: A validation study. *American Journal of Psychiatry, 152(9)*, 1302-1308.

# A Tale of Two Cities (and Two Programs): The Rise and Fall of Alcoholism and Drug Dependence Treatment at Mayo Clinic and Timberlawn Hospital, 1975-2000

Edgar P. Nace, MD
Robert M. Morse, MD

**SUMMARY.** Two personalized accounts describe the authors' perceptions of drastic changes in their treatment centers. The growth and decline of the programs is traced in terms of treatment, education, and financial dimensions. *[Article copies available for a fee from The Haworth Document Delivery Service: 1-800-HAWORTH. E-mail address: <getinfo@haworthpressinc.com> Website: <http://www.HaworthPress.com> © 2002 by The Haworth Press, Inc. All rights reserved.]*

**KEYWORDS.** Alcoholism, drug dependence, treatment, education, Mayo Clinic, Timberlawn

Edgar P. Nace has focused his career upon the addictions but with ample attention also to personality disorders, Vietnam veterans, and impaired physicians. His national leadership has been invaluable in clinical, research, and educational pursuits. The 1972 opening of Mayo Clinic's addiction unit was headed by Robert M. Morse who insisted upon integrating it into the psychiatry residency training and making it as "mainstream" as possible. His work resulted in the program becoming respected as a comprehensive diagnostic and treatment center where complex medical and psychiatric disorders could also be treated. The impaired physician was also an emphasis.

[Haworth co-indexing entry note]: "A Tale of Two Cities (and Two Programs): The Rise and Fall of Alcoholism and Drug Dependence Treatment at Mayo Clinic and Timberlawn Hospital, 1975-2000." Nace, Edgar P., and Rober M. Morse. Co-published simultaneously in *Alcoholism Treatment Quarterly* (The Haworth Press, Inc.) Vol. 20, No. 3/4, 2002, pp. 211-226; and: *Alcohol Problems in the United States: Twenty Years of Treatment Perspective* (ed: Thomas F. McGovern, and William L. White) The Haworth Press, Inc., 2002, pp. 211-226. Single or multiple copies of this article are available for a fee from The Haworth Document Delivery Service [1-800-HAWORTH, 9:00 a.m. - 5:00 p.m. (EST). E-mail address: getinfo@haworthpressinc.com].

## INTRODUCTION

All involved in treatment of alcohol and drug problems over the years have witnessed the recent deterioration of this system. Edgar P. Nace and Robert M. Morse have been intimately involved in addiction treatment since the "golden era" in the 1970s. Originating sophisticated residential programs based on a medical-psychiatric model, they also incorporated AA and community resources. The Timberlawn and Mayo Clinic units became known for their high quality, devotion to education and research, and also their promotion of treatment for impaired physicians. Each program, however, has suffered dramatically due to the managed care revolution in treatment coverage, the Timberlawn Hospital being forced into bankruptcy. The authors take us through this ebb and fall with personalized accounts.

## THE TIMBERLAWN EXPERIENCE (EDGAR P. NACE)

The decade of the 1980s arrived with substance abuse treatment capacity expanding and riding the crest of developments carried over from the 70s. Employee Assistance Programs were increasing in number and influence; insurance benefits for inpatient treatment (not outpatient treatment) were available and data substantiating the effectiveness of treatment emerging. An important thrust for the acclaim and acceptance of substance abuse treatment was a First Lady's revelation of her own drug problem. Betty Ford's acknowledgement of her struggle with chemical dependency struck a sympathetic chord in the American public and gendered support for early case finding and intense treatment.

Further evidence that substance abuse treatment had come of age was found in academic circles. The University of Texas Medical Branch in Galveston, the oldest medical school west of the Mississippi, established a substance abuse program within its academic Department of Psychiatry. I was recruited in 1981 to develop this program. A small inpatient unit was established at one end of the psychiatric floor. When a new psychiatric facility was completed one year later, a floor was dedicated to substance abuse treatment. The chair of the department, Robert M. Rose, MD, was supportive of efforts to recruit professional counselors including those with a personal history of recovery. Thus, a multidisciplinary treatment team was established involving licensed chemical dependency counselors (both recovered and otherwise), social workers, nurses, psychologists, and psychiatrists. Of particular importance was the opportunity for medical students and psychiatry residents to rotate through this unit and work closely with men and women of all ages and backgrounds who were embarking on the effort to recover from alcohol or drug dependence. A true teaching moment had arrived in regard to substance abuse issues. The program was a success financially for the department, and, through the efforts of the program coordinator, John Sheehan, a grant was obtained to establish an EAP program at the University of Texas Medical Branch. This enabled us to assist the large number of employees and professionals within the medical center as well as their families when a substance use disorder or other psychiatric disorder was present.

After three years at the University of Texas Medical Branch I was contacted by Dr. Jerry M. Lewis, II to establish a substance abuse program at Timberlawn Psychiatric Hospital. Timberlawn was founded in 1917 and, interestingly, had the chart of the very first patient–a man who suffered from both cocaine and alcohol addiction. Timberlawn was a conservative long-term treatment institution with heavy emphasis on psychodynamically-oriented psychotherapy and an intense therapeutic milieu. It was throughout the 1980s a premier psychiatric hospital in the United States. The quality of its medical staff and other professional disciplines and the capacity for the hospital to draw patients from across the United States was impressive. The decision to bring in a psychiatrist from outside the system to start a new program was one that the hospital considered carefully and at length. One issue was whether my selection as the psychiatrist to establish this program should incur the title of Chief of Service or Staff Psychiatrist. My input to this question was very simple. If Timberlawn was going to take this step to establish a substance abuse program, it should make a full commitment and have a "Chief of Service." The board of the hospital–all psychiatrists–agreed and in 1984 the first phase was initiated. This phase was an evening intensive outpatient program of six weeks duration. Starting with an outpatient program may have been ahead of its time but, in fact, no inpatient beds were available at the hospital. The hospital's capacity for 220 patients was filled and a waiting list existed. A new building was going to be constructed for the substance abuse program as well for an acute psychiatric unit. These plans, although they hit the drawing board, never materialized because by the end of the decade of the 80s, it was clear that managed care was significantly impacting inpatient treatment. Nevertheless, a unit was obtained exclusively for the substance abuse program upon the completion of a new adolescent building. The old adolescent building was refurbished and the inpatient substance abuse program, including detoxification capacities, was opened. A day hospital and IOP program complimented the unit. Patients were expected to be on inpatient status of 4-6 weeks and a special effort was made to develop an impaired physician's program. This met with better than average success. Further, a specific adolescent substance use program was developed about 1986 and thrived for the next several years. Involvement with the families of adult and adolescent substance abuse patients was a paramount aspect of the program and a very capable social work and counseling staff provided educational and group and individual psychotherapy modalities for family members. The Timberlawn program gradually allowed patients to have increasing duration of time at home in graded fashion to assess each individual's capacity to follow through with weekend passes such as attending a local AA meeting and to report back as to how family relationships were proceeding and, in particular, how they felt in regard to urges or cravings for alcohol or drugs. Patients who had a comorbid psychiatric disorder, which was at least 50% of the patients, were treated with medication as appropriate. Because of my interest in research and through the recruitment of a staff psychologist, Dr. Carlos Davis, we were able to conduct research with particular emphasis on the incidence of personality disorders in substance abusing patients and to what extent personality disorder impacted treatment outcome. The program was listed as one of the nation's 100 best programs.

The Timberlawn program was an enriched, intense, psychotherapeutic model with a degree of patient governance and a strong connection to AA principles and the AA community. It took time and patience to overcome the suspicions of the local AA community regarding a well-known psychiatric hospital's efforts to treat alcoholics and drug dependent patients. There had been many affluent and influential individuals treated at Timberlawn but whose alcoholism or other drug problem had been given short shrift. This was an image problem that needed to be overcome. As we held in-house AA meetings as well as sent patients to community AA and NA meetings, confidence in our approach and recognition of our support for AA principals were established. It was also during this time that AA members seemed to be increasingly aware that some, indeed a sizeable number, of AA members would require antidepressant medication or perhaps Lithium or other mood stabilizers. Compared to a decade or two earlier there was less of a tendency in AA meetings to discourage a person from properly utilizing a psychiatric medications. This was a welcome change as such poor advice often was a disaster for patients.

These few years of flourishing, enriched, intense, long-term treatment were exciting, and effective for the large majority of patients who participated. It was rewarding for staff who could enjoy the resources of the institution and the opportunity to work in a multidisciplinary team. Again, the substance abuse program at Timberlawn provided another teaching opportunity as the hospital psychiatry residency program was well established and residents spent at least a month on the inpatient unit and gained skill in the understanding and treatment of individuals with substance use disorders. Parenthetically, the onslaught of managed care was such that the Timberlawn residency could not be sustained and was discontinued in the mid-1990s.

By the late 1980s, the rumblings of the managed care era were heard over the horizon. A moment stands out in my mind–a nurse from a managed care company arrived on our inpatient unit and challenged our treatment of a patient. She was quite haughty and continued to visit periodically and insist on rapid discharge into a less intensive modality, i.e., outpatient. As a treatment team we were indignant at this intrusion and it took, at least for me, three years to face the reality of this enormous social change and the resulting extreme pullback in resources for substance abuse treatment. I do recall that prior to the substance abuse treatment efforts being dramatically reshaped by managed care, executives at Texas Instruments in Dallas had been complaining loudly about adolescent treatment at Timberlawn. Their complaint was that adolescents were kept too long, it was too expensive, and they were tired of paying for it. The devastation of substance abuse treatment was parallel to a similar effect on adolescent treatment units.

The psychiatrist-in-chief of Timberlawn Psychiatric Hospital, Doyle Carson, MD, put a considerable effort into accommodating to the managed care era. In some respects this seemed to be successful as the hospital was able to enter into contracts with managed care companies and sustain a flow of patients. However, the long inpatient stays were essentially over and a short-term psychiatric unit was established in 1990–something that had not even been contemplated five years earlier (other than for substance abuse). The demise of Timberlawn continued throughout the 1990s and the hospital went into bankruptcy and was sold to a chain hospital and is now managed by an outside entity. The character of the hospital underwent significant changes as a result of this process. Could it have been handled differently? Possibly, but only if the board of the hospital had the will to accommodate to the sparser resources from insurance sources. I left Timberlawn at the end of 1992. The hospital went into bankruptcy about 18-24 months later. Many of the former psychiatrists of Timberlawn, including myself, felt that a more fiscally responsible approach might have precluded this unfortunate change.

A substance abuse unit survived and continues today. But as is characteristic of psychiatric hospitals substance abuse units, it is for brief stays involving primarily detoxification. Patients then are put into IOP or, possibly for a brief period of time, day hospital.

From 1993 until 1998 I witnessed through my affiliation with another private psychiatric hospital in the Dallas area as well as my more extensive involvement with the Charter Hospital Corporation, enormous pressures to compete for patients, and to gain approval for services, to develop essential utilization review processes and to continuously trim back staff and program features in order to meet diminishing revenues. While I was with the Charter Behavioral Health System I noticed that the census of the hospital was well correlated with the number of cars in the parking lot. As the census increased there were more staff brought in and as a contraction of census occurred nursing staff and others were laid off if only temporarily. This accordion-like effect in the staffing precluded effective team building and damaged staff moral. Psychiatric hospital administrators in the era of the 1990s were under enormous pressure to meet the bottom line. As medical director of the Dallas Charter Hospital for several years, I worked with several "generations" of administrators who for one reason or another the corporation felt were not doing enough to make the entity profitable or some cases were let go secondary to "personality conflicts" with the higher ups. Across the latter half of the 1990s everything that had been learned about constructing a sensitive and positive milieu for the treatment of individuals with psychiatric and/or substance use disorders was being thrown to the wind. Staff were not nurtured nor necessarily rewarded for longevity. Crisis management seemed to be the operative mode and policies and procedures were directed toward defensive strategies such as avoiding law- suits, minimizing rejection of approval for treatment, and avoiding suicidal incidents. By the end of the 1990s it was clear that managed care was not only wiping out inpatient treatment of substance use disorders but was highly suspicious of partial or day hospital approaches. A whittling away of coverage for the latter continued and intensive outpatient remained the only sure viable treatment effort to be approved. It hardly needs to be mentioned that the capacity of an individual with a chronic relapsing disorder, with denial and other pathological defenses, will not quickly catch on to what he or she needs to do to turn around the course of his life and arrest the addictive process. Brief stays of a week or less on a high turnover inpatient unit focusing primarily on detoxification do not provide a holding pattern sufficient to impact denial and bring a person beyond compliance into fuller acceptance of their "powerlessness over drugs." The need to quickly transfer to a intensive outpatient program resulted in many patients falling through the cracks and simply dropping out of treatment before they could be inculcated into the benefits of working a 12-step program or attending to their substance use disorder in some other constructive way. This became very demoralizing for most of us who had participated in the "golden era" of substance abuse treatment, i.e., the early 1970s through the late 1980s.

Stepping back from these tumultuous changes may allow us to gradually gain a better perspective. The pendulum swung from essentially an open ticket to treatment to a very tight, stingy, resource limited model. Regretfully, irrational efforts to match the patient to treatment were not occurring during the golden era nor was it occurring in the brutal restrictions of the managed care era. During the era of open availability of treatment, inpatient treatment was the gold standard. That is, a gold standard was reflected by the insurance structure itself. Inpatient coverage was abundant. Outpatient coverage was very sparse. Corporations or labor unions that referred patients for treatment of alcoholism or drug abuse expected us, as clinicians, to put them into an inpatient setting for at least four weeks. If we had other ideas, such as merely using an outpatient program, we were considered to not know what we were doing as it was by and large assumed that the intense inpatient approach was essential to accomplish positive results. We have learned as a result of the changes in the closing decades of the 20th century that a variety of approaches to substance use disorders can be effective. The issue is to match the treatment to the patient's needs and to be flexible. Today, there remain many patients whose recovery would be more certain and more quickly accomplished if the old fashioned thirty-day inpatient program were available. For most it is not available and we struggle with a range of outpatient possibilities from day hospital, intensive outpatient or office-based treatment.

As the turmoil destroyed the free-standing substance abuse treatment centers, such as Parkside and the Charter Behavioral Health System, positive forces were beginning to slowly emerge which, I believe, have not yet reached full fruition, but will continue to develop and have a favorable impact on substance abuse treatment and ultimately provide a positive counterforce to the diminished social resources put forth by American corporations. I am referring to the developing pharmacologic strategies that are helping some patients with substance use disorders. Naltrexone and Acamprosate are two examples and other possible anti-craving or blocking drugs can be expected to be developed. In addition, the increased capacity of psychiatry to fully and confidently address substance use disorders has grown. In 1985 the American Academy of Addiction Psychiatry was founded and has had a membership of psychiatrists ranging from 750-1000 across the last 15 years. This organization spearheaded the effort for the American Board of Medical Specialties through the American Board of Psychiatry and Neurology to establish full credentials in addiction psychiatry by the process of "added qualifications" which is a sub-specialty board status. There are now at least thirty addiction psychiatry fellowships available in training centers across the country. More has to be done to further the skills of the psychiatrist in substance use disorders but each psychiatry residency today is required to offer training in the field of substance abuse. This is a change from even ten years ago.

From my perspective I have encouraged psychiatrists to gain confidence and competency in office-based treatment of substance abusing patients. I currently chair the Texas Society of Psychiatric Physicians' Task Force on Addictive Disorders and we have put forth treatment guidelines for office-based detoxification from alcohol, opiates, and anxiolytic/sedatives/hypnotics. Further, we are encouraging the general psychiatrist, i.e., the psychiatrist who does not have special extra training in the addictions field, to participate in continuing medical education activities so that their capacity to identify and initiate treatment within an office context is strengthened. This process of office-based treatment is occurring in parallel at the national level as an effort is underway to expand opiate dependence treatment through utilization of Buprenorphine dispensed by qualified physicians as an alternative to federally regulated Methadone maintenance programs. The success of this endeavor remains to be seen but early pilot projects have been encouraging.

The last twenty years have born witness to remarkable changes in the delivery of alcoholism and other drug treatment services. The early years were exciting, and fulfilling, yet ultimately proved more costly than social resources would tolerate. A rapid reaccommodation was necessary by those working in the substance abuse field. This led to the elimination of large treatment system enterprises such as Comp-Care, Parkside and Charter. Further, many of the nation's outstanding psychiatric hospitals have had to close for fiscal reasons or have been severely compromised in their efforts to provide sustained quality treatment. Yet, out of the ashes of the old system newer visions are emerging. I have referred to the increased capacity of psychiatric physicians to respond and to the broader range of available pharmacologic treatment. I would be remiss to not add the by now widely accepted recognition that the majority of individuals with substance use disorders have a comorbid psychiatric disorder which requires treatment in synchrony with the substance use disorder. This has been an important breakthrough resulting from large scale epidemiologic studies such as the Epidemiologic Catchment Area Study and the National Comorbidity Study.

Across these changes Alcoholics Anonymous and its offspring Narcotics Anonymous have remained steadfast in reaching out to the suffering alcoholic or drug dependent individual. I believe that physicians, including psychiatrists, have a greater respect for 12-step programs today. They are certainly more aware of 12-step programs and are more knowledgeable as 12-step programs receive greater visibility in our society. I am hopeful that physicians in the primary care specialty as well as psychiatrists will continue to develop their capacity to identify, intervene, and initiate treatment with patients presenting with substance abuse or substance dependence. A final take home message from the experience of the past two decades seems to me to come back to the principle that we diligently assess and diagnose patients and accurately determine what treatment is needed. We have patients who need a long-term protected structured residential treatment such as was available decades ago in a few state hospitals. Twelve to eighteen months of such treatment often allowed a sizeable percentage of "skid row" alcoholics to resume a constructive lifestyle. This niche treatment needs to be available again. Similarly, an intermediate residential hospital length of stay should be available for certain patients, albeit the minority of patients. The range of outpatient modalities will be adequate for a majority of patients with substance use disorders if they are able to continue participation for sufficient lengths of time and if such programs can regain some of the enrichment seen 20 years ago in inpatient units, i.e., a strong family dimension, and supportive integration with an Employee Assistance Program.

### *THE MAYO CLINIC EXPERIENCE (ROBERT M. MORSE)*

As treatment programs for addictive disorders[1] combat the many restrictions on care for patients and clients in the early 21st century, it is not uncommon to reflect back on the "golden era of treatment," usually referring to the 1970s through the early 1980s. At that time medical insurance uniformly covered treatment costs including, and even recommending, residential stay. Health care professionals were becoming more interested in and more sophisticated about these disorders. Employee assistance programs (EAPs) were influential in referring workers with behavioral problems for evaluation and subsequent treatment. Outcome studies were beginning to show substantial improvement one or two years after treatment. It was even becoming popular to consider entering the addiction field as a genuine career goal! For various reasons most of us did not anticipate the rather severe effect upon these programs by managed care organizations which began to influence treatment in the 1980s.

Minnesota, the "Land of 10,000 Lakes," was dubbed "Land of 10,000 Recovery Programs," referring to its nationwide reputation as a source of respected treatment programs almost all developed around the "Minnesota Model" of treatment (Morse, 1991). Originating at Wilmar State Hospital in the 1950s and spearheaded by later to be well-known professionals, such as psychiatrist Nelson Bradley and psychologist Dan Anderson, this model had several distinct features (Curson, 1991). These generally included the use of lay counselors (themselves recovering from addiction), group therapy, daily lectures, a multiprofessional staff, therapeutic milieu, family involvement, a 12-step AA program and orientation, and prescribed reading. This model was based upon the then revolutionary concept that alcoholism is a primary illness, which can be treated directly and behaviorally.

Thus, it is not too surprising that a young psychiatrist, well trained but in a conventional psychiatric medical model, might eventually be influenced by the evolving alcoholism treatment programs in his state. Serving a 2-year assignment to the Zumbro Valley Mental Health Center in Rochester, Minnesota, from 1966 to 1968, I was asked to begin an alcoholism treatment program to help meet some of the community needs. Having little interest in this disorder but possessing one admirable trait, the willingness to ask for help, I began to look around. Ray Island and Vern Kuluvar were alcoholism counselors both recovering themselves, at the same mental health center and eventually prided themselves in being able to show a young psychiatrist what it was really like! I soon became deluged with alcoholic patients, began to follow them individually and in a group therapy setting, and surprisingly began to see some recover! More surprisingly, some patients returned to thank me for urging them into treatment even against their wishes! Clearly, this was an interesting disorder which did not seem to fit well with the concepts I had been taught about alcohol and drug problems.

Returning to the Mayo Clinic, the site of my psychiatric training, I continued my alcoholism interests as a consultant to the mental health center program. Eventually Dr. Richard Steinhilber, then chair of the Mayo Department of Psychiatry, said "Dammit Morse, if you are going to talk about this problem all the time, why don't we do something about it?"–and gave me the green light to proceed with planning. The planning phase was exhilarating, exciting and, at the same time, frustrating. Having learned a bit about the Minnesota Model programs, I was aware that this approach would contradict a number of our traditional psychiatric ideas and approaches to alcoholism and the addictions. Thus, we would either have to sell this approach to our department or, perhaps better yet, demonstrate its effectiveness.

An exciting part of the planning process was getting to know some prominent, independent thinking, pioneering professionals who invariably went out of their way to lend a hand to our project and offer ongoing assistance. We were able to visit the Georgian Clinic in Atlanta, Georgia, the Johnson Institute in Minneapolis and Vern Johnson, the Northwestern Hospital program with Reverend Phil Hanson, and the Minneapolis VA program with Dr. Richard Heilman. We were most impressed and became close friends with Dr. Dan Anderson of Hazelden in Center City, Minnesota, and Dr. Nelson Bradley of the Lutheran General program in Chicago. Psychiatrist Bradley was an open-minded energetic man, not at all concerned by the diffusing of professional identities in his program but, at the same time, insisting on maintaining a medical model which allowed him to treat serious psychiatric disorders on site. Dan Anderson, president of the most well known treatment facility in our country, was a modest, bright and open-minded psychologist who seemed pleased to have us spend as much time at his facility as we desired. I cannot overemphasize the important of these contacts as reassuring support for a then rather shaky idea!

After deciding that the Minnesota Model was the most appropriate and currently effective model for treating addictions, we set out to recruit a nursing and counselor staff. Ray Island joined us from the Mental Health Center and Al

Iverson from Wilmar State Hospital also became one of our counselors. The new staff began regular meetings for orientation, education and morale building. To begin the long process of a program acceptable in the multispecialty arena of Mayo, we benefited from the active interests of a select few physicians. Most notably, the late Dr. John Higgins, a respected gastroenterologist, spent countless hours of his own time both helping promote the program and devoting clinical time to examining our patients. The alcoholism treatment unit (ATU) in 1972 opened at the Colonial Building of Rochester Methodist Hospital, one of the two Mayo Medical Center hospitals. In the context of an unwritten policy that any patient hospitalized with the active diagnosis of "alcoholism" should be transferred to the locked psychiatric ward, it is not surprising that hospital staffing for our program started out a bit askew. In addition to nurses, a secretary and receptionist, we were provided with three burly male aides, no doubt to handle the anticipated disruptive behavior of our patients! Fortunately, they were not needed for this purpose.

Coincidentally, with the opening of the ATU was the beginning of Mayo's medical school. Prior to this Mayo had focused its educational efforts exclusively upon graduate physicians training in many specialty areas but now had decided to open its own undergraduate medical school. We were fortunate in being able to get a foot in the door from the very beginning as far as medical student education. Our first presentation to the new medical students included a session where recovering alcoholics told their story of drinking, multiple problems and subsequent recovery. They then led small discussion groups with the students. This proved to be an excellent way of introducing medical students to the positive side of alcoholism, i.e., that recovery does occur. Unfortunately, our teaching opportunities later became somewhat irregular but the medical school has remained committed to providing ongoing addiction education.

Of equal importance was the commitment of Mayo's Department of Psychiatry and its resident education program, then under the auspices of the late Dr. John Graf, to require addiction training for all Mayo psychiatric residents subsequently trained. This allowed us to have at least two young psychiatrists helping to staff our unit at any one time. And the concept of a counselor/physician team began to evolve. With an initial capacity for 22 patients, each of two teams was responsible for 11 patients. Each patient was involved in two group therapy sessions per day, staffed by the counselor and physician jointly and occasionally with a nurse co-therapist. In addition to providing therapy, the counselor/physician team became an excellent means of cross-fertilization and education for our young physicians. They began to learn, both formally and informally from the counselor, addiction concepts rather than only read about them. The counselors, on the other hand, became more sophisticated with psychiatric disorders and psychological management.

Along with the counselor/physician team, our "medicalized Minnesota Model"[1] included daily on-site supervision by a staff psychiatrist with experience in the addictions, a formal psychiatric interview for each admitted patient, a comprehensive general medical examination by a Mayo physician, and specialty medical or surgical consultation as required with the belief that many conditions could be treated concurrently with the ongoing treatment for addiction. For example, we were able to treat such conditions as peptic ulcer disease, hypertension, rheumatoid arthritis, and diabetes mellitus quite easily during the hospital residential treatment program which averaged about four weeks in length. Concurrent psychiatric treatment, the popularized "dual diagnosis" idea, was also successfully initiated. Recognizing that the chief limiting factor for treating psychiatric disorder in our setting was the overt behavior of the patient, e.g., a floridly psychotic schizophrenic or manic individual would need transfer to the psychiatric unit, we were able to treat schizophrenia in remission, anxiety and panic disorder, major depression, chronic pain syndromes, etc.

The ATU became the ADDU (alcoholism and drug dependence unit) within a couple of years, reflecting accurately our experience that most alcoholic patients were using, if not abusing, other drugs and increasingly drug dependent patients themselves were referred for treatment. The ADDU benefited greatly from its position as an integral program of the Mayo Medical Center. With its multiple specialty focus and deserved reputation for excellence in diagnosis and clinical care, Mayo offered us resources most other addiction program could only dream about. Of course, there was some early skepticism about whether or not a Minnesota Model program could operate in this context, offering simultaneous medical and psychiatric care without detracting seriously from the focus upon addition.

And indeed it was often a delicate balance which tilted either way at times but generally proved effective and stimulating to staff.

Fortunately for us, we were able to subscribe to the three Mayo goals of striving for excellence in clinical practice, education and research. We have alluded to our clinical practice model and also to our commitment to both medical school and physician training. From the outset we also attempted to provide enough scientific detachment to pursue clinical research on an ongoing basis. Subsequently, over a period of years, we were able to demonstrate that outcome from our efforts compared very favorably with that from other reputable treatment institutions, including the Hazelden Treatment Center. In several outcome studies, roughly two-thirds of our patients were doing well one year after discharge, defining "well" as complete abstinence from drugs of dependence or at worst a brief relapse (no more than two or three days) with no return to the addictive behavior (Morse, Martin et al., 1984). This favorable outcome included those who had been simultaneously treated for medical and psychiatric disorders. We were also able to show that female patients did as well as males in our coeducational model despite the fact that we treated about two men to every one woman and did not have a "special" program for women. Patients with a "chronic pain syndrome" had a similarly positive outcome from the addictive standpoint (Finlayson, Maruta et al., 1986). We were greatly aided in work with the latter patients by staff from our Pain Management Center under the direction of Drs. David Swanson and Toshihiko Maruta.

Attempting to find a simple yet valid screening test for alcoholism, we experimented with a version of the Michigan Alcoholic Screening Test (MAST). At that time the MAST was an interview instrument only. We were able to demonstrate that our version, nine items more than the MAST, was valid when used as a self-administered test of 35 items. This was the origin of our Self-Administered Alcoholism Screening Test (SAAST) (Swenson, Morse, 1975).

It also began a long-standing working relationship with excellent psychologists such as Drs. Wendell Swenson and L. J. Davis, which allowed us to have ongoing clinical research projects.

Other research from our staff showed that physicians, treated identically with other patients in the ADDU, had a substantially higher rate of recovery when contacted one to five years after treatment (Morse, Martin et al., 1984). We had become a regional and national resource for evaluating and treating impaired physicians with excellent direction by one of our staff psychiatrist, Dr. Bob Niven, who later went on to direct the National Institutes of Alcohol Abuse and Alcoholism (NIAAA). During the 1970s we were also benefited by a fine relationship with the Impaired Physician Program of the state of Illinois, then under the direction of Dr. Jim West. Dr. West later became the medical director of the newly formed Betty Ford Center in California.

A final example of clinical research helping to promote treatment change, has to do with the evolving issue of whether or not alcoholic and other addicted patients should try to stop smoking during their treatment or whether or not this addiction should even be addressed. Dr. Richard Hurt, now director of Mayo's Nicotine Dependence Center, led an interesting clinical study in which alternate patients were entered into a brief nicotine cessation program while being treated for alcohol or drug addiction. A control group went through the usual ADDU program at the same time but without attempts to stop smoking. Following these patients one year later, we were pleased to find that the outcome from alcohol and drug dependence did not differ between the two groups and remained at the relatively high level of about 60+ percent (Hurt, Eberman et al., 1994). Disappointingly, however, less than 10 percent of those who attempted to stop smoking were actually able to do so. These findings helped us decide that it was appropriate to offer smoking cessation therapy for our inpatient addicts should they wish, as there should be no detraction from treatment of their primary addiction.

As cost of treatment became an increasing concern in the 1980s, managed care insurance programs came on the scene. We were initially in agreement with them that some addicted patients need not have expensive 4-week residential care and that they might benefit either from reduced length of treatment and/or outpatient care only. On the other hand, we agreed with managed care providers that there were some patients who not only would require four weeks of care but even longer lengths of stay should we individualize for severity of their conditions as they were suggesting. Unfortunately, the latter situation never materialized and we were faced with rather severely shortened lengths of stay for all of our patients! This, of course, was greatly damaging to our program, one of the few which had been able to evaluate and treat complex associated disorders along with the addiction. It became less and less feasible to provide the thorough care we had been doing. We were asked to care for patients with complex problems with a shorter stay, fewer staff, reduced costs, increased efficiency, improved outcome and with greater patient satisfaction–clearly an impossible task (Morse, 1995)! Furthermore, we knew that there were seldom if ever any "quick fixes" in chemical dependency/addiction programing. The typical addict denies or minimizes his or her condition. When told that an inpatient treatment stay of seven to ten days is "adequate," this reinforces the denial and defense system. Contrary to other medical conditions where the healing process will naturally continue upon dismissal, the newly abstinent addict is quite different. Relapse is almost certain without immediate and serious affiliation with ongoing daily recovery program. Attempts to mitigate these problems and find an effective treatment approach continues.

We were privileged to develop several special programs over our initial years, again usually fashioned through affiliation with our Mayo Medical Center colleagues. To promote contact with our patients and to recognize recovery efforts, we began an annual reunion weekend. This generally included an informal evening program, a morning didactic session featuring several staff members and topped off by a dinner dance at a local hotel. The dinner speaker was generally a well-known celebrity in the chemical dependency field. This event was uniformly a positive experience for returning patients and a morale booster for our staff!

In the 1970s we became a national career teacher location with Dr. Bob Niven receiving the federal grant and myself functioning as his sponsor. Under this rather farsighted program, a faculty member from each of some 40 or 50 medical centers around the country was selected to be partially sponsored by

NIAAA in turn for being given dedicated time to be educated about and then teach in the addiction field. Several of the career teachers have gone on to national leadership positions.

With medical education as an important part of our function, we were urged to try a new approach in the early 1980s by Ms. Mary Adams Martin, a social worker with the ADDU program. Mary had been a central figure in other community educational efforts and, as a devotee of the arts, wondered if we might invite Mr. Jason Robards to perform the soliloquy from Eugene O'Neill's *The Iceman Cometh* for Mayo physicians and staff. O'Neill's chief character was a drinking alcoholic who personified the defense system of most alcoholic people. Through her own perseverance, Mary was eventually able to organize such a production. With brief didactic presentations followed by Robards' performance, over 1,000 attendees were both entertained and educated by this new format! We unfortunately did not measure attitudes and/or behavior before and after the program and thus cannot be very scientific about its effects. But from anecdotal feedback it was an enormous success.

We added a formal Addiction Psychiatry Fellowship to Mayo's psychiatry residency program and continue to attract fellows interested in making this a subspecialty focus. With the American Board of Psychiatry's "added qualifications," exam specialty in Addiction Psychiatry is now available. Special training in this field has become quite desirable.

The effectiveness of required clinical training in the addictions was demonstrated by a recent finding published in an article describing a point prevalence study of alcoholism in Mayo hospitals, primarily authored by Dr. Terry Schneekloth (Schneekloth, Morse et al., 2001). Outpatients on the medical and surgical units were surveyed by the SAAST screening test on one particular day. Comparing the screening test findings with the ability of clinical staff to identify and diagnose alcoholism in their patients, psychiatry was the only unit with 100 percent concordance. All of the SAAST-identified alcoholics were also identified by psychiatry staff. This reflects, we believe, the fact that clinical addiction training is not mandated at Mayo by any specialty except psychiatry.

The disappointing finding of the above study, that only 7 percent of the SAAST-identified alcoholic patients received a discharge diagnosis of alcohol abuse or alcohol dependence, accurately reflects the continuing challenges in this field. We believe that attitudes of physicians and other health care providers are likely the major explanation of these findings of persistent low levels of recognition and treatment of the addictions. There is evidence to suggest that attitudes demonstrated by our 1975 study of 927 general physicians continue to this day (Morse, Mitchell et al., 1975). The majority of those physicians tended to view the alcoholic person as weak-willed, immature and undependable. Add to this the opinion of the general public, which physicians often mirror, that these problems are self-inflicted and we have substantial evidence of the continuing stigma attached to this field of medicine. Despite the difficulties facing us as caregivers, however, there are numerous suffering patients all about us who deserve the best. They deserve accurate and comprehensive identification, diagnosis and treatment. Let's continue the effort (McElrath, 2001)!

## NOTE

1. For purposes of this discussion, "addictive disorders" is an all-encompassing term, which includes chemical dependency, substance abuse and dependence, alcoholism and the multiple drug dependencies.

## REFERENCES

Curson DA (1991). Private Treatment of Alcohol and Drug Problems in Britain. *British Journal of Addiction*; 86:9-11.

Finlayson RE, Maruta T, Morse RM, and Martin MA (1986). Substance Dependence in Chronic Pain: Experience with Treatment and Follow-Up Results. *Pain*; 26:175-180.

Hurt RD, Eberman KM, Croghan IT, Morse RM et al. (1994). Nicotine Dependence Treatment During Inpatient Treatment for Other Addictions. *Alcohol Clinical and Experimental Research*; 18:867-872.

McElrath D (2001). The Quiet Crusaders. Hazelden Foundation, Center City, Minnesota.

Morse RM (1991). Medicalizing the Minnesota Model. *Professional Counselor*. 33-35.

Morse RM (1995). The Uneasy Alliance Between Managed Care and Clinical Services. *Front Lines* (OCT) 1.

Morse RM, Martin MA, Swenson WM, and Niven RG (1984). Prognosis of Physicians Treated for Alcoholism and Drug Dependence. *JAMA*; 251:743-746.

Morse RM, Mitchell MM, Martin MA. Physician Attitudes Toward Alcoholism: A Positive Trend? In: Seixas FA (Ed) Currents in Alcoholism, San Diego.

Schneekloth TD, Morse RM, Herrick LM, Suman VJ, Offord KP, and David LJ (2001). Point Prevalence of Alcoholism in Hospitalized Patients. *Mayo Clinic Proceedings*; 76:460-466.

Swenson WM, and Morse RM (1975). The Use of Self-Administered Alcoholism Screening Test (SAAST) in a Medical Center. *Mayo Clinic Proceedings*; 50:204-208.

# Broadening the Base of Treatment
## for Alcohol Problems,
## a 1990 Report for the Institute of Medicine:
## Personal Reflections

### Robert D. Sparks, MD, FACP

**SUMMARY.** These reflections on the 1990 report for the Institute of Medicine provide an abbreviated summary of the methods used to prepare the original report. A few of the significant observations and recommendations of the IOM report are highlighted. Considerations are offered for a need to determine the impact of the report. *[Article copies available for a fee from The Haworth Document Delivery Service: 1-800-HAWORTH. E-mail address: <getinfo@haworthpressinc.com> Website: <http://www.HaworthPress.com> © 2002 by The Haworth Press, Inc. All rights reserved.]*

Robert D. Sparks, after post-graduate studies, was appointed to the faculty of Tulane's School of Medicine and held several administrative positions, concluding as Dean, during the period 1959 to 1972. After 1972 he held the positions of Chancellor of the University of Nebraska Medical Center in Omaha, NE, and Vice President of the University of Nebraska System, Program Director and then President and Chief Programming Officer of the W. K. Kellogg Foundation. He directed the Addiction Treatment Services of the Battle Creek Adventist Hospital of Battle Creek, MI, and was President of the California Medical Association Foundation until retiring in 1997. He served on the Board of Directors of the National Council on Alcoholism and Drug Dependence, including holding the offices of Treasurer, Vice-Chairman and Chairman. He was elected to the Institute of Medicine of the National Academy of Sciences in 1986.

[Haworth co-indexing entry note]: "Broadening the Base of Treatment for Alcohol Problems, a 1990 Report for the Institute of Medicine: Personal Reflections." Sparks, Robert D. Co-published simultaneously in *Alcoholism Treatment Quarterly* (The Haworth Press, Inc.) Vol. 20, No. 3/4, 2002, pp. 227-231; and: *Alcohol Problems in the United States: Twenty Years of Treatment Perspective* (ed: Thomas F. McGovern, and William L. White) The Haworth Press, Inc., 2002, pp. 227-231. Single or multiple copies of this article are available for a fee from The Haworth Document Delivery Service [1-800-HAWORTH, 9:00 a.m. - 5:00 p.m. (EST). E-mail address: getinfo@haworthpressinc.com].

227

**KEYWORDS.** Institute of Medicine, alcohol problems, study, base of treatment

The report, *Broadening the Base of Treatment for Alcohol Problems*, was completed in the late 1980s and published in 1990 by the National Academy Press. It was a pleasure for me to serve as Chair of the committee appointed by Dr. Samuel O. Thier, then the President of the Institute of Medicine [IOM], to formulate a response to a request set forth in Public Law 99-570 [PL-99-570], Section 4022 that was enacted on October 17, 1986. The report was to be prepared by the National Academy of Sciences [of which the IOM is a unit] and presented subsequently to the Congress of the United States. The Director of the National Institute on Alcohol Abuse and Alcoholism [NIAAA], then Dr. Enoch Gordis, was charged by PL 99-570 to arrange for a study by the National Academy of Sciences to respond to the items enumerated by the legislation. In summary, they wanted a report on research knowledge and experience about alternative approaches and mechanisms for treatment and rehabilitative services for persons with alcoholism or alcohol abuse in the U.S. and other appropriate countries. The concerns extended to a desire for information about costs, quality, effectiveness and appropriateness of such care and how the services were funded in private and public mechanisms. The legislation asked for recommendations for policies and programs of research, planning, administration, and reimbursement for the treatment of individuals affected adversely by their use of alcohol. Dr. Gordis urged particular attention to eight issues ranging from consideration of available or developing treatments through validity of outcome measures. He hoped we could give improved definitions of patient types and methods of treatment including settings of treatment, the possibilities for treatment-matching, and consideration of controlled drinking proposals. He, too, sought advice about existing studies or forms of treatment that might be replicated.

Members of the committee in addition to me were: Thomas F. Babor, Robert W. Blum, Chad D. Emrick, Jim Francek, Edward Gottheil, Merwyn R. Greenlick, David C. Lewis, G. Alan Marlatt, Thomas F. McGovern, Mark V. Pauly, Barbara Ross-Lee, Harvey A. Skinner, Cynthia P. Turnure, Roger Dale Walker and Constance M. Weisner. Our committee's work was capably aided by Study Staff: Frederick B. Glaser, Herman I. Diesenhaus, Leah Mazade, Barbara A. Kelley, Fredric Solomon and Elaine Lawson. All the members of the committee were actively engaged in the field of treatment and study of alcohol problems and addictions. Few members of this committee had worked with each other or had collaborated in preparation of similar reports. Recognizing the diverse backgrounds and experiences of the committee members, we did agree upon some procedural assumptions that guided our deliberations and preparation of the report. On page 3 of the report, we observed that:

> *Each member of the committee was understood to have not one but two special roles to fulfill in the work of the group. First, each was to bring the benefit of his or her professional experience in dealing with alcohol problems. Second, every member also had a duty to function as an informed and responsible citizen in carrying out the committee's work. It was hoped that such an emphasis would encourage committee members to rise above special interests, current controversies, and loyalties to particular constituencies.*

Later on page 5, we noted that:

> *Points of contention were put forward and discussed in professional and agreeable exchanges. Where such disagreements proved to be significant, the chairman played an active role in working out a satisfactory resolution. Compromise was usually effected through this process. In the few instances in which disagreements persisted, they are noted in the text.*

I did paraphrase these operating guidelines as: *we agreed to disagree agreeably in respecting the contribution of every individual on the committee and the staff who participated in the discussions.* From the beginning we understood that any persisting disagreement from the majority view on a specific point or part in the report would be presented adequately for the dissenter. As we stated in the report, such conflicting opinions or observations were very few. I believe that this approach in no way diluted the contributions made by the report, and, in fact, aided the significance of the report.

In the years after our report was presented, we individually, and collectively on one occasion in 1996, wondered how the report could have been improved and what the effect of our report had been. Had the process we used resulted in the best product in the form and content of the report? How many people had read any part of the report, let alone the entire 609 pages? What was the reaction of any reader? Had our work predicted a future about care of persons with alcohol abuse or alcoholism? Had new policies resulted from the report? Had the book been referenced in writings in the field? Had the book been cited by authors of articles on addictions or abusive use of alcohol or other chemicals? Certainly questions such as these have crossed my mind many times in the 12 years since the report was published. I know my fellow members of the IOM committee have similarly pondered such questions about the benefits or lack of benefits of our report.

The vision we set forth in the report guided our thoughts as we addressed the several broad questions that had been posed to us. On page 6 of the report we briefly summarized our view

> *of the probable structure toward which treatment for alcohol problems seems to be evolving. That structure is a treatment system in which a broad community-wide treatment effort is coupled closely with a comprehensive specialized treatment effort. The role of community agencies in treatment would include the identification of individuals with alcohol problems, the provision of brief interventions to a portion of those identified, and the referral of others to specialized treatment. Specialized treatment would emphasize comprehensive pretreatment assessment, the matching of particular individuals to specific treatment interventions, and the regular determination of the outcome of treatment. Assuring the continuity of care and providing for the feedback of outcome results in the reformulation of matching guidelines are also viewed as important functional elements of the emerging treatment system. The most fundamental recommendation of the committee is that this vision be shared, tested, refined, and implemented.*

The report did urge earlier identification of persons with significant psychological, physical or social problems consequent to the excessive consumption of alcohol. Increased availability of community programs and resources were expected to develop in the view of our committee. A recent meeting I attended in California of a group wishing to advocate for new funds from selected portions of the alcohol industry whose products were used heavily by "underage drinkers" revealed the desire to achieve goals set forth in our IOM report. Their proposals included a continuing need for early detection of individuals with alcohol problems and the use of community facilities and programs with appropriate levels and intensity of care. The discussions and recommendations in that meeting echoed the spirit and intent of many elements of our IOM report. How many similar actions are underway now or started earlier by other groups in California or other states?

At this moment we do not have a methodically collected body of information to answer my questions about the possible effects of the IOM report. It would be useful for the Congress and the National Academy of Sciences to have objective answers to such questions. The benefit from such information would not only be for the assessment of the impact of the report, *Broadening the Base of Treatment for Alcohol Problems*, but also for the process by which such reports are formulated and used by a variety of other organizations and individuals in the fields of policy formulation in addition to the Congress. The one attempt this committee made to obtain such information was from a follow-up meeting held at Brown University on September 27-29, 1996. The sessions were informative to members of the committee but frustrating for public presentation because funding was only available for a convening of the committee and preparation of a brief report. An extensive report from that follow-up session was not possible because of the absence of adequate funding to support the editing and publishing needed to provide a report of the essential elements of the meeting.

David Lewis, a member of the IOM Committee, has had a continuing project since the IOM report, titled "Physician Leadership on National Drug Policy [PLNDP]," to try to redirect national policy on addictions toward greater attention and funding for treatment and prevention of addictions. He observed to me recently:

> *No question that the timeliness of our book lives on. It's obvious from the discussions here and subsequent discussions that the book is relevant to-day—in many ways more relevant today than when it was published. In retrospect, the controversy that we encountered trying to set standards for screening and referral has occurred but our formulation for standardization was benign compared to the assault on costs by managed care and behavioral carve-out firms. I think "our vision" still holds up quite well. The PLNDP project encounters the generic issues we addressed all the time because we're focused on a public health approach to medical problems.*

These two observations are anecdotal but suggestive that at least our IOM report did anticipate changes in the management and care of individuals who have suffered from their consumption of alcohol products. It would be desirable to have more objective observations about the report's effects. Such an endeavor would require a substantial effort with the necessary financial support. Subjective responses of other members of the committee would provide a valuable contribution toward responding to questions I posed earlier in this personal reflection. Absent available funding for the objective evaluation, I will poll the members of the IOM committee to request any information they could provide me about outcomes from our report. With permission of members of the committee, I hope to submit a sequel to this "Personal Reflection." It is my hope that I will be able to provide a collective reflection on *Broadening the Base of Treatment for Alcohol Problems* that will provide a more valuable contribution than this "Personal Reflection."

## REFERENCES

*Broadening the Base of Treatment for Alcohol Problems*, The National Academy Press, National Academy of Sciences, Washington, DC. 1990.

Personal communication from Dr. David C. Lewis, Professor of Medicine & Community Health, Center for Alcohol & Addiction Studies, Brown University, Providence, RI 02912.

# Treating Alcohol Problems:
# A Future Perspective

William L. White, MA
Thomas F. McGovern, EdD

**SUMMARY.** In this closing article commemorating the twentieth anniversary of the publication of *Alcoholism Treatment Quarterly* (ATQ), the editors offer their own thoughts about the future treatment of alcohol problems in the United States. The review includes twenty-two predictions that topically span the organization and staffing of the treatment field, the central ideas that undergird the field, and the future of clinical technologies used to treat alcohol problems. *[Article copies available for a fee from The Haworth Document Delivery Service: 1-800-HAWORTH. E-mail address: <getinfo@haworthpressinc.com> Website: <http://www.HaworthPress.com>* © 2002 by The Haworth Press, Inc. All rights reserved.]

**KEYWORDS.** Future, trends, client characteristics, treatment technology, aging of workforce

---

William L. White is Senior Research Consultant at Chestnut Health Systems, and has more than 30 years of experience in the addictions field as a clinician, clinical director, researcher and trainer. He has authored more than 100 articles and monographs, and seven books, including *Slaying the Dragon–The History of Addiction Treatment and Recovery in America.*

Thomas F. McGovern has worked in the addictions field for more than 25 years as a teacher, author and researcher. He has been deeply involved in the professionalization of the alcoholism treatment field. He has served as Editor of *Alcoholism Treatment Quarterly* for the past fifteen years.

[Haworth co-indexing entry note]: "Treating Alcohol Problems: A Future Perspective." White, William L., and Thomas F. McGovern. Co-published simultaneously in *Alcoholism Treatment Quarterly* (The Haworth Press, Inc.) Vol. 20, No. 3/4, 2002, pp. 233-239; and: *Alcohol Problems in the United States: Twenty Years of Treatment Perspective* (ed: Thomas F. McGovern, and William L. White) The Haworth Press, Inc., 2002, pp. 233-239. Single or multiple copies of this article are available for a fee from The Haworth Document Delivery Service [1-800-HAWORTH, 9:00 a.m. - 5:00 p.m. (EST). E-mail address: getinfo@haworthpressinc.com].

## *INTRODUCTION*

The authors of the articles in this publication commemorating the 20th volume of ATQ hint at many things to come in the future treatment of alcohol problems. They envision a treatment field that is more ethically centered, evidence based, recovery focused, community linked and more clinically nuanced for those with special characteristics and needs. In this final article, the editors of this collection offer their own thoughts about the future treatment of alcohol problems in the United States. This review includes predictions that topically span the organization and staffing of the treatment field, the central ideas that undergird the field, and the future of clinical technologies used to treat alcohol problems. It is their hope that this list will stir discussion about the most critical issues in the future treatment of alcohol problems.

## *INFRASTRUCTURE AND CULTURAL CONTEXT*

*Prediction 1:* The federal/state/local partnership created by the Comprehensive Alcoholism Prevention and Treatment Act of 1970 (known as the Hughes Act) will be challenged by the growing restigmatization, demedicalization and recriminalization of severe alcohol and other drug problems. We believe this partnership and the treatment system it sustains will survive due to support from new and renewed grassroots recovery advocacy groups and increased responsiveness of local treatment programs to a broad spectrum of alcohol-related problems.

*Prediction 2:* The federal investment in an alcohol problems research infrastructure will reap significant rewards in the coming decades. For example, we anticipate that new understandings of the neurobiology of alcohol dependence will reap rewards in terms of new clinical tools for assessment and treatment, the most significant of which may be the ability to distinguish alcohol problems of biological and non-biological origin and the introduction of fundamentally new pharmacological adjuncts to treatment.

## *ORGANIZATION*

*Prediction 3:* The integration of the treatment of alcohol and other drug problems–arguably one of the major professional achievements or (according to some) the worst mistake of the past 25 years–will progress in the next decades with a full integration of the treatment of nicotine addiction alongside the treatment of other drug addictions. The overextension of the concept of addiction to other problem areas will spur a redefinition of the boundaries of the field, distinguishing the use of *addiction* as a medical concept versus the personal use of the concept of *addiction* as an organizing metaphor for behavioral change.

*Prediction 4:* The categorical segregation of the treatment of alcohol problems will be severely challenged in the next two decades as alcohol treatment programs are absorbed into larger umbrellas of "behavioral health" and "human services." While such integration promises a more consumer-friendly service process and a better stewardship of community resources, our fear is that the field of alcoholism treatment could disappear while the illusion of its presence continues.

## PROBLEM DEFINITION

*Prediction 5:* Multi-pathway models of understanding and intervening in alcohol problems will replace more traditional, single-pathway models. These prevailing models will detail how alcohol problems spring from multiple etiological pathways, unfold in diverse patterns with varying courses/outcomes, and are resolved through diverse clinical interventions and innumerable pathways and styles of long-term recovery. This conceptual shift will require that treatment agencies shift from offering a "program" to offering a wide menu of services that are uniquely combined and sequenced based on the needs and readiness for change of each client/family.

*Prediction 6:* The next two decades will witness attempts to integrate the emerging public health and medical/clinical models of understanding and responding to alcohol problems. We feel the integration of the former, which places emphasis on the economic, social and political ecology of alcohol problems, and the latter, which emphasizes the role of the individual as the source and solution to alcohol problems, has great potential.

## CHANGING CHARACTERISTICS OF TREATMENT CONSUMERS

*Prediction 7:* Differences between community and clinical populations will widen with the multiple problem client/family (greater problem severity and psychiatric co-morbidity and fewer recovery assets) becoming the norm within publicly funded treatment programs. This will create a growing dichotomy between individuals who can resolve alcohol problems with recovery self-management tools (e.g., manuals and online recovery support services) or brief professional intervention versus those who will require multi-agency models of sustained recovery management. The latter clients will require a broader menu of services (far beyond acute models of detoxification and symptom stabilization) delivered over a much longer period of time.

*Prediction 8:* Escalating life expectancies and the demographic aging of the "war babies" will spark growing concern about the problem of late-onset alcohol problems. We anticipate that the prevention and treatment of such problems will become a major specialty within the alcohol problems field.

## THE PROFESSIONALIZATION OF TREATMENT PROVIDERS

*Prediction 9:* The recognition of addiction medicine as a recognized specialty will continue, but will be offset by greater involvement of primary physicians, physician assistants, and nurse practitioners in the treatment of alcohol problems. The further professionalization of addiction medicine will be hampered by the recent restigmatization and demedicalization of alcohol problems and the resulting marginal status associated with this arena of medical practice.

*Prediction 10:* The continued professionalization of the role of the addiction counselor (e.g., the licensure movement) will be balanced by new roles (recovery coaches, recovery support specialists) that will bring greater numbers of recovering people back into the field. Some will interpret this latter trend as a deprofessionalization of the field while others will view this as a renewal process and a needed reconnection of treatment and recovery.

*Prediction 11:* Professional roles in the field, dominated by men when the first issue of ATQ was published, will be increasingly filled by women. This feminization of the field will add momentum to address the special needs of women impacted by alcohol problems.

## TREATMENT TECHNOLOGY

*Prediction 12:* The organizing mantra of the next decade will be the call to bridge the gap between clinical research and clinical practice in the resolution of alcohol problems. The failure to achieve this goal could threaten the very future of the field; the achievement of this goal could move treatment from the status of a folk art to a science-guided endeavor. Some of the most promising applications include new identification and engagement technologies, a new generation of global assessment and service planning instruments; new pharmacological adjuncts to treatment; evidence-based, manual-guided therapies; and sustained recovery management protocols.

*Prediction 13:* The next decade will witness the widespread application of disease (recovery) management technologies from primary medicine to the treatment of severe and persistent alcohol problems. We believe that the shift from an exclusively acute model of intervention to a continuum of interventions that include the option for sustained recovery management will mark one of the most significant technical advancements in the history of the field. This breakthrough marks the marriage of the relapse prevention technologies of the alcohol field with techniques used in primary medicine to manage chronic disorders like diabetes, asthma, and hypertension.

*Prediction 14:* Research findings will compare and contrast explicitly religious and spiritual frameworks of recovery from explicitly secular frameworks. Although hoped-for treatment matching effects have not been robust in existing studies, there may be matching effects related to these broader frameworks.

*Prediction 15:* There will be a movement to push the breakthroughs in knowledge about special populations of clients from the enclave of the demonstration project to the mainstream of the field. It is time these breakthroughs in understanding and technique were moved from the status of loosely attached appendages to the field to the very heart of the field, e.g., front line clinical practice in non-specialty programs.

## PROFESSIONAL ETHICS

*Prediction 16:* There will be a significant movement in the next decade to get the treatment field ethically recentered. This movement will include developing new ethical decision-making models, upgrading organization codes of professional practice, and advanced training to enhance ethical sensitivities and ethical decision-making skills. A major focus of this work will be on the development of ethical standards related to the field's business practices–an arena we view as one of continued vulnerability for the field.

*Prediction 17:* New roles that focus on harm reduction, pre-treatment/engagement, and sustained recovery support will call for a reevaluation of traditional definitions of appropriateness related to ethical conduct, particularly those governing relationship boundaries. This will emerge as an area of intense debate within the field and call for heightened supervisory support for persons filling these roles.

## RECOVERY AND COMMUNITY

*Prediction 18:* The treatment field will face in the next decade what it has never faced in its history: a strong consumer/constituency movement. This new recovery advocacy movement will demand inclusion of recovering people and their families in the planning and evaluation of treatment services. This movement will demand lower thresholds of engagement, higher thresholds of extrusion, and a greater focus on building long-term recovery support services for individuals and families.

*Prediction 19:* The locus of treatment will expand beyond the institutional/office environment to the natural environment of each client. "Systems interface" will become the rule rather than the exception as alcohol treatment agencies enter into an increasing number of service delivery partnerships with public health, mental health, child welfare, criminal justice, educational, occupational and welfare institutions. Treatment and recovery support services will be offered in a wider variety of settings–health care clinics, churches, community centers–but they will also be much more likely to be delivered within neighborhoods and homes. Work with clients enmeshed in drug/criminal cultures will focus on guiding the client into a relationship with an alternative culture of recovery and organizing such cultures where none exist.

*Prediction 20:* There will be increased demands for the field to shift its research focus from one of pathology to one of resilience and recovery. More specifically, there will be calls to generate new service technologies based, not on studies of the problem, but on studies of the myriad solutions that already exist in the lives of individuals and families in communities across America. There will be calls to plot the long-term pathways, stages and styles of recovery and to delineate these findings across such factors as gender, age, ethnicity, and clinical profiles. Advocacy for this resilience and recovery research agenda will generate parallel calls for strengths-based models of assessment and intervention.

*Prediction 21:* The growing "varieties of recovery experience" will continue to manifest themselves within the growing diversification of mutual aid structures. As these structures become more geographically accessible, the communities of recovery with whom treatment programs will be collaborating will be greater in number and more diverse than anyone could have anticipated, confirming in local communities across the country A.A. cofounder Bill Wilson's 1944 observation that "the roads to recovery are many."

## ACHILLES HEEL: THE AGING OF THE FIELD

*Prediction 22:* The rapidly approaching loss of long-tenured clinical and administrative leaders will constitute one of the most significant challenge to the future integrity and existence of the field. If major efforts are not implemented to address the issues of leadership development and leadership succession, much of the field's history, core values and technical knowledge will be lost, and the field will be vulnerable to colonization by more powerful forces within its operating environment. The mantle of leadership of the alcoholism treatment field is about to be passed: Will there be a new generation of prepared leaders there to accept it?

## A CLOSING THOUGHT

If there is a legacy of this past twenty years it is most fittingly the fact that there are hundreds of thousands of individuals and families in recovery today whose lives were touched by professionally-directed treatment services. For the past twenty years, ATQ has detailed the interventions that have made such transformations possible. It is hoped that twenty years from now, ATQ will be again celebrating the reality and methods of such recoveries.

# Index